COMPUTE!'s
Using *Microsoft Excel* on the IBM

Elna R. Tymes with Charles Prael

COMPUTE! Books

Greensboro, North Carolina
Radnor, Pennsylvania

Editor: Lynne Weatherman

Copyright 1988, COMPUTE! Publications, Inc. All rights reserved.

Reproduction or translation of any part of this work beyond that permitted by Sections 107 and 108 of the United States Copyright Act without the permission of the copyright owner is unlawful.

Printed in the United States of America

10 9 8 7 6 5 4 3 2 1

Library of Congress Cataloging-in-Publication Data

Tymes, Elna.
    COMPUTE!'s using microsoft Excel on the IBM/Elna R. Tymes with Charles Prael.
      p.   cm.
    Includes index.
    ISBN 0-87455-147-1
    1. Accounting—Data processing. 2. Finance, Personal—Data processing. 3. Microsoft Excel (Computer program) 4. IBM microcomputers—Programming. I. Prael, Charles E. II. Title.
    III. Title: Using microsoft Excel on the IBM.
HF5679.T96 1988
005.36'9—dc19   88-25695
                                                                                                                                                   CIP

The author and publisher have made every effort in the preparation of this book to ensure the accuracy of the information. However, the information in this book is sold without warranty, either express or implied. Neither the author nor COMPUTE! Publications, Inc. will be liable for any damages caused or alleged to be caused directly, indirectly, incidentally, or consequentially by the information in this book.

The opinions expressed in this book are solely those of the author and are not necessarily those of COMPUTE! Publications, Inc.

COMPUTE! Books, Post Office Box 5406, Greensboro, NC 27403, (919) 275-9809, is a Capital Cities/ABC, Inc. company and is not associated with any manufacturer of personal computers. *Wordstar* is a registered trademark of MicroPro, International, Inc. *Lotus 1-2-3* is a registered trademark of Lotus Development Corporation. *Excel* and *Windows* are trademarks and *Microsoft* and *Multiplan* are registered trademarks of Microsoft Corporation.

Contents

Foreword	v
Acknowledgments	vii
Chapter 1: Introducing *Excel*	1
Chapter 2: Getting Started	13
Chapter 3: Entering Data and Creating Worksheets	37
Chapter 4: Working with Files	65
Chapter 5: Editing What You Have	91
Chapter 6: Formulas and Functions	143
Chapter 7: Printing	207
Chapter 8: The Database	229
Chapter 9: Graphs and Charts	251
Chapter 10: Using Macros	293
Chapter 11: *Excel* **and Other Programs**	345
Appendix A: Shortcut Key Quick Reference	355
Appendix B: The Models in *Excel*	361
Appendix C: Using the Clipboard and Control Panel	375
Index	383

Foreword

Welcome to *COMPUTE!'s Using Microsoft Excel on the IBM*. Among its multitude of powerful financial, database, and statistical features, *Excel* lets you link data between worksheets, graph the data using one of the many chart formats available, and easily create and run macros for routine tasks.

With power comes complexity, and that is what makes a friendly, comprehensive guide like *COMPUTE!'s Using Microsoft Excel on the IBM* so important.

But, while the book completely covers information for the *Excel* novice, the experienced user will be at home here, too. From manipulating databases to creating macro functions (virtually a programming language in itself), *COMPUTE!'s Using Microsoft Excel on the IBM* grows with you as your *Excel* skills increase.

Besides databases, graphs, and macros, separate chapters are also devoted to printing, formulas and functions, and using *Excel* with other programs. Of special interest is the section concerning linking *Excel* files to the external world. *Excel's* windowing and workspace capabilities are also discussed, along with using *Excel* in a network where files can be shared with other users.

So relax. Packed with hundreds of step-by-step examples and clear illustrations, *COMPUTE!'s Using Microsoft Excel on the IBM* will ease your learning process, and help you create and analyze spreadsheet data faster than you ever thought possible.

Acknowledgments

No book gets done in a vacuum. Production of a book like this takes cooperation and help from a number of people, in an assortment of ways. We wish to thank:

Bill Gladstone, Waterside Productions, superagent.

Stephen Levy and Lynne Weatherman, COMPUTE! Books, for steady counsel and cooperation under stress.

The unnamed crew who run the *Excel* Help desk at Microsoft, for cheerful, on target help whenever we had a problem.

David Harvey, for defusing a major interruption.

Bob Fry, for moral support and straight answers to programming questions.

Chapter 1
Introducing *Excel*

Microsoft *Excel* is a spreadsheet program that incorporates graphics and a number of features that allow you to share data with other programs. Built into the spreadsheet are powerful functions and macro programming commands with which you can develop more complex and automated spreadsheets as you get used to the program.

Excel also has a variety of database features that let you create and modify records, sort your data, and query it with criteria you specify.

What's a Spreadsheet?

Think about planning a budget for an event you and a committee will offer one weekend several months from now. How do you know how much to ask as a registration fee? How will rooms and meals be handled? Will all the payments arrive at once, or will they come in over a period of time? Will you need to pay all your event-related bills at once, or will payments need to be made at separate times?

Most budgets for an event such as this can't be handled as a single income-and-expense statement. They require several months' worth of budgets, each one showing a carryover of income and expenses from the last period. You can allocate certain income and expense items to each month, knowing you'll be spending most of the event money right around the time of the event. However, you also know the money must be in the account before the event so you can spend it. That means your committee will have to devise a way to get income before the expenses start to accumulate. You may even be able to generate a bit of extra income by putting money not immediately needed in some interest-bearing account and letting the interest help pay some of the bills.

You and your committee devise a strategy whereby a publicity blitz will create the money you need for the first month's expenses. Here's a sample worksheet showing your committee's four-month plan for the event:

	May	June	July	August	Total
Income					
Registration	700	440	300	560	2,000
Room fees	2,000	1,500	1,025	1,000	5,525
Meal package	300	225	125	200	850
Interest	0	12	23	31	66
Total Income	3,000	2,187	1,473	1,781	8,441
Expenses					
Rooms	500			4,900	5,400
Meals	250			600	850
Speaker fees				1,000	1,000
Decorations				100	100
Publicity	50	50		35	135
A/V equipment				75	75
Snacks			75	300	375
Mailing	50	10	10	100	170
Phone	10	10	10	10	40
Total Expenses	860	70	95	7,120	8,145
Difference	2,140	2,117	1,378	−4,339	296

If you know what your costs are likely to be, you can estimate registration and other fees. That's where the ledger sheet and calculator approach come into the planning process. A spreadsheet is an electronic version of such ledger sheets and calculators. It allows you to experiment with different assumptions and quickly see the results.

For instance, in the spreadsheet above, let's say you and your committee have assumed there will be about 100 people attending. Based on that number, you've set your registration fee at $20 per person. What would happen if you raised it to $25 per person in order to cover costs for a dance band and hall rental for one night?

With an electronic spreadsheet such as *Excel*, you could simply change the registration assumptions to reflect the extra $5 per person, insert the expense lines for the band and the hall rental, and watch the spreadsheet calculate the results:

	May	June	July	August	Total
Income					
Registration	875	550	375	700	2,500
Room fees	2,000	1,500	1,025	1,000	5,525
Meal package	300	225	125	200	850
Interest	0	12	23	31	66
Total Income	3,175	2,297	1,548	1,921	8,941
Expenses					
Rooms	500			4,900	5,400
Meals	250			600	850
Speaker fees				1,000	1,000
Decorations				100	100
Publicity	50	50		35	135
A/V equipment				75	75
Snacks			75	300	375
Mailing	50	10	10	100	170
Phone	10	10	10	10	40
Hall rental				200	200
Band				300	300
Total Expenses	860	70	95	7,620	8,645
Difference	2,140	2,117	1,378	−5,699	296

Hey, that's terrific! Does that mean you can just plug in a new value here and there and let the spreadsheet do the calculating for you?

Yes. With a full-function spreadsheet such as *Excel*, you can construct a spreadsheet with formulas and built-in functions so that you can play "what if?" with your data as much as you need, letting the program display the results for each new set of assumptions.

Excel's power lets you run multiple-year analyses of real-estate portfolios, or statistical analyses of several years' worth of population changes, or monthly budget forecasts broken down by department, or sensitivity analysis on market-share data. Then, when you have a set of data you want to show someone else, you can turn it into any of seven different kinds of charts, formatted in whatever way best suits your needs. Or, if you prefer, you can enter your data directly into a graph.

And because number-crunching seldom is done in a vacuum, you can share your spreadsheet files with a co-worker, perhaps one who doesn't even have *Excel*. As long as the destination program can recognize one of the types of files that *Excel* is capable

Chapter 1

of producing, your spreadsheet file can be given to your co-worker on a floppy disk or be sent electronically, then used at its destination.

But to give you a feel for the kinds of things you can do on a simpler level, consider your revised budget (above). Wouldn't it be great if you could keep track of all the registration data with *Excel*, too?

You can. Look at the worksheet in Figure 1-1, set up so that you also can use it as a working database. Note that as you update your database, you can transfer figures from the totals for each column directly to the working budget for the event.

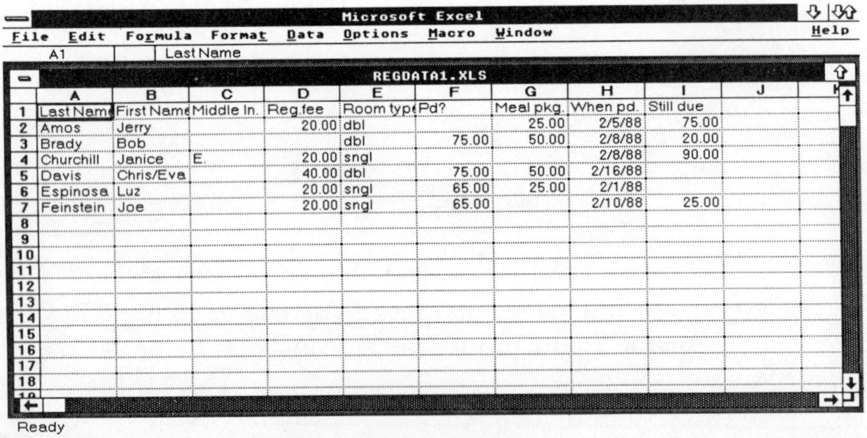

	A	B	C	D	E	F	G	H	I	J
1	Last Name	First Name	Middle In.	Reg.fee	Room type	Pd?	Meal pkg.	When pd.	Still due	
2	Amos	Jerry		20.00	dbl		25.00	2/5/88	75.00	
3	Brady	Bob			dbl	75.00	50.00	2/8/88	20.00	
4	Churchill	Janice	E	20.00	sngl			2/8/88	90.00	
5	Davis	Chris/Eva		40.00	dbl	75.00	50.00	2/16/88		
6	Espinosa	Luz		20.00	sngl	65.00	25.00	2/1/88		
7	Feinstein	Joe		20.00	sngl	65.00		2/10/88	25.00	

Figure 1-1. Spreadsheet as Registration Database

Because people sometimes see relationships between numbers better when they're presented in graphic displays such as charts rather than in columns of numbers, you might also choose to turn your budget into a pie chart, to show your committee how much is being spent for each category.

Since your rooms and meals are basically billed at cost, you don't have to include them. The registration fee and any incidental income let you pay for the program, and that's what your committee would probably be more concerned about. Figure 1-2 is a chart showing how that money would be spent, based on the second budget.

Introducing Excel

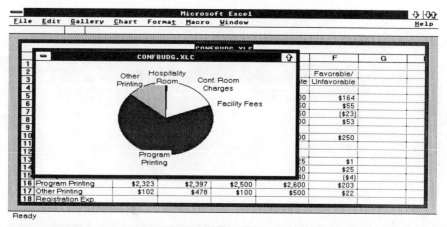

Figure 1-2. Chart of Program Budget Items

Each of these two sets of auxiliary data, the registration database and the chart, can be stored as separate files and be viewed and printed, or they can be modified whenever necessary. Data in each of the files can be used with other *Excel* files so that the whole group becomes interactive.

And that's part of what makes *Excel* so powerful. It's easy to learn and to use, and a grasp of even the simplest concepts in spreadsheets lets you be productive right away.

What's on the Screen?

When you start *Excel*, a blank worksheet appears on your computer screen (Figure 1-3). The lines at the top and the bottom of the screen contain information that varies according to what you're doing. Your data goes in the middle part, the one with columns labeled A–J and rows labeled 1–17. The bars at the top and bottom of the screen contain several different types of data, sometimes showing you what you've done, sometimes telling you options that are available to you, and sometimes giving you status or error messages.

Chapter 1

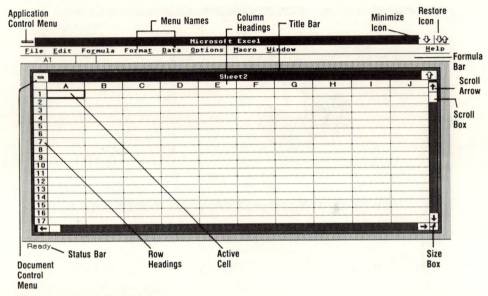

Figure 1-3. Blank Worksheet

Generally, you won't need to be involved with the Application Control bar and its menu, or the Document Control bar and its menu, in your initial work with *Excel*. Most of the menus you'll work with are in the Menu bar, which is the bar containing the words *File*, *Edit*, *Formula*, *Format*, *Data*, *Options*, *Macro*, *Window*, and *Help*. Choosing any of these words results in a pull-down menu appearing on the screen (Figure 1-4).

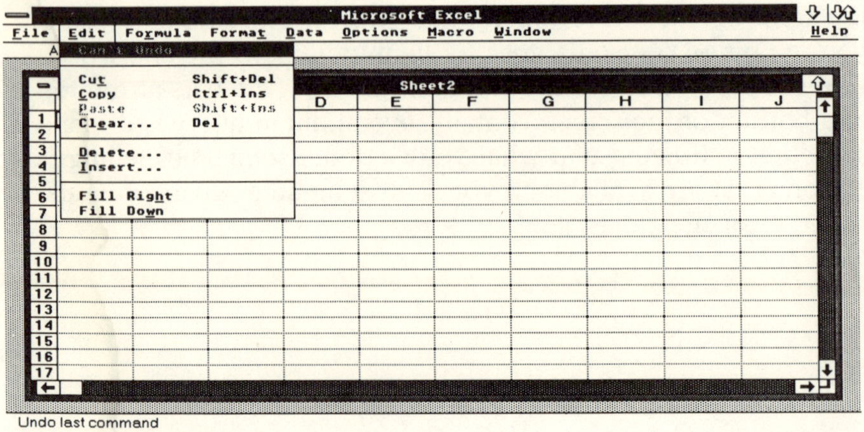

Figure 1-4. Edit Menu

The next bar below the Menu bar is the Reference area, which contains information about the active cell, the kind of activity you can perform (entering data or canceling what you've typed), the contents of the active cell if you have data or a formula entered in it, and where you are in your current typing of data.

The dark bar below that shows the title of the current spreadsheet file. If you have several files active at once, you may see their titles as if the files were pages stacked one on top of another (Figure 1-5).

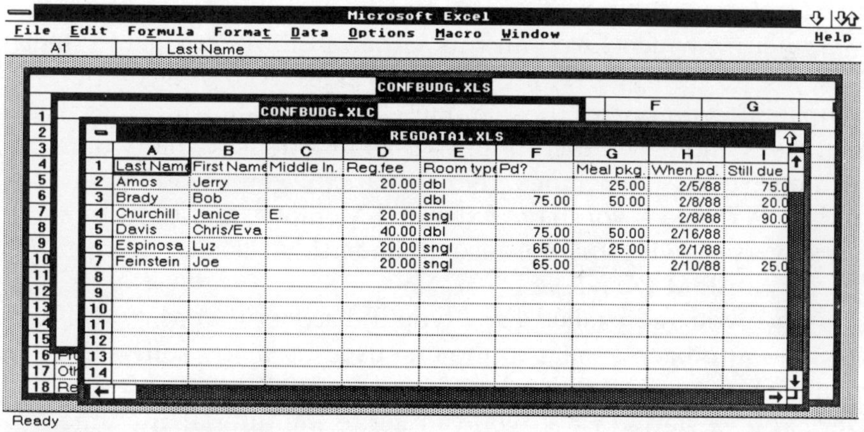

Figure 1-5. Several Open Files

The shaded bar to the right side of the worksheet is the scroll bar that lets you move backward and forward through your file. The shaded bar below the screen is another type of scroll bar, one that lets you move to the right or left within your worksheet. Both are especially useful if you have a mouse installed on your computer.

The bar at the very bottom of your screen is the Status bar. It shows information about the currently selected command and describes the current state of your workspace within *Excel*. The left side of the Status bar is the message area, which displays information about commands, dialog boxes, and processing information. You may see messages here about the current mode and about what *Excel* is doing behind the scenes; other information includes warnings about nondefault settings you have chosen.

The right side of the Status bar is the keyboard indicator

Chapter 1

area, which indicates whether you've selected some key with a special function: Caps Lock, Num Lock, the over-type key (Ins), and so on.

The arrows and angle at the bottom right corner of the screen are related to the size of the worksheet area on your screen and the placement of it relative to the center of the screen. Later in this book, you'll see how to change the size of a worksheet on your screen and how to move it around.

What You Get with the Package

When you open the Microsoft *Excel* package, you find several disks and several books. The disks were designed for the type of computer on which *Excel* can run: either an IBM Personal System/2–Series, an IBM PC AT, a Compaq Deskpro 386, or a computer compatible with one of these models. Your package includes 3½-inch disks and/or 5½-inch floppy disks in a density that works with one of these machines. (Note that *Excel* can't work on an IBM PC XT unless you have Extended Memory, and even then it works very slowly. It is not recommended that you try to run *Excel* on an IBM PC XT.)

Once you've installed *Excel*, you'll discover that Microsoft has taken an approach similar to the one used by many software manufacturers: providing a built-in tutorial with the software. Once you've started *Excel*, you can get to the tutorial any time you want by selecting the Help menu from the Menu bar and choosing the Tutorial.

The tutorial is usually stored on disk when you install *Excel*, which means that you can get to it any time you need a refresher on some point. The tutorial has six general parts. You can choose any of them and see lessons on how to use *Excel*. The lessons also offer several alternatives for learning, including screens of information, some exercises, and even some hints on what to do if you can't figure it out by yourself. As a rule, you can skip from topic to topic as the need strikes you.

The Feature Guide, also available from the Help menu, gives you more data, arranged differently from the way the Tutorial presents it. With it, you can get instant information about how to state a command or how to use a feature, for example.

Generally, each section has a quick introduction, a demonstration of how to use the feature(s) discussed, a "side trip" showing some of the options and procedures, and some hands-on examples.

And, if that's not enough, when you press F1, you get an index, arranged alphabetically, of Help topics.

Then, of course, there are the manuals. The *Reference Guide* is arranged alphabetically by topic, with a complete discussion of the topic and any options that may apply. There are also cross-references to other topics that may provide related information. The Functions and Macros manual is basically a reference manual that lists each of the functions and shows how to use them. Plus, it contains several chapters about the macro functions available within *Excel* and demonstrates how to use macros.

Additionally, there are two other manuals. *Getting Started and Quick Reference* is the one you'll use when you begin the Tutorial and again later when you want just a quick reminder about how to do things within *Excel*. The *Sampler and Idea Book* provides some examples of how to use *Excel* for reporting, financial analysis, tracking data, planning and forecasting, scientific equations, and automating your work.

You can also sign up for ongoing support; just call the Microsoft Customer Support number—(206) 882-8089 in Washington and Alaska, or (800) 426-9400 elsewhere. However, to be eligible for the support program, you must register your copy of *Excel* using the registration card that comes with the package.

What Can You Do with a Spreadsheet?

Earlier in this chapter, you saw how *Excel* could help you plan a simple weekend conference. Can it do more?

Definitely.

Consider the schedule in Figure 1-6, created with *Excel*. It shows different job requirements, when they're needed, and who's going to fill them.

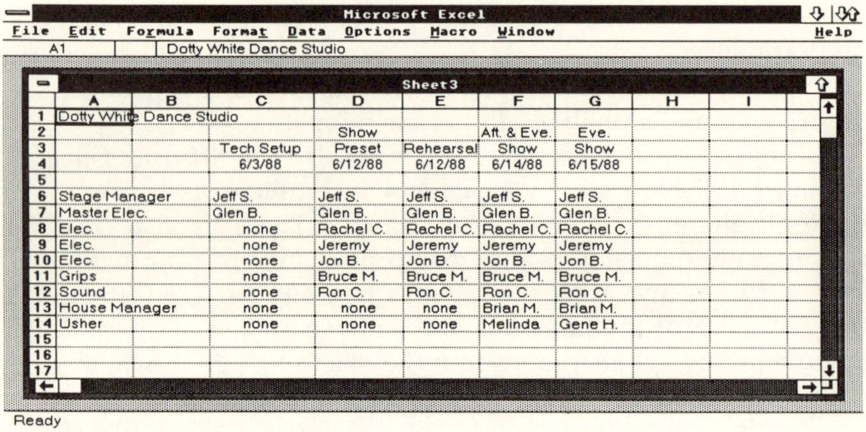

	A	B	C	D	E	F	G	H	I
1	Dotty White Dance Studio								
2				Show		Aft. & Eve.	Eve.		
3			Tech Setup	Preset	Rehearsal	Show	Show		
4			6/3/88	6/12/88	6/12/88	6/14/88	6/15/88		
5									
6	Stage Manager		Jeff S.	Jeff S.	Jeff S.	Jeff S.	Jeff S.		
7	Master Elec.		Glen B.	Glen B.	Glen B.	Glen B.	Glen B.		
8	Elec.		none	Rachel C.	Rachel C.	Rachel C.	Rachel C.		
9	Elec.		none	Jeremy	Jeremy	Jeremy	Jeremy		
10	Elec.		none	Jon B.	Jon B.	Jon B.	Jon B.		
11	Grips		none	Bruce M.	Bruce M.	Bruce M.	Bruce M.		
12	Sound		none	Ron C.	Ron C.	Ron C.	Ron C.		
13	House Manager		none	none	none	Brian M.	Brian M.		
14	Usher		none	none	none	Melinda	Gene H.		
15									
16									
17									

Figure 1-6. Stage-Crew Schedule

How about devising a calendar? You can produce calendars automatically with the Calendar macro by using the CALENDAR. XLM macro sheet on the Library disk; see Figure 1-7. This macro inserted six holidays into the annual calendar, but you could add others. The calendar was annotated by means of the Formula Note command.

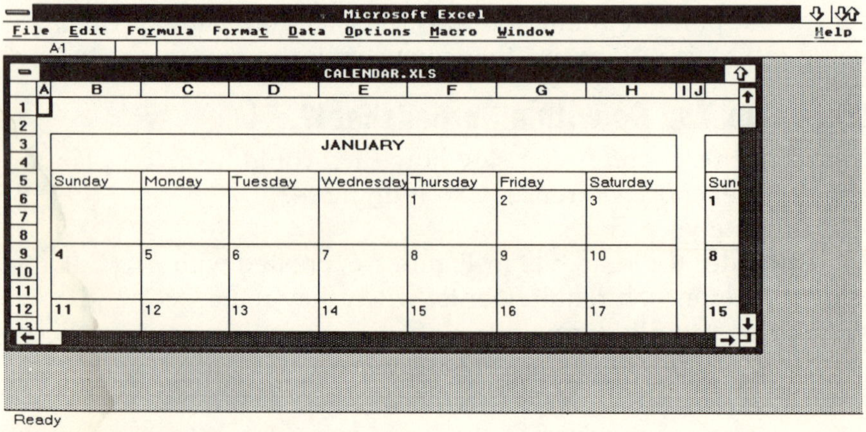

Figure 1-7. Calendar Produced by *Excel*

Of course, you've already seen how you could use data from an *Excel* worksheet to produce a chart. Figure 1-8 contains another example, showing the average monthly rainfall in the U.S. over a one-year period.

Introducing Excel

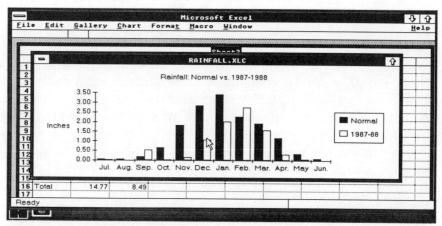

Figure 1-8. Average Monthly Rainfall

"What about financial analysis?" you ask. "How can *Excel* help me do that?" One of the very best applications of a sophisticated spreadsheet results from its ability to do what-if analysis on numbers. And helping you see the results of different financial options is one such application.

Suppose you're considering buying a piece of income property and holding it for 18 months before selling it. What are the factors that could influence your net profit? There are several, but just to keep things simple, let's look at mortgage interest rates and appreciation levels in the area as important factors. Figure 1-9 is a summary of the results of some what-if assumptions in those categories.

	A	B	C	D	E	F	G	H	I
1	Real Estate Workup								
2									
3	Basic Assumptions		Purchase Price		$180,000				
4			Hold Period		18 months				
5									
6	Total Payoff								
7					Mortgage Interest Rate (annual)				
8			8%	9%	10%	11%	12%	13%	14%
9		10%	5400	2700	-2.9E-11	-2700	-5400	-8100	-10800
10	Appreciation	11%	8100	5400	2700	0	-2700	-5400	-8100
11	of Value	12%	10800	8100	5400	2700	0	-2700	-5400
12	per year	13%	13500	10800	8100	5400	2700	0	-2700
13		14%	16200	13500	10800	8100	5400	2700	0
14		15%	18900	16200	13500	10800	8100	5400	2700
15		16%	21600	18900	16200	13500	10800	8100	5400
16		17%	24300	21600	18900	16200	13500	10800	8100
17		18%	27000	24300	21600	18900	16200	13500	10800

Figure 1-9. Possible Outcomes, Real Estate

Suppose you're setting up a small business. You need some idea of what kind of capital you'll need to invest before the business can stand on its own feet, and you'll also need ongoing help in the form of billing and invoicing statements for individual customers, monthly income statements, statements of accounts receivable and accounts payable, salary and tax worksheets, and a host of accounting and finance forms. Can a spreadsheet help you there?

Absolutely. The models in the back of this book will show you some sample worksheets you can adapt to your own situation and use with *Excel* in a business. With *Excel*, you can also have these worksheets "talk" to each other, sharing data and updating figures whenever needed. And easily, too.

Summary

You're about to be introduced to the nuts and bolts of *Excel*, a powerful spreadsheet program from Microsoft. This introductory chapter has given you a brief overview of some of the things you can do with *Excel*, and how to learn from the information that's included in the package.

Chapter 2
Getting Started

Microsoft *Excel* for the IBM AT, PS/2, and compatible computers is one of the most powerful spreadsheet programs available on the market today. Yet it has been designed to be easy to use and easy to learn.

Installing *Excel*

If you have a hard disk:

- Put the Setup disk in the floppy disk drive that the computer regards as drive A, and at the C: prompt type

    A:SETUP

- Then press the Enter key.

Excel's Setup program will guide you through the steps you need to take to install the program on your hard disk and configure it to recognize the equipment you're using. When the Setup program has finished, you'll be told which directory *Excel* is in and how to access it. If you've used the defaults, you'll be expected to type the following:

    CD\WINDOWS

and press Enter, then type

    EXCEL

and press Enter.

The first command results in your changing to the *Windows* directory, in which the *Excel* program and supporting subprograms are stored. The second command causes the *Excel* program to start, with the result that you'll see the opening screen.

If you are working with floppy disks:

Chapter 2

- Put the Setup disk in the drive your computer recognizes as drive A, and, at the A: prompt, type

    SETUP

- Then press the Enter key.

Excel's Setup program will guide you through the steps necessary to install the program correctly on your floppy disks. When you've finished with Setup, type

    EXCEL

and press Enter. The program displays the opening screen.

A Quick Tour

In Chapter 1 you got a general idea of what is on the *Excel* opening screen. In this chapter, you'll learn more about the screen and the special functions of some of the keys on your keyboard.

Commands and Menus

You get *Excel* to do things for you by issuing commands. These commands are grouped under the keywords shown at the top of the screen, in the Menu bar. You invoke the keyword by either touching it with the mouse pointer and dragging it down, or by pressing the Alt key and typing the underlined letter in the keyword. You can also invoke the keyword by pressing the Alt key and using the right- and left-arrow keys to highlight the word you want. In any case, once *Excel* knows which keyword you want, it displays the menu of related commands.

If you're used to the *Lotus 1-2-3* style of invoking commands, you can also press the / key, which works the same way that pressing the Alt key does.

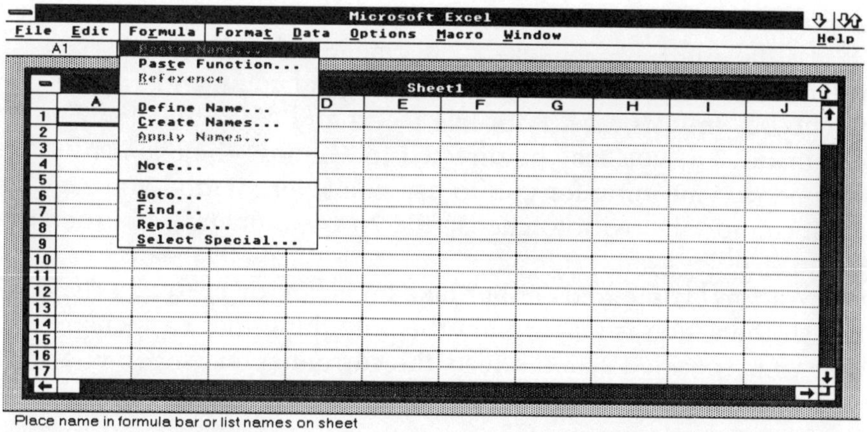

Figure 2-1. Formula Menu

    Figure 2-1 is an example of what menus look like. The shaded bar indicates the option you want. The Status bar, at the bottom, indicates which action will be taken if that command is selected. Initially, the shaded bar is over the top item, but you can use the mouse pointer or the arrow keys to move the shaded bar to any of the other commands shown. You can also bypass the actions of the shaded bar by typing the underlined letter of the command you want.

    When you press the Enter key or release the mouse pointer, the option indicated by the shaded bar is the one *Excel* acts upon. If you've typed a letter, *Excel* takes the related option.

    What happens next depends on what that command does. The commands with ellipses following them (such as Paste Function. . .) have dialog boxes that prompt you for further information. We'll look at dialog boxes in a moment.

    Some commands shown in lighter characters, such as Reference and Apply Names. . . appear in the example shown in Figure 2-1. The lighter typeface means that these options aren't available to you at the moment—usually because some other situation needs to occur first. In the example in Figure 2-1, the Paste Name. . . function, while in the shaded box, is nonetheless not available and is shown in a lighter typeface since no names had been created for this spreadsheet when the menu was called.

    If you press the Enter key while one of the lighter-shaded commands is highlighted, *Excel* warns you with a beep.

    Throughout this book, when you're to choose a particular

menu and command, you'll be directed to do something like "Press the Alt + F + N keys." This means to press the Alt key, then the underlined letters in the menu and command you need to choose—in this case, F for File menu and N for the New File command. Or, you may be directed to "Choose the File New command," meaning for you to use whatever method you are most comfortable with to choose the New command from the File menu.

All *Excel* commands either take an action or present a dialog box. If the action is taken, then the only thing that happens is that your specified action affects the current spreadsheet, and it reappears on your screen.

Dialog Boxes

A dialog box is a box of choices that appears on your screen, overlaying your current work. It is a bit like a command menu, but it offers more options, allowing you to make some very specific choices about how something is to work.

To give you an idea of how a dialog box works, let's take a look at the Fonts dialog box, available when you choose the Format Fonts command.

The Fonts dialog box lets you choose from four different appearances of ten-point Helvetica: normal, bold, italic, or bold italic. These choices are shown in the Fonts box. You can use up to four fonts in a worksheet, and these can be any combination of sizes and styles for one or more fonts.

Notice the buttons to the left of each of the choices. The dark button is the one that will be activated if you make a choice. You can use a mouse or the arrow keys on your keyboard to choose either the default (in this case, normal ten-point Helvetica), or one of the other choices. Your choice applies to the material on your worksheet that you've already selected, be that one or more cells or individual characters within a cell.

The longer bars on the right are to be used when you've finished choosing the items on the dialog box that have buttons associated with them. Standard for most of the dialog boxes are bars that say *OK* and *Cancel*. If you choose the OK button (you can use the mouse pointer to choose it, or you can highlight it using the Tab key and then choose it by pressing the Enter key), the highlighted choice is taken. In the example shown in Figure

2-2, the selected material will be displayed (and printed) in ten-point Helvetica, normal print.

If you choose the Cancel bar, any choices you may have made in the dialog box (without pressing the Enter key) will be ignored, and you'll be returned to your worksheet. You can choose the Cancel bar by clicking on it with your mouse, by moving the highlight to it with the Tab key and pressing Enter, or by pressing the Esc key.

This dialog box has another option: the Fonts⟩⟩ bar. If you choose this (select it with your mouse, use the Tab key to highlight it and then press the Enter key, or type the letter *o*), you'll see an expanded Fonts dialog box (Figure 2-2).

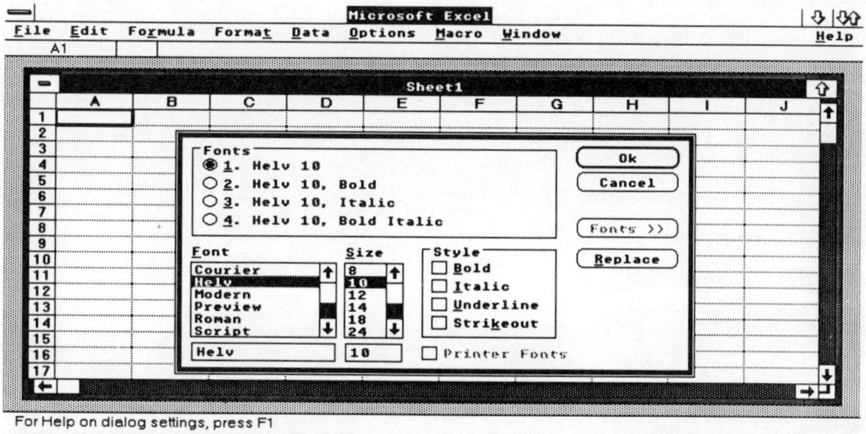

Figure 2-2. Expanded Fonts Dialog Box

This expanded version gives you more choices. Like many dialogs, it's subdivided into more boxes, each with a list of choices.

In this case, the lower Fonts box shows you other typefaces that you can use. You can install more fonts with the Control Panel, which is discussed later in this chapter. Each font listed is a particular typeface and comes in a variety of sizes and styles.

If you have a mouse, click or drag on the arrow on the right side of the list box to highlight the selection you want. If you're using a keyboard, press Alt and the key for the underlined letter or number to move to a list box or to a check box. Then press the up- and down-arrow keys to move from selection to selection within a list box.

Under the list of typefaces and sizes are two blank boxes, called *Text boxes*. Your selection goes here. In some dialog boxes, if you highlight the item you want in the list, it appears in the box. In other cases, you'll have to type what you want.

A text box uses some special editing techniques:

Action	Key Used
Move one character to the right or left, including text that continues beyond border of text box	Right- or left-arrow
Extend selection one character right or left	Shift + right- or left-arrow
Move to beginning of text line	Home
Extend selection to beginning of text line	Shift + Home
Move to end of text line	End
Extend selection to end of text line	Shift + End
Erase character to left	Backspace
Erase selection or character to right	Del
Copy selection to Clipboard	Ctrl + Ins
Move selection to Clipboard	Shift + Del
Paste contents of Clipboard	Shift + Ins

The Style box shows a different method of choosing. This box shows check boxes, a method available when you can specify one or more of the choices shown. To move around a Style box and select something, use the mouse to click on the box or boxes you want; or use the arrow keys to move up or down the list, and then press the space bar to choose the items you want.

Once you've specified what you want, choose the Replace button. If you don't like your choices or you've changed your mind, choose the Cancel button. However, note that Cancel can't undo any changes you've made previously—it only cancels the command and closes the dialog box. To undo something you've chosen to replace, go back through the steps outlined above and choose the original font, size, and style.

The process described above for the Font dialog box applies to the other dialog boxes, with individual variations depending on content. Almost all have both an OK and Cancel button. Most have choices arranged in lists, with buttons to indicate which ones you want. Some have bars where you must type something—a word to match, for instance, in the Formula Replace dialog box, or the word you want to use as a password in the Options Protect dialog box. Some have check boxes that you can turn on or off, such as those found in the Format Border dialog box.

Short Menus vs. Long Menus

Once you've become familiar with the menu structure of *Excel*, you can choose the Short Menu version. This gives you a list of the most commonly used commands—the ones you'll probably use on a routine basis for worksheets, macros, and charts.

Figure 2-3 shows an example of the full menu for File. Figure 2-4 shows an example of the same File menu in the shorter version.

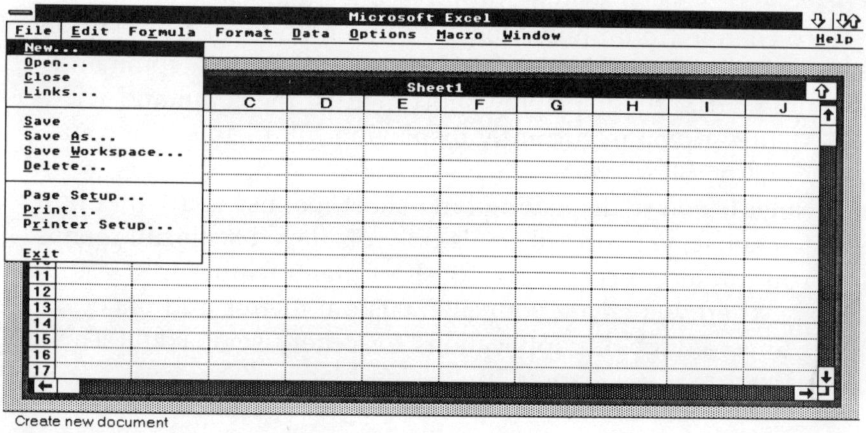

Figure 2-3. File Menu, Full Menu Option

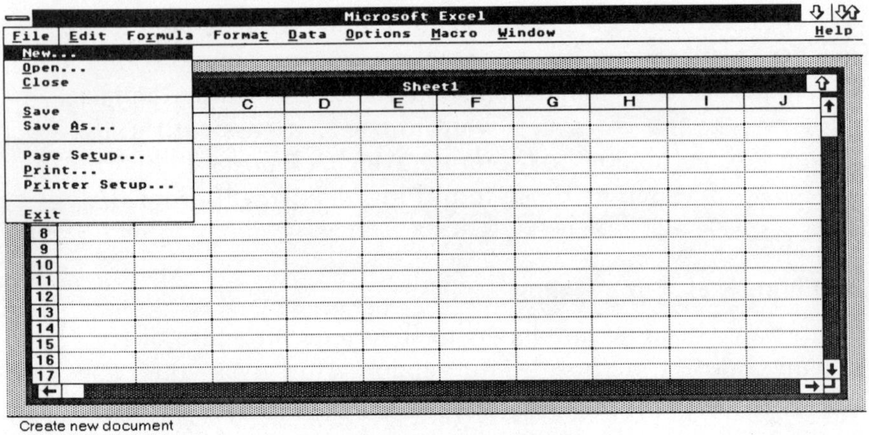

Chapter 2

Figure 2-4. File Menu, Short Menu Option

The full menu contains everything on the short menu plus all the commands for more specialized tasks such as linking to a network file, or special search-and-replace techniques.

To change from Short Menus to Full Menus, or from Full to Short, use the Options menu and choose the bottom command. (If you're currently displaying short menus, the command will be Full Menus; if you're currently displaying full menus, the command will be Short Menus.)

Note: If you're displaying only short menus, you won't be able to choose a command that's only displayed with full menus.

You can also incorporate the short-menu feature into your display when you create your own custom menus and dialog boxes to go along with applications for other users. You'll learn more about that in Chapter 10, "Using Macros."

Control Menus

There are two extra menus which are not always obvious when you press the Alt key. They are accessed through the lines that look like handles in the upper left corner of the screen and the upper left corner of the worksheet. These lines actually are prompts for the key you press along with the Alt key in order to see these menus.

The one in the upper left corner is *Excel*'s symbol for the space bar; press Alt + space bar and you'll see the control menu that appears in Figure 2-5.

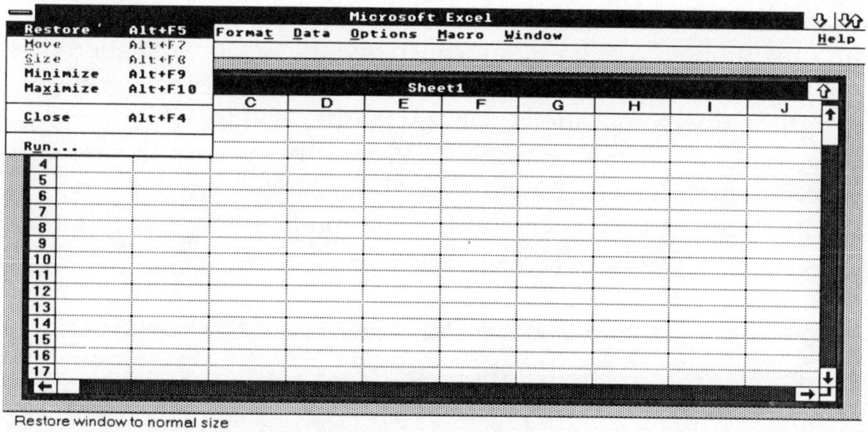

Getting Started

Figure 2-5. Control Menu—Applications

This menu lets you control an application window. Its companion, the Document Control menu, lets you control the window for an individual document.

These control menus can get very confusing if you begin to play around with them before you understand the concepts behind windows. What follows will give you a brief overview of what they do; you may also need to spend a fair amount of time reading about them in the *Excel Reference Manual*.

By doing this exercise (working with a new, blank spreadsheet), you'll see how to use the control menus. If you have anything on your screen at this moment, save it and close it; then open a new file.

Press Alt + space bar; then choose Size (type the letter *S*, or move the shaded bar so that it's over Size, and press Enter). Once you get used to using the Control commands, you can go straight to the command without using the menu—just type Alt and press the function key for the command you want. That's what Alt + F5 means, for instance; it's the shortcut key for the Size command.

On the middle of your screen is a four-headed arrow, which means that *Excel* wants to know which edge you want to alter. Let's move the left edge of the screen over to the right about a column's width.

Press the right-arrow key. This creates a small arrow at the left edge of the screen.

Use your mouse to drag the arrow to the right one column

Chapter 2

width. If you're using a keyboard, use the right-arrow key to do the same thing. Notice that as you move the arrow, a shaded line appears from the top to the bottom of the screen. This marks where the new applications window border will be when you press the Enter key. Also notice that the other part of the arrow appears when this line moves away from the left edge. Keep moving this line until it is over the column line between columns A and B. The result looks like Figure 2-6.

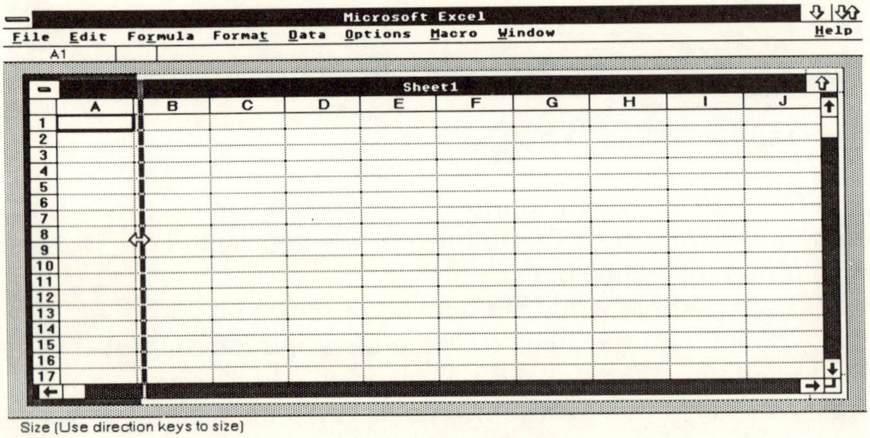

Figure 2-6. Moving the Left Edge of the Window

You can continue to move this edge to the right or left, if you like. The position the edge is in when you press the Enter key is where the left edge of your workspace will be for any worksheets you construct during this session of *Excel*. If you exit to DOS and come back, you'll find the standard-size worksheet in use, even if you saved your experimental version with an adjusted size.

If you haven't done so, press the Enter key. Your screen will probably look like the one in Figure 2-7.

Getting Started

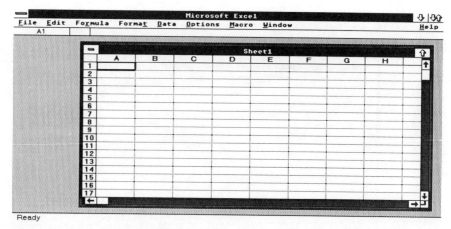

Figure 2-7. Worksheet with Adjusted Size

You can adjust any of the four borders of your work area with the Size command. Just follow the steps outlined above.

At this point, the Restore command you saw on the Control menu won't restore your worksheet to its earlier size. The Restore command refers only to actions taken by the last Maximize or Minimize command.

To restore your worksheet to its original size, press Alt + space bar and choose the Size command again. Since you want to restore the left edge to its former position, press the left-arrow key, or with your mouse drag the four-headed arrow to the left edge. Next, move the two-headed arrow to the left, all the way to the left edge of the screen. Then press the Enter key. Now your screen looks the way it did originally.

The document window is controlled through an identical menu, but to get to it you press Alt + Hyphen (-). The document control menu works best when you have two or more files open, such as two worksheets. To see what it does, first open a new file (choose the File New command); then repeat the process described above. You won't be able to position the shaded line exactly on the column line between columns A and B, so choose something close by.

Notice that when you press the Enter key, the current worksheet is shifted to the right, but the worksheet under it remains positioned at the left edge of the workspace on your screen. Your screen may now look something like the one shown in Figure 2-8.

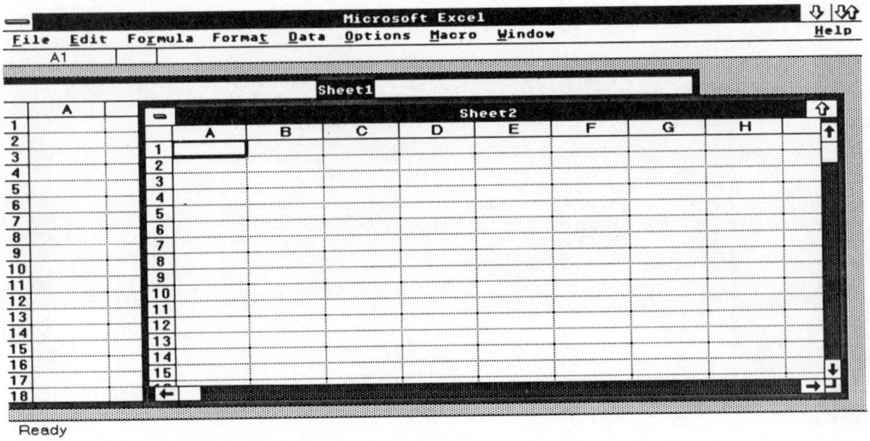

Chapter 2

Figure 2-8. Two Worksheets, One Sized

The purpose of this set of commands is to let you work with more than one window on your screen at a time. This may come in handy when you're constructing something fairly elaborate: One part of your screen shows some data in worksheet form, while another has a chart, and a third has some explanatory text. Each portion can be assembled in a separate window and sized appropriately with the document-control commands.

If you want to use a particular window size as a default for all of your subsequent work, save the current settings with the File Save Workspace command, and use the default filename and extension shown in the dialog box.

Info Menu

You can get detailed information about the active cell (the one containing the highlighted cursor) by using the Info Window, available on the Window menu. The Info Window lets you see the cell address, any formula in the cell, the value this formula produces, the format settings for the cell, any protection that has been applied to the cell, any notes attached to the cell, and both the list of cells that refer to this cell (precedents) and the list of cells that this cell refers to (dependents).

The Info window is especially useful in debugging a worksheet, particularly one that uses macros or one that has formulas or other data manipulation that isn't obvious to another user. When used in conjunction with the Formula Find command, it helps you find specific cell information rapidly.

To use the Info window, be sure that Full Menus is the option currently in effect; then choose the Show Info command from the Windows menu. You'll see a box drop down over the upper right corner of your screen, as in Figure 2-9, containing data about the active cell.

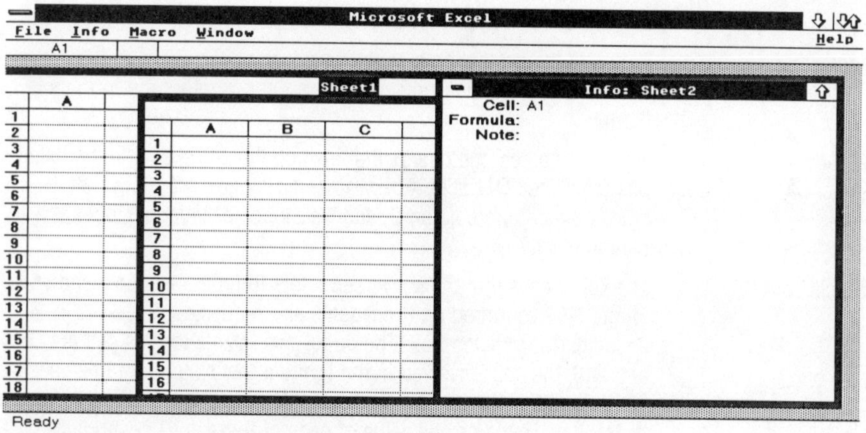

Figure 2-9. Info Window

If you want the Info window to disappear, choose the Show Document command on the Window menu.

You can use the Control commands to move or adjust the Info window just as you would any other window.

The top bar of the Info window shows the name of the worksheet for which it is displaying information.

When the Info window is on your screen, notice that the commands available on the Menu bar have also changed. When you choose Show Info, you still have access to all the File, Macro, and Window commands, but you also have a set of Info commands on their own separate menu.

These commands let you specify what you want to display in the Info window. Initially, this window displays three types of data about the active cell: the cell address, the formula, and any notes attached to the cell. You can specify any or all of the Info options, so it's possible to see all nine types of data in this window.

To choose the type of information you want, select the Info menu. Below are the choices you'll see.

Info Menu Choice	Description
Cell	The address of the active cell
Formula	The formula (if any) used in this cell (the same as what's displayed in the formula bar)
Value	The value produced by the contents of the active cell
Format	The format settings for the current cell; includes number format, alignment, font, borders, and shading
Protection	Refers to the protection mechanisms currently in use with the active cell; includes whether the cell is locked and whether the formula is hidden
Names	Refers to named cell ranges that include the active cell (In the example above, cell D17 is part of two named ranges: March, which includes the data in column D, and Net_Income, which includes the data in row 17.)
Precedents	The list of cells that the active cell refers to (In the example shown in Figure 2-9, we turned on Precedents and requested All Levels in the accompanying dialog box. The direct precedents for this cell are D6 and D16, the cells involved in the formula that's stored in this cell. Those would be shown if we selected the Direct Only option in the dialog box. However, the value of each of these cells depends on formulas, too, so the All Levels option lists the cells involved in those formulas, as well.)
Dependents	Lists the cells where the results shown in the active cell are used (As with Precedents, there are direct and indirect dependents, and you can choose Direct Only or All Levels in a dialog box.)
Note	The text of any notes you've appended to this cell (Here is one of the best features of an advanced spreadsheet: the ability to add comments to a cell explaining what you've done and to have those comments travel with the cell if the cell gets moved. You won't see the notes unless you specifically ask for them.)

A special tip about using notes: You create a note for a particular cell with the Formula Notes command, which is covered in Chapter 5. You can scroll through all the notes for this worksheet with the Formula Select Special command, which is also covered in Chapter 5.

Chart Menus

There's a complete set of menus you don't see unless you specifically issue a command to work with charts. Generally, you won't want to work with them unless you have a set of data you'd like to chart or you already have an existing chart which you wish to change.

To see some of your data in chart form, select the data (by pressing F8 and choosing the appropriate cells), and choose the File New command.

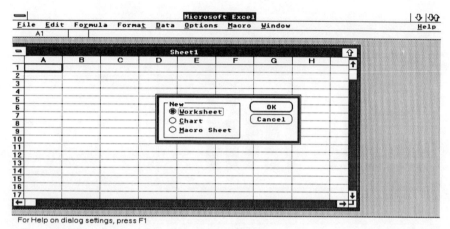

Figure 2-10. File New Dialog Box

You want to create a chart, so choose the Chart button and then press the Enter key. *Excel* uses its default values to arrange the selected data in chart form, as in Figure 2-11.

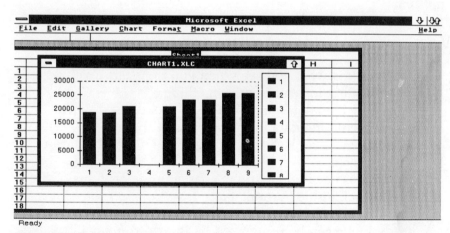

Figure 2-11. Chart from Selected Data

Charts occupy an application window and can be moved and sized with the control commands.

Notice the menu bar at the top of the chart window. Each word represents a set of menus covering commands that pertain

Chapter 2

to charts. Some of the menus, such as the File and Macro menus, are fairly similar to menus for worksheets. Some, however, are quite different. Figure 2-12 contains the Gallery menu.

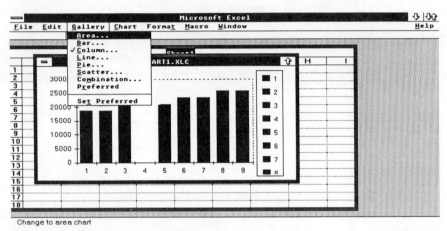

Figure 2-12. Gallery Menu, Chart Window

Chapter 9 is devoted to working with charts, so this is enough detail about them for now.

Modes

Excel has several modes of operation, each allowing you to perform a different category of actions.

> *Ready mode* is what you see when you first start *Excel*, when it is waiting for you to do something.
> *Enter mode* is the ordinary data-entry mode, used when you're entering data in the active cell.
> *Point mode* lets you select cell ranges when you're entering formulas.
> *Edit mode* is used when you're changing the contents of the active cell in the Formula bar.

Ready mode can be recognized by the word *Ready* in the Status bar at the bottom of the screen, either when you have a blank worksheet on your screen or when you've opened one of your files but haven't started using it. The Formula bar is not active. The moment that you start entering data anywhere or that you change to Edit mode, the word *Ready* disappears from the Status bar, and is replaced with the name of the mode that's appropriate to what you're doing.

Enter mode is so simple you may not even notice it. Enter mode is the mode you're in the moment you start typing anything in a cell. The Formula bar is activated, and you can use the movement selection keys to go from cell to cell. When you've finished entering data in a cell, either press the Enter key, click the enter box with your mouse, or press an arrow key to indicate where you want the next active cell to be. In Enter mode, you can use the backspace key to erase mistakes if you haven't yet pressed the Enter key, and you can press the Esc key to cancel your entry.

Point mode is entered from Enter mode and is only used for constructing a formula. The Status bar displays the word *Point* and the Formula bar is active. To use Point mode, make sure the insertion point is immediately after one of the following characters:

$$= (, + - * /$$

Next, select the cell or cell range you want to use in your formula. If you're using a keyboard, use the arrow keys to select the first cell in your range. Then type a colon, and use the arrow keys again to select the last cell in the range. The selected cells appear with a dotted line, or marquee, around them, and the cell references for these cells appear in the Formula bar.

If you're using a mouse, click and drag through the range you want. The range affected will appear in the Formula bar.

Once the reference is there, type the next character or finish the formula by pressing the Enter key or clicking the enter box. Point mode disappears when the next character is entered.

Edit mode is used to change the existing contents of the active cell. You can get to Edit mode from either Enter or Ready mode. Once you enter Edit mode, the word *Edit* appears in the Status bar.

To enter Edit mode, press F2 or, with a mouse, click in the Formula bar. Use the arrow keys or your mouse to position the insertion point where you want to start making corrections. Type new characters if you want to insert them, or use the Backspace key to delete characters. If you want to switch to Enter mode before completing the entry, press F2 again. When your editing of

Chapter 2

the cell is complete, press Enter or click the Enter box with your mouse.

Using *Excel* with a Keyboard

Excel is designed to work with either a keyboard or a mouse. If you don't have a mouse, you'll want to look at this section. The next section discusses moving around the screen with a mouse.

The Help section within *Excel* has a special Help Keyboard subsection that provides a lot of information on using the keyboard with *Excel*. Since it's available any time you're using *Excel*, use it as a reminder whenever you have difficulty with keyboard matters.

Moving Around the Worksheet

The following list describes how to move one cell at a time.

Action	Key Used
Move up a cell (or row)	Up-arrow
Move down a cell (or row)	Down-arrow
Move right a cell (or column)	Right-arrow
Move left a cell (or column)	Left-arrow

Some keys allow you to move by a distance larger than one cell at a time. To move the active cell by more than one cell at a time, follow the steps in the following table.

Action	Key Used
Move to start of row containing active cell	Home
Move to end of row containing active cell (last occupied column of worksheet)	End
Move to start of data	Ctrl + Home
Move to end of data	Ctrl + End
Move by one block of data right, left, up, down	Ctrl and appropriate arrow key

Selecting Data

You can use special keys to select data—data that you want to move or copy or change in some way. When you select a cell or range of cells, *Excel* highlights it on your screen, and notes its coordinates for subsequent action.

Action	Key Used
Select a cell	None—active cell is automatically selected
Extend the selection one cell up, down, right, or left	Shift or F8 and the appropriate arrow key
Extend the selection one block of data up down, right, or left	Ctrl + Shift and the appropriate arrow key
Extend the selection to the beginning of the row	Shift or F8 and Home
Extend the selection to the end of the row (last occupied column of the worksheet)	Shift or F8 and End
Select entire rows containing selected cell or range	Shift + space bar (**Note:** Do not use F8 here; when you press the space bar after pressing F8, the data in the active cell is replaced by a selected cell or range.)
Select entire columns containing selected cell or range	Ctrl + space bar
Extend selection to start of data	Ctrl + Shift + Home
Extend selection to end of data	Ctrl + Shift + End
Extend selection to start of window	Shift + Home (Scroll Lock should be on.)
Extend selection to end of window	Shift + End (Scroll Lock should be on.)
Select entire worksheet	Ctrl + Shift + space bar
Collapse selection to single cell	Shift + Backspace

Moving Within a Selection

For a range selection or for multiple selections within a range, you can use the keys as listed in the table below.

Action	Key Used
Move down one cell in the selection	Enter
Move up one cell in the selection	Shift + Enter
Move right one cell	Tab
Move left one cell	Shift + Tab
Move to the next corner of the area	Ctrl + . (period)
In a multiple selection, move to the next area	Ctrl + Tab
In a multiple selection, move to the previous area	Ctrl + Shift + Tab

Scrolling Within an Active Window

If you have more than one window active, you can move around within the active window with the keys listed in the table below. You'll need to turn on the Scroll Lock key first, however, so that the movement keys indicate movement, not selection.

When the Scroll Lock key is on, you'll see *SCRL* on the right side of the status bar. Remember to turn it off when you're finished moving around within the window.

Action	Key Used
Move one row up or down	Up- or down-arrow
Move one column right or left	Right- or left-arrow
Move one window up or down	PgUp or PgDn
Move one window right	Ctrl + PgUp
Move one window left	Ctrl + PgDn
Move back to display the active cell	Ctrl + Backspace

There are also shortcut keys that are convenient alternatives to choosing most of the commands in *Excel*. They're listed in the Quick Reference Guide in Appendix A.

Using *Excel* with a Mouse

If you're using a mouse with *Excel*, you'll want to look at this section.

All *Excel* tasks work with the keyboard. However, using a mouse makes certain tasks less difficult. A mouse makes it easy and efficient to choose commands and select options in a dialog box, to move and select cells or ranges in a worksheet or chart, to manipulate windows (sizing, moving, enlarging, shrinking, and closing), and to manipulate objects in a chart.

For instance, look at the sample screen in Figure 2-13.

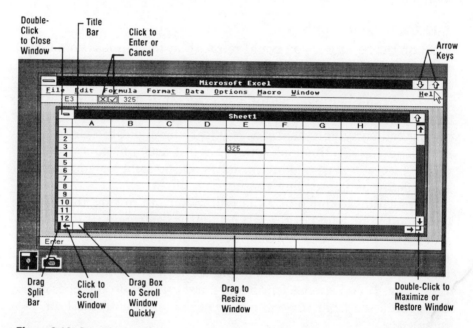

Figure 2-13. Sample Screen

Click the arrow keys to maximize, minimize, or restore the size of the window.

Click the check to enter or the X to cancel the current contents of the formula bar.

Drag the title bar to move the window.

Double-click the hyphen in the upper left corner of the worksheet to close the window.

Drag the split bar in the bottom left corner of the worksheet to split the window into panes.

Click the arrow in the bottom left corner of the worksheet to scroll the window.

Drag the scroll box next to the arrow to speed up scrolling.

33

Drag the bottom bar to size the window (make it larger or smaller).

Double-click the angle icon in the lower right corner to maximize or restore the window.

There are a number of special pointers that are used with a mouse to move around the screen and take certain actions. For a thorough discussion, see the Mouse section of the *Excel* reference manual.

The Undo Command

Wouldn't it be nice if you could retract that thoughtless comment you made last night? How about the gaffe during a business meeting last week?

Excel can't help you with those errors, but it can help you retract that command you just issued by pressing the wrong key, or that cell entry you just made. By learning about the Undo command early in the book, you'll have at least one tool you can use in case you start making mistakes on the samples you'll be constructing in subsequent chapters.

The Undo command on the Edit menu can reverse the last command you issued or the last cell entry you typed. It won't work with the File Delete, Data Delete, or Data Extract commands. It also won't work if you've done something else in the meantime—in particular, something for which you pressed the Enter key. If you choose Undo and *Excel* can't undo the operation, you'll see *Can't Undo* in a gray or lighter face on the Edit menu.

When you choose the Edit menu, you'll see the Undo command in the top bar. Usually the word *Undo* will be paired with whatever command you just issued, such as Paste or Justify.

Generally, the Undo command lets you retract whatever you've typed in the formula bar after you've entered a formula or value in a spreadsheet cell. It also lets you retract all commands on the Edit menu, the Apply Names and Replace commands on the Formula menu and the Paste List option in the Formula Paste Name dialog box, the Justify command on the Format menu, and the Parse and Sort commands on the Data menu.

And if you decide that you really *did* want things the way they were before you selected the Undo command, you can retract the Undo command. The top bar on the Edit menu will say *Redo*, paired with the command that Undo reversed. Choose this command and you'll be back where you were before you issued the Undo command.

Summary

This chapter has given you a brief overview of *Excel* and has shown you what you need to do to get started. Later chapters demonstrate how to use *Excel* to create, modify, and store worksheets, charts, and databases.

Chapter 3
Entering Data and Creating Worksheets

To enter data into an *Excel* worksheet:

- Use the mouse or the cursor keys to move the highlighted cursor to the cell in which you want data to appear.
- Type the data. When you enter data into an *Excel* worksheet, *Excel* displays it in the Formula Bar until you press either the Enter key or one of the directional cursor keys.
- Press the Enter key.

Data in an *Excel* worksheet can be one of several types:

Numeric	Integers, decimals, percentages, currency, date and time values.
Text	Anything entered in a format other than integer, decimal fraction, or scientific notation—for example, Price, JANUARY, 125 Elm Street, "15633".
Logical values	TRUE, FALSE, true, false. These are values that indicate whether a condition exists. *Excel* can evaluate an expression in terms of its truth and store the result as a logical value. You can also enter TRUE or FALSE as data, and *Excel* treats the entry as a logical value. *Excel* also recognizes 0 and 1 as logical values.
Error values	#NUM!, #VALUE!. These are values that are generally produced as error messages when you've entered something that makes it impossible for *Excel* to calculate the formula for that cell. You can enter these if you need to; usually any calculation that references a cell containing an error value will also produce an error value.

Chapter 3

For the most part, data you enter in an *Excel* spreadsheet will be numbers and text. However, you can change the appearance of your data with formatting actions so that it only works in certain kinds of operations and not in others. For instance, if you enter the number

1001001010

and format it as currency, that cell entry ceases to become available as a percentage.

This chapter discusses how you enter data to create a spreadsheet, and what you can do with the spreadsheet once it's made. Chapter 5 shows you how to edit what you've entered, and Chapter 6 shows you how to manipulate your data with formulas and functions.

Creating a Simple Spreadsheet

Let's construct a simple spreadsheet to give you a feel for using one. (A detailed explanation of these concepts follows in the sections below.)

Suppose you took a business trip that had you flying for a meeting in another city, where you had dinner with a client, stayed in a hotel room overnight, met with the client again in the morning, and flew home. You need to submit an expense report to your company to get reimbursed. The following describes what you can do to present that information on a spreadsheet.

- With a clear worksheet on your screen and the active (highlighted) cell in A1, type a title indicating the date and purpose of the trip. For example, type *June 15, 1988 Meeting with Distribution Services* and then press the Enter key.
- Press the down-arrow key twice so that the active cell is in cell A3. Type the word *Expenses* and press the Enter key. To give yourself a bit of room, press the down-arrow key twice again so that you're in cell A5.
- On the next three rows, you'll enter your expenses for travel and hotel room. Use column A for the category label and column B for the numbers. In A5, type the word *Airfare*, and press the Enter key. Press the down-arrow key so that you're in A6, and then type the word *Hotel*. This time, just press the down-arrow key; it's a shortcut for pressing the Enter key and

Entering Data and Creating Worksheets

an arrow key. In A7, type the words *Car rental* and press the down-arrow key.
- Now to enter the figures. Move the active cell to B5 and enter the amount of an airplane ticket: *276.46.* Press the down-arrow key so that you are in B6 and type the figure for the hotel bill: *83.31.* Press the down-arrow key again and type the car rental figure, *42.55,* in B7; then press the down-arrow key.
- You need a tally line, and then you need to add up those figures. A tally line will be a row of underlines, since Excel thinks that a minus sign is an arithmetic operator. In B8, type _____ and press the down-arrow key. In B9, type the formula =B5+B6+B7. (Don't forget the equal sign. Formulas are discussed in detail in Chapter 6.) When you press the Enter key, the result of the formula appears in B9.
- Your company will also reimburse you for meals, which you'll enter in rows 11, 12, and 13. Type the labels *Dinner, Breakfast,* and *Lunch* in A11, A12, and A13, respectively. Dinner with your client cost $65, so type the figure *65.00* in B11. Notice that it appears as an integer; we'll correct that shortly. Type the figure *5.50* in B12 and *7.50* in B13.
- Type a tally line in B14 and press the down-arrow key. In this case, to add up the meal figures, we'll use the SUM function. In B15, type =SUM(B11:B13). (This is the function *Excel* uses to add numbers. Functions are also discussed in Chapter 6.) When you press the Enter key, the result appears in B15.
- The figures will look better if we format them as dollars and cents. Move the active cell to B5 and press F8 to select cells that will be formatted. Press the down-arrow key so that all the cells from B5 through B17 are highlighted. (We'll put a total figure in B17, so that should be formatted as well.) Now choose the Format Number command, and when the dialog box appears, choose the *$#,##0.00* format. Notice that the meal figures change to dollars and cents.
- All that remains is to display a total cost for the trip. In A17, type the abbreviation *Tot.Exp.* (since any more characters would spill over into column B). In B17, type the formula =B9+B15 and press the Enter key.

   You now have a completed expense report which can be printed and handed in. You can also save the worksheet as a file so that it's available if you ever need a backup copy.

39

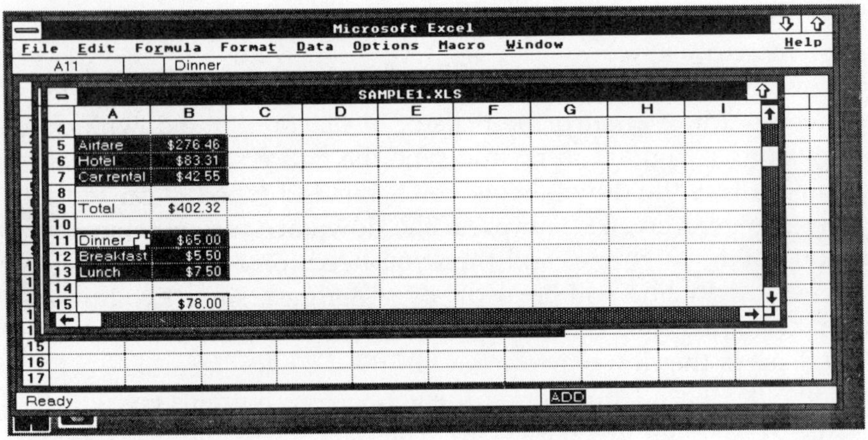

Chapter 3

Figure 3-1. Sample Spreadsheet

Cells and Ranges

A new worksheet shows you 170 cells in which you can enter data, arranged in 10 columns and 17 rows.

    A cell, located at the intersection of a row and a column, is the basic unit of a worksheet. You enter and store data in cells. *Excel* has a total of 256 columns, usually labeled as A through IV (A, B, C, . . . Z; AA, AB, AC, . . . AZ; BA, BB, BC, . . . BZ; . . . IV); and it has 16,384 rows, numbered 1 through 16,384. Simple multiplication shows that there are a maximum of 4,194,304 cells available in an *Excel* worksheet. However, you'll only see some of them at any one time through the *window* on your screen.

    A cell is addressed by its row and column coordinates. Normally, the A1 address style is used: The leftmost column is column A, the next is column B, and so forth, and the top row is 1, the next row is 2, and so forth. The cell four columns from the left edge and six rows down is known in this address style as D6.

    Another address style is permitted in *Excel:* the R1C1 style. With this style, columns are addressed by number, too. An *R* is required before each row number and a *C* is needed before each column number. You can choose this address style on the Options menu.

    There are two kinds of referencing allowed in *Excel: relative* and *absolute.* A relative reference, the default, is one made to another cell a given number of rows and columns away from the current cell. Using a relative reference is like telling someone the nearest gas station is three blocks to the right and one block up.

When you type a formula or issue a command that uses a relative reference to identify another cell, that original cell (D5, which was over three and up one, and is now E14) is used regardless of whether you insert or delete rows or columns.

An absolute reference is to a specific cell, and it will never change regardless of how much moving around occurs in the rest of the spreadsheet. It's a bit like telling someone the gas station is at the intersection of Highway 9 and Stevens Creek Road. An absolute reference is indicated by adding a dollar sign ($) in front of the column letter and row number. For instance, if you're sure you're never going to change the location of what's currently in B15, a formula in another cell might make an absolute reference to that cell by specifying $B$15.

You can mix relative and absolute references. Where you need to keep a row reference absolute but the column reference relative, for example, you may have a cell reference such as C$7.

An example of an absolute column but relative row reference would be $G15.

Selecting and the Active Cell

The active cell is the one where you can currently enter data; it is indicated with a heavy border.

The border (sometimes called a highlight) indicates the cell is selected for activity. You can select more than one cell—for copying or moving, for formatting, or for printing, for instance. If you select more than one cell, the first cell is considered the active cell, and the others are displayed in reverse.

Entering Numbers

When you type a number into a cell, *Excel* recognizes it as a number if it's in one of the formats found in the following table.

Format	Example
Integer	123, −123
Decimal fraction	1.23, 0.123, −.123
Scientific notation	1.23e1, 123E−4

Unless you enter a number in one of the above formats, *Excel* thinks you've entered text.

Chapter 3

However, you can include as a number any of the following characters:

( ) $ %

all of which are used to describe different kinds of numbers, or expressions which can be evaluated as numbers.

You can use + or − signs to indicate positive or negative values, and you can use commas in numbers you enter, such as 1,000,000.

When you type a number, its appearance depends on how the cell into which it is entered has been formatted. We'll look at the number format options available under *Excel* shortly. With no formatting, *Excel* assumes a General format, displaying numbers as accurately as possible given the width of the cell and the number you entered. If you enter a number with a $ or %, the cell format automatically changes to reflect currency or percentages. If you enter a date or time number in one of the appropriate date or time formats, the cell formatting is changed to reflect that type of formatting.

Data Series

You don't have to enter all of your data if you know that subsequent cells in the same row or column will increase or decrease in regular increments, or steps.

Excel's Data Series command, on the Data menu, lets you fill a selected range of cells with numbers or dates.

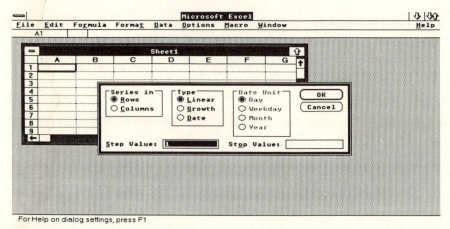

Figure 3-2. Data Series Dialog Box

42

Type the starting value in the first cell of the series, select the row or column you want filled, and choose Data Series. Then you'll see the dialog box shown above.

This is very handy when you're constructing a worksheet with regularly spaced headings, such as an annual budget with columns for each month's projected income and expenses. For instance, suppose you have one month's figures of an annual budget. Type the data on a blank *Excel* spreadsheet as shown in Figure 3-3.

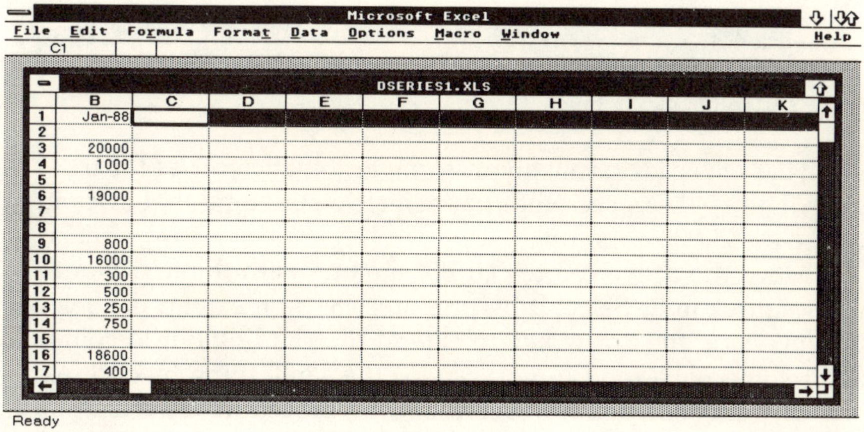

Figure 3-3. Worksheet Before Using Data Series

With the Data Series command, you can direct *Excel* to label the columns for subsequent months. In our spreadsheet, select the row of column headings, row 1, by pressing the F8 key and extending the selection to column M, using the right-arrow key to move the shading to the right.

Then, in the Data Series dialog box (press Alt-D and then choose Series), choose the Month increment and press the Enter key. Since the January information was entered in one of *Excel*'s acceptable date formats, the subsequent columns will show monthly headings for the other months in the year. Now the spreadsheet looks like Figure 3-4.

43

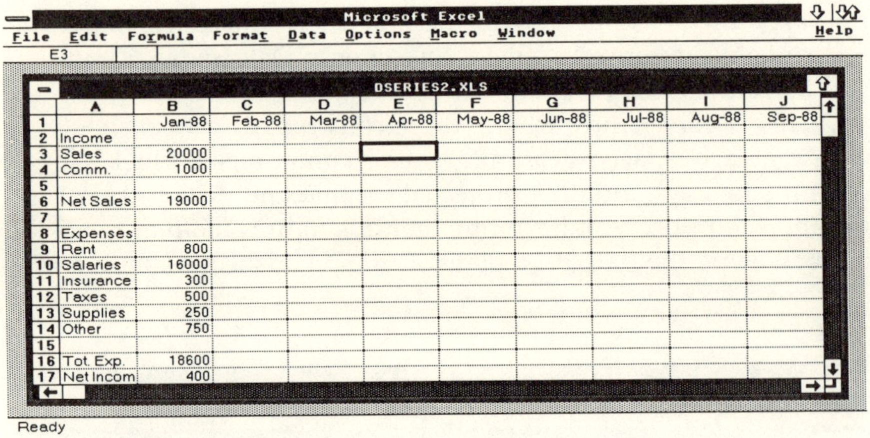

Chapter 3

Figure 3-4. Automatically Entered Column Headings

That was easy. How about some automatic entries for the sales figures? Let's see what happens if we assume that sales increase by $5,000 a month.

Move the active cell to cell B3, the one with the first month's sales figures in it. Select it by pressing F8; then extend the selection by using the arrow key to extend the shading out to column M. If you have a mouse, you can do the same thing by clicking and dragging the pointer. Use the same procedure described above to get the Data Series dialog box, and enter 5000 as the Step Value.

You can use this feature to extend numeric assumptions and assumptions about dates and times. The Type option in the dialog box lets you specify Linear growth, in which the step value is added to each cell in turn to produce the value of the succeeding cell. There's also Growth, in which the step value is multiplied by the value of each cell in turn to produce the value of the succeeding cell. The Date choice lets you work within any of the acceptable date or time formats.

What's Actually Stored

A cell entry in *Excel* can be as many as 255 characters. The standard width for a cell is 8 characters, but a cell can hold more if the characters are any combination of letters and numbers (some letters take up less space than do numbers).

If you enter a number that's too big to fit in the cell according to the usual number formats, *Excel* tries to convert it to scientific notation and display it that way. For instance, if you enter the number

    12345678

into a cell, you'll see that it just fits. However, try entering the number

    123456789

and what you'll see in the cell is 1.23E+08. What you'll see in the formula bar at the top of the screen, however, is exactly what you entered: 123456789.

If, on the other hand, you format the cell into which you type that number as one of the currency formats ($#,### for example), you'll find the character string ######### in the cell where you type the long number.

When you see that character string, it means that *Excel* has tried to fit your number into the cell according to the format you're using and has failed. As with scientific notation, the actual number shows up on the formula bar regardless of what appears in the cell.

These examples are typical of the way *Excel* tries to display your data as you type (or format) it, but the program ends up displaying it differently if the number's original form doesn't fit the current cell limits. The actual contents of the cell remains as you have entered them, and that's what *Excel* uses in formulas, functions, and other manipulations.

When *Excel* manipulates your data—for instance, through multiplication or division—the result may have more decimal places than either of the operands. Where possible, *Excel* rounds off the result so that it can be displayed in the appropriate cell.

However, you may wish to impose some of your own limits on this. For instance, if you've been calculating the amount of interest due on a loan with monthly payments, you're likely to come up with a result that has five or more places after the decimal. Yet you pay only in dollars and cents, expressed as $x.xx.

Rounding errors, small though they may be at any point, can cause problems in the long run. If you use the Precision as Displayed option available on the Options Calcluation menu, *Excel* translates $45.434145 into $45.43 and $67.464802 into $67.46, and

Chapter 3

it stores them that way. In the following table, you can see what happens when this option is used and then what happens when it is not.

	Precision as Displayed:		Left Alone:	
	Entered	Displayed	Entered	Displayed
	$45.434145	$45.43	$45.434145	$45.43
	$67.464802	$67.46	$67.464802	$67.47
Sum:		$112.89		$112.90

Entering Text

As you've discovered by typing the sample shown in Figure 3-3, you can type text into any cell or set of cells on your worksheet. What you type appears in the formula bar and is entered into the currently active cell regardless of the width of that cell. It also appears in adjacent cells to the right until *Excel* encounters a cell that is not empty.

Be aware, however, of the way *Excel* interprets the first character of a string. If your text string starts with a number, *Excel* attempts to evaluate the entire text string as a number. If it can't, *Excel* stores the string as text. To be sure the number is stored as text, start the string with a set of double quotation marks.

Text will also continue into adjacent cells as long as they contain no values. For instance, if you type a long sentence into a cell of standard width, you'll see the entire sentence in the formula bar at the top of the screen whenever the active cell cursor is on that cell. However, only the first few characters will appear in the cell. How many characters appear in the cell is a function of individual character widths: If there are a lot of *i*'s, *l*'s, and *t*'s in your sentence, there will be more characters in the cell, but if there are several wide characters (such as *m*'s and *w*'s), there will be fewer.

See Figure 3-5 for an example.

Entering Data and Creating Worksheets

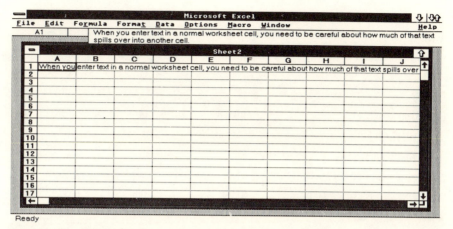

Figure 3-5. Text in a Cell

You can apply any of the editing commands and functions to text that is stored in any cell on a worksheet. Details about how to edit a worksheet are given in Chapter 5, "Editing What You Have."

Formatting Options

Excel lets you display your data and text in a variety of formats. You can also choose how text and data are aligned, specify the width of columns and the height of rows, choose font and font size (including adding as many as four fonts of your own), add borders or shading to cells, and protect data in cells from accidentally being changed. Each of these options is discussed in this section.

Number Formats

The Format Number command tells *Excel* how you want to display numbers, dates, and time. You can choose from the 21 formats supplied with *Excel* or create a custom format of your own.

The Format Number command generates a dialog box with the choices listed. Scroll through the list to see all of the formats. Several number formats are listed in the following table.

Chapter 3

Format	Positive	Negative	Percentage
General	1	−1	0.1254
0	1	−1	0
0.00	1.00	−1.00	0.13
#,##0	1	−1	0
#,##0.00	1.00	−1.00	0.13
$#,##0; ($#,##0)	$1	($1)	0
$#,##0; [RED]($#,##)	$1	($1)*	0
$#,##0.00;($#,##0.00)	$1.00	($1.00)	$0.13
$#,##0.00;[RED]($#,##0.00)	$1.00	($1.00)*	$0.13
0%	100%	−100%	13%
0.00%	100.00%	−100.00%	12.54%
0.00E+00	1.00E+00	−1.00E+00	1.254E-01

Several date and time formats are listed in the next table.

Format	Example
m/d/yy	4/15/88
d-mmm-yy	15-Apr-88
d-mmm	15-Apr
mmm-yy	Apr-88
h:mm AM/PM	2:45 PM
h:mm:ss AM/PM	4:55:35 PM
h:mm	16:55
h:mm:ss	16:55:35
m/d/yy h:mm	4/15/88 23:59

There a few things to note about number formats and colors. If your system can display colors, you can specify negative numbers in colors other than red (the default when the format chosen uses a color). In addition to red, allowable colors are black, white, green, blue, yellow, magenta, and cyan. You can change these with the Format Number command by editing an existing format or typing one of your own. That will be discussed in a bit.

To format a number, select the cell or cells you want formatted, choose Format Number, and select a format from the list shown in the dialog box (Figure 3-6).

Entering Data and Creating Worksheets

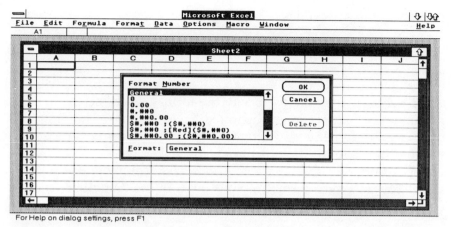

Figure 3-6. Format Number Box

Use your mouse or the arrow keys to scroll through the list of formats; select the one you want and then choose the OK button. *Excel* assigns the format to the cells selected. The format is then stored with the cell data.

For instance, let's experiment with the sales figure in cell B3. Make B3 the active cell, and choose the Format menu (press Alt + T or choose it with your mouse). You'll see the box shown in Figure 3-9.

Now choose the sixth format—the one that shows numbers as $#.##0 ;($#,##0). When the box disappears, notice that the sales figure now has a dollar sign in front of it. Any number you put in this cell from now on will appear this way unless you change the format.

Try another format. Repeat the process to get the Format Number box, but this time choose the eighth selection: $#,##0.00 ;($#,##0.00). When the box disappears, notice that you get *Excel*'s message about data being too wide to fit in the cell (because of the added dollar sign, comma, period, and cents digits).

If you want just integers on your worksheet, choose the first or second options. The General option will allow decimals later on, but 0 will show all values as integers.

Creating Your Own Format

You may need to show data in a format that isn't on *Excel*'s list. For instance, if you want to format a set of cells to show phone

49

numbers with area codes, you can type

###-###-####

in the Format Text box.

Excel uses a picture to specify the format. Each picture has a maximum of four sections, separated by semicolons. The first three are for numeric values that are positive, negative, and zero; the fourth section (if there is one) is for text.

The Microsoft *Excel Reference Guide* has a complete discussion about how to type a format of your own, in the "Number" section.

Text Formats

The Format Text command refers to text within a chart, which is dealt with in Chapter 8, "Graphs and Charts." However, you can type paragraphs into your worksheet and have them appear on a finished worksheet just as if you were using a word processor.

Generally, questions about formatting text on a worksheet fall into two categories: alignment, and fonts and font sizes.

Because you're in a worksheet, you can use many of the cell-formatting techniques that are available, such as adding borders or shading, or changing the effective spacing of lines of text by changing the row height.

Further, with the windowing option, you can type text into another part of your worksheet and then open a window in a screenful of numbers and formulas, thus showing the text in a *pane* in one corner of your worksheet.

Alignment of Data and Text

Where the data or text appears in your cells is a function of alignment. You may want all your text to be left-aligned (which *Excel* uses as a default). You may want all of your numbers right-aligned (which some number formats allow). Or you may want some data centered within a cell.

Number formats dictate how a number is aligned, but, generally, numbers are right-aligned. However, if you have numbers with decimal places, you may find that the decimals are not aligned, since the numbers to the right of the decimal point dictate where the decimal point appears.

For instance, look at the following column of numbers:

$125.66
5
23%
3.14159
2.01E+08

All of the numbers in the list are right-aligned, the default used with *Excel* numbers, unless you specify something else. To align the decimal points within a column of numbers, use the Format Numbers command and pick formats with the same number of decimal places.

To align text, use either the Format Alignment or the Format Justify command from the Format menu.

The Left, Right, and Center choices are obvious: Text is either aligned at the left or right edge of the cell or it's centered within the cell width. General alignment for text means that it is left-aligned. Since it's a default value, it also means that any numbers are right-justified, and logical and error values are centered.

For instance, on our sample, the column headings are the month names, all of which are left-justified. Let's right-justify them. Select the month names (make sure they're all highlighted); then choose the Format menu. Next, choose Alignment, and, in the dialog box, choose Right. When you press the Enter key, all the month names are right-justified.

The Fill option lets you type one character and have *Excel* repeat that character across the cell or cell range selected. This is particularly useful when you're drawing a line of dashes or asterisks across several columns.

Changing Column Width

It may be necessary for you to change the width of a column—for instance, because a number can't be displayed in the format you've chosen. (You'll see ######### in the cell instead of numbers.)

To change the width of a column, select any cell in it. You don't have to select the entire column, but changing the width of any cell in the column changes the width for all cells in that

Chapter 3

column, including any that may be hidden. Next, choose Format Column Width. You'll see the dialog box pictured in Figure 3-7.

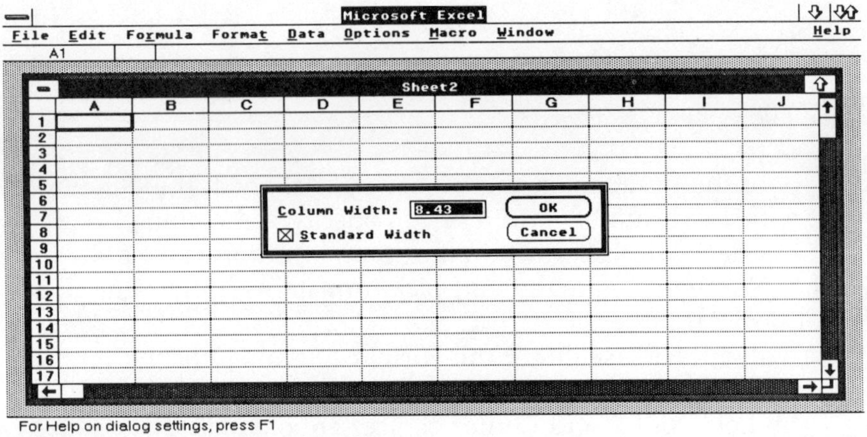

Figure 3-7. Column Width Dialog Box

The current width is shown as the number of characters for Column Width. Type the number you want here, or use your mouse to point to the line to the right of the column heading you want to change, and drag until the column is as wide as you want.

If you want to change a column width back to its default value of eight characters, choose Standard Width.

You can have a column as wide as 255 characters or as thin as a decimal fraction of 1. If you specify 0 for the number of characters, the entire column is hidden, which means you can enter data into any cell in the column but it won't be displayed either on your screen or if you print the spreadsheet.

You can also change the width of all the columns on your spreadsheet by selecting an entire row (all the way out to column IV) and then applying the Format Column Width command.

Changing Row Height

You may wish to change the default height of a particular row so that it can accommodate the font and size of the characters you're using.

You can do that with the Format Row Height command. Row height is measured in points; a point is 1/72 inch.

After you've changed the row height, you don't see any

change to your worksheet until you've also changed the font size. However, once you have selected a larger font, the entire worksheet looks different.

For instance, when the row height of Row 1 of our sample worksheet is changed to 18 points (from the standard 13 points), the size of the top row changes. However, nothing else changes on the screen until you also select a larger size for the default typeface being used. *Excel*'s default typeface and size is Helvetica 10-point; when you increase the type size to 18 points, you get a screen that looks like the one in Figure 3-8.

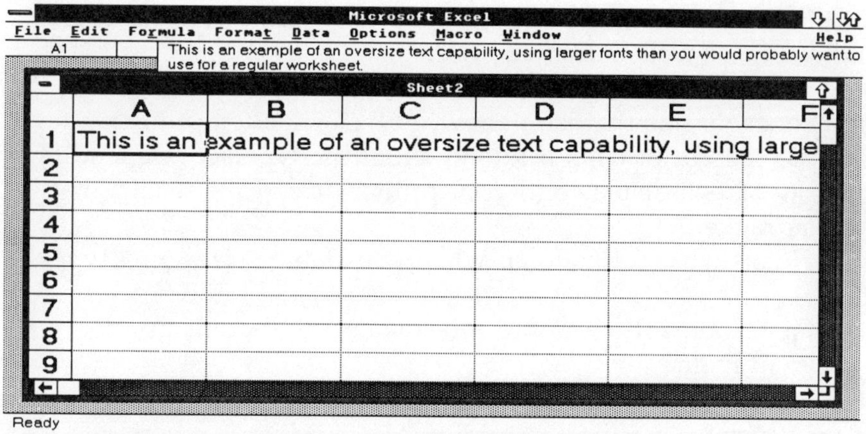

Figure 3-8. Larger Row Height, Larger Characters

The Row Height command applies only to the row the cursor is in. It works in conjunction with the font size you've chosen as a default for the entire worksheet and the font size you've chosen for this particular row of cells. This allows you to have worksheets that feature a different size of type for headings or notes from the one you're using for the rest of the data.

For instance, you might choose to make the column headings of our sample worksheet 12-point, leaving the rest of the worksheet alone.

A word of warning: If you change the row height in expectation of using a larger type size, allow for larger width of characters, too. If the larger characters don't fit in the existing column width, you'll see the standard ##### indicator, which means the data is too wide to fit the current column.

Chapter 3

Selecting Fonts and Font Size

Excel offers a number of fonts and font sizes, allowing you to turn an ordinary sheet of paper with numbers and headings into an interesting report or chart.

The Format Font command lets you change the font for the entire worksheet, for a single cell, or for any range of cells. A font consists of one typeface in one size. You can use up to four different fonts on a single worksheet and can change to any of those installed on your computer.

As installed on your AT or AT-compatible computer, *Excel* provides eight typefaces, each available in a number of sizes.

Each typeface is also available in bold, italic, underline, and strikeout, as well as normal style.

While you can specify any size for the typefaces available, if you choose a size that isn't shown, *Excel* will attempt to show that size based on what it knows about the typeface. Depending on your screen display and your printer driver, the results may appear ragged.

Here's what can happen when you change sizes on a typeface.

First, look at the sample spreadsheet in 10-point Courier shown in Figure 3-9.

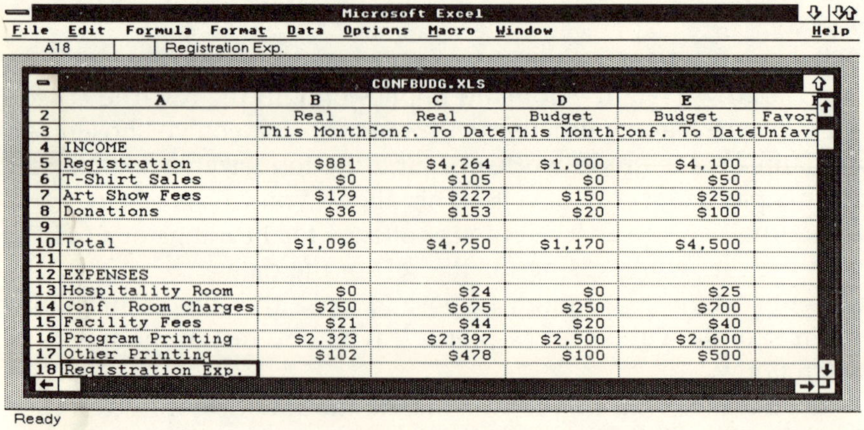

Figure 3-9. Sample Spreadsheet, 10-Point Courier

Figure 3-10 shows what it looks like when you specify 24-point, a size that's not listed.

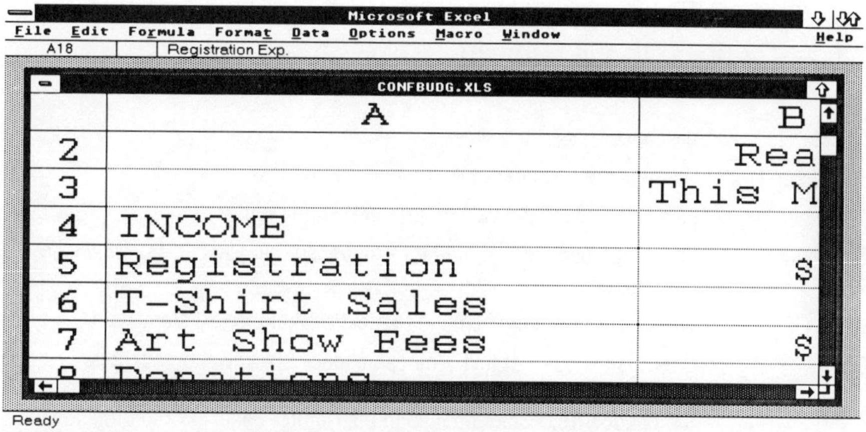

Figure 3-10. Sample Spreadsheet, 24-Point Courier

    The fonts listed when you use the Format Font command are those that your printer driver is designed to print. If you change printers, go through the Install process again to load the appropriate fonts; they'll show up in the Font dialog box.

    The Font dialog box has two lists. The first one shows the fonts (typefaces and sizes) that can be used on the current worksheet. While you can choose others, remember that only four different fonts can be used with any one worksheet.

    To change to one of the listed fonts, use the arrow keys or your mouse to select the button next to your choice. Then press the Enter key. If you don't want to change anything, choose the Cancel option (use the Tab key to highlight it).

    If you want to change to another font, one that isn't listed, use the Tab key or your mouse to choose the Fonts option, and press the Enter key.

    When you choose the Fonts option, you'll see the second set of choices—the typefaces and sizes installed with the current printer driver. The font currently in use is highlighted. The size choices available for the highlighted typeface are shown in the Size list.

    The Printer Font box shows whether the fonts displayed are those your printer is designed to print or the ones that can be handled by your monitor. If the Printer Font box is on, the fonts displayed are linked to the abilities of your printer; if it's off, the fonts displayed are screen display formats. You can get an idea of your printer's capabilities by turning on the box.

Chapter 3

If you have installed a color monitor, you'll also see further lists, as outlined in the following table.

Choice	Description
Background	Controls the appearance of the area behind text.
Automatic	Lets *Excel* select the background pattern for you.
Transparent	Leaves the background area transparent so that you can see what's behind the text.
White Out	Whites out a rectangle behind the text so that the text stands out.
Color	Controls the color of text. You can choose black, white, red, green, blue, yellow, magenta, cyan, or Automatic. If you choose Automatic, *Excel* uses the Window Text Color defined in the Control Panel. (For information about using the Control Panel, see Appendix D.) If you print a chart with the Automatic option chosen, text prints as black regardless of what color has been picked in the Control Panel. The background for text with Automatic color always prints white.
Patterns	Displays the Format Patterns dialog box and carries out any changes you've made in the Format Font dialog box.
Scale	Displays the Format Scale dialog box and carries out any changes you've made in the Format Font dialog box.
Text	Displays the Format Text dialog box and carries out any changes you've made in the Format Font dialog box.

Adding Borders and Shading

You can add solid border lines and/or shading to cells in your spreadsheet with the Format Border command. This is not the same thing as the gridlines you normally see on your worksheet. Borders and shading are especially useful for adding emphasis to certain areas of your worksheet or for visually separating blocks of data. Gridlines, which you normally see on the screen, can be turned on or off with the Options Display command or, when you're printing, with the File Page Setup command.

Protecting Your Data

Picture this.

It's late in the afternoon, and you have a few more changes to make to a spreadsheet you've been working on for the last few days. You're tired. Numbers are swimming in front of you, but just a few more changes will finish things off. You enter your changes and save the file.

Ten minutes later, something bothers you, and you decide to retrieve the file and see whether you made the changes you thought you did. Oh, no! Somehow you've managed to enter data into a cell that contained an incredibly complex formula, and the data has overwritten the formula. The rest of your calculations are probably off, since several subsequent calculations depended upon the result that would have been in that cell.

This has the makings of one of those workaday personal disasters. Since you've saved the file, you can't use the Undo command. If you've been saving your efforts with different filenames, you can retrieve the most recent past version, and work on that. If you're like most of us, though, you haven't.

There is a way to prevent this kind of disaster from happening in the future. The Format Cell Protection command, in conjunction with the Options Protect Document command, lets you selectively protect your cells so that further entry into a specific cell is inhibited. This same command also lets you hide and lock cells so that others can neither see nor change the contents.

When you use this option, you lock the cell. This means that unless someone deliberately unlocks the cell, its contents cannot be changed, deleted, or overwritten.

Locking a cell means that you're keeping others from accidentally changing the contents. If, for instance, you have a constant that needs to be used elsewhere in the spreadsheet and it's located in a cell adjacent to one where someone can enter data, you may want to lock the cell containing the constant. Or if you're using a text string or formulas over and over, with just the data changing whenever anyone uses the spreadsheet, you may want to lock the cells containing the text string or formulas so that they don't accidentally get overwritten.

To lock a cell or cells, specify the cell or cell range you want locked; then choose the Format Cell Protection Command. The dialog box looks like the one in Figure 3-11.

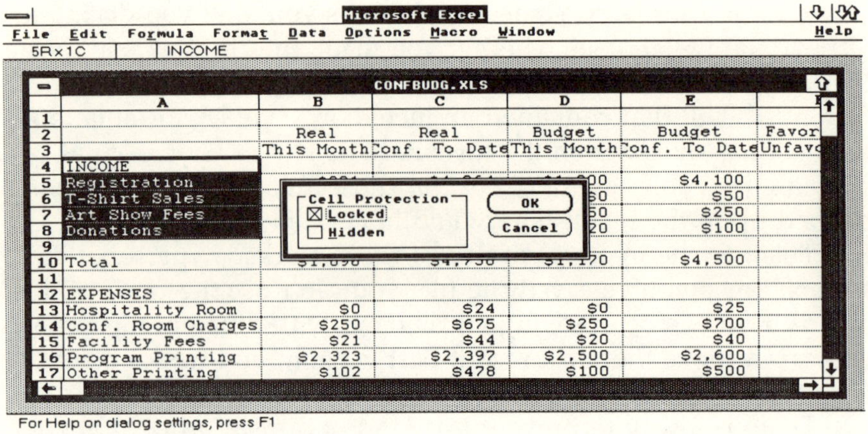

Chapter 3

Figure 3-11. Cell Protection Dialog Box

In this example, *Excel* has assumed that you want the cells locked and has turned on that option. If you also want them hidden, use the Tab key or the mouse to move the highlighting to Hidden, and press the space bar to put an X in the box. In either case, once you have the options the way you want, press the Enter key.

You'll also have to turn on the protection option by locking the entire worksheet with the Options Protect Document command. The Contents option is already turned on when you see the Options Protect Document dialog box, and you'll have to give a password. Once that is done, the cells you've locked may not be changed until you give the password and unlock the spreadsheet. If anyone tries to change locked cells, they'll get a warning message.

Naming Cells and Ranges

Sometimes it's easier to work with values that you can refer to by name instead of by cell address. This is a particularly valuable feature if you start moving data around, so that it becomes difficult to remember where a particular variable is stored.

Case in point: If you're working with a cashflow statement, it may help you pinpoint net income by group if you refer to each type of income and expenses by name rather than by cell address, as in the example below.

    Group1NetSales
    Group2NetSales

Group1PhoneExp
Group2Travel

Excel gives you a wide variety of features that encourage the use of names as applied to individual cells or cell ranges. The main commands related to names are on the Formula menu, which lists the following commands.

Command	Definition
Define Name...	Lets you define a single name.
Create Names...	Lets you use use existing text to name several rows or columns.
Apply Names...	Lets you search through a selected range of cells and replace all references to a cell or cell range with the name you've given that cell or cell range.
Paste Name...	Lets you see the names you've already used and paste one of them into the formula you're currently working on.

Naming Guidelines

To use a name for a cell or range, follow these guidelines:

- The first character must be a letter. Any other character can be a letter, number, period, or underline. The name must not look like a cell reference (B24 or R5C2).
- No spaces are permitted. When you're typing the name, use upper- and lowercase letters, or separate text strings with a period or underline.
- A name may be as many as 255 characters long.

When you name a cell or cell range, *Excel* offers some suggestions: Choose a name selected from text in the active cell or the one above or below it, and use the absolute reference of the active cell. You're free to accept *Excel*'s suggestion or use a name of your own.

Defining a Name

To name a cell or cell range, select it by using the F8 key and the arrow keys or by clicking and dragging the mouse so that the cell(s) you want to name are highlighted.

Choose the Formula Define Name command and, in the Name box, either accept the proposed name or type what you want. In the Refers To box, accept the proposed cell reference or

Chapter 3

type what you want to link to the name, starting with an equal sign (=). When the name and reference are the way you want them, choose the OK button. This adds the name and reference to the current list of names that is stored with the worksheet.

For instance, let's name the sales cell in our working example, the one in B3. With the active cell in B3, choose the Formula menu (Alt + R), and on it choose Define Names. A dialog box like the one in Figure 3-12 appears.

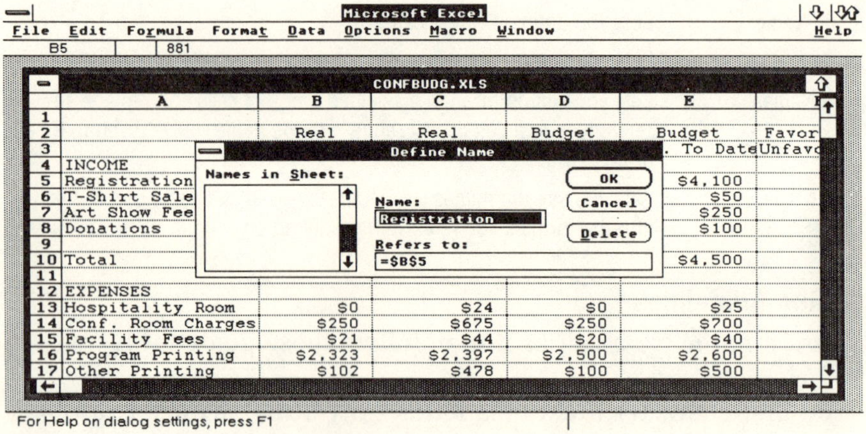

Figure 3-12. Define Names Dialog Box

Notice that *Excel* has suggested the name *Sales*. In the Refers To line, *Excel* indicates the absolute reference for this cell, $B$3. Accept these by pressing the Enter key. From this point on, if you want to type a formula involving B3 you can use the name *Sales* instead of the cell address.

Create Names

What if you have a number of cells to name, all with different names? That's what the Create Names command is all about. With this command, *Excel* takes its suggested names from text in the top or bottow row of the selected range, the left or right column, or any combination of the four.

To use the Create Names command, select the range you want, including the text you'll be using as names, which should be in the top or bottom row or the left- or rightmost column of the range.

Choose the Formula Create Names command, and, when the

box appears, choose the location of the names: Top Row, Bottom Row, Left Column, and/or Right Column. When you've finished telling *Excel* where to look for the names, choose the OK button. If any of the new names you've indicated are already in use, *Excel* asks you if you want to replace the previous definition.

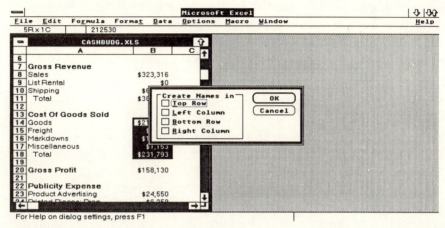

Figure 3-13. The Create Names Dialog Box

Viewing Existing Names

If at any time you want to see the current names in use, choose the Formula Paste Names command. The dialog box lists the current names in use in alphabetical order so that you can check the name you have in mind against the ones you've already used. If you want to see the specific reference for each name, move the active cursor to a portion of the worksheet you won't be using *before* choosing the Formula Paste Names command. Then choose the Formula Paste Names command and the Paste List option. Starting at the current active cell, *Excel* pastes a table showing the name and reference associated with each name.

Naming a Formula or Value

You can also name a formula or a value without having the formula or value actually in a cell. This can be particularly useful if you're going to be using the same formula or value over and over in one worksheet, but there is a chance that its value may need to change the next time you use the same worksheet.

For instance, if you are doing a mortgage-payment calcula-

Chapter 3

tion that involves, among other things, computation of a monthly payment, plus an amortization schedule, plus a payoff before the loan is due, and you'd like to see how the cashflow works with a selection of mortgage rates, use this approach.

To name a formula or value without its necessarily being in the spreadsheet, use the Formula Define Name command. When the dialog box appears on the screen, ignore the Names list (except to make sure that the name you want to use isn't listed there). Type the name of your value or formula in the Name box, and in the Refers To box, type the value or formula. Then choose the OK button.

Changing a Name

When you want to change the value or formula associated with that name, simply go back to the Formula Define Name command and specify a new value or formula.

You can also change the name associated with any cell, range, formula, or value any time you need to. Since a name is accessible any time you use the Formula Define Name command, just highlight the name you want to change and retype it so that it's correct.

If you want to delete a name, follow the same procedure, and when the name is in the Name box, choose the Delete button.

Note: If you choose the Cancel button, *Excel* can't restore any names you've deleted. Once you've deleted a name, it's gone, and you have to recreate it if you want to use it.

Using Names

Once you've named something on your worksheet, you can use it anywhere it's needed, either by typing the name or by using the Formula Paste Name command.

For instance, if you're typing a formula, stop at the point where you'll use the name and choose Formula Paste Name. When the dialog box appears, choose the name that refers to what you want. (The address, formula, or value associated with that name will appear in the Refers To box.) Then choose the OK button, and the name is pasted into your formula.

Note: When you paste an existing name into a formula or a location, *Excel* makes any cell reference into an absolute address.

It's possible to make pasted names refer to relative references, but it's chancy.

If you want to use a name that's defined on another worksheet, follow the conventions for linking to another worksheet. Once you have the Formula Define Name box on your screen, type an equal sign, followed by the filename of the other worksheet, followed by an exclamation point, followed by the name of the cell or the range, formula, or value you're after. For instance, to use the value Cost_of_Goods from the worksheet INVENTRY.XLS, type

=INVENTRY.XLS!Cost_of_Goods

and choose the OK button. *Excel* imports the value onto your current worksheet and lists the linked name along with the other names.

Applying Names

Once you've defined a name, you can use the Formula Apply Names command to look through your worksheet and replace all occurrences of the reference linked to it with the new name. For instance, if you have used PRICES as the name for the range B5:B12 (remember, when you name it, it's stored as $B$5:$B$12), you can use the Formula Apply Names command to replace all references to B5:B12 with the name PRICES.

To apply names on a worksheet, select the range within which you want to apply names. If you want to affect the entire worksheet, choose a single cell; then choose Formula Apply Names. You'll see a dialog box with the names already in use listed. Choose the name or names you want applied by holding down the Ctrl key while using the up- or down-arrow key, and press the space bar to add or delete names (names chosen appear in dark bars; names not chosen appear against a light background). Once the names have been chosen, select the options you want.

If you choose the Options button on the dialog box, the complete dialog box, in addition to choosing the names you want to use, will let you instruct *Excel* to use the names regardless of reference style (Ignore Relative/Absolute), have *Excel* pick up the range names of the referred-to cells if an exact match can't be found (Use Row and Column Names), and (with Full menus

Chapter 3

turned on) use or ignore existing row and/or column names in a specified order (Omit Column Name. . ., Omit Row Name. . ., and Row Order).

Excel has an excellent tutorial and indexed description on disk that illustrates how to apply names. It's in the "Auditing and Documenting Your Worksheet" section of the Features Guide, available on the Help menu. It's worth taking a look at for a more detailed explanation.

Saving Your Work

Saving your work at any time is a breeze—it takes only a couple of keystrokes to guarantee your latest work won't be lost.

Use the File menu to save your work.

The options you'll apply most often for everyday use are two of the four options in the middle, Save and Save As. Both save the current version of your worksheet; Save assumes you want to store it on the default drive and directory under the filename that it previously had, while Save As lets you save the current spreadsheet under a new name, directory, and/or drive.

When you select the File Save command, *Excel* simply saves the current worksheet with the name that you used to retrieve it. The current worksheet stays on the screen, ready for you to continue your work.

When you select the File Save As command, *Excel* shows you the current filename and gives you the option of changing the name, directory, or drive.

There's more detail about file operations, including more information on saving your files, in the next chapter.

Summary

This chapter has given you an introduction to entering and working with data. You've learned about cells and ranges, entering numbers and text and how *Excel* stores both, formatting your work, using names to work with your data, and a bit about saving your work.

Chapter 4
Working with Files

A file is the basic entity in which your data is stored. While you're typing data into cells on the screen, *Excel* is creating a file within the computer's memory. When you save it, you create a file on whatever disk and/or directory you specify, and in either the default format or one that you specify.

Excel gives you a number of options for working with your files, all of which are accessed through the File menu.

The table below describes what the commands on the File menu allow you to do.

Command	Description
New...	Open a new file.
Open...	Open a previously created and stored file.
Close	Close the currently open file.
Links...	Open supporting files that are linked to the current file.
Save	Save the current file.
Save As...	Save the current file under a filename/directory/format that you specify.
Save Workspace...	Save a list of all windows and files open at the time, as well as saving all open files.
Delete...	Delete the file you specify.
Page Setup...	Control the appearance of the printed document; Setup settings are saved with the file.
Print...	Print the file according to Setup specifications.
Printer Setup...	Identify the printer you want to use.
Exit	Save the current file and then quit *Excel* and return to the directory prompt.

Each of these commands is explained in more detail later in this chapter, along with some other topics.

Filenames and Directories

The *filename* is the unique descriptive name you give to each of your files. A filename consists of the name itself and an exten-

Chapter 4

sion. The name can be as many as eight characters—including the letters A through Z, the numbers 0 through 9, and these characters:

~ ' ! @ $ % ^ & ( ) - _ ' [ ]

A filename must start with an alphabetic character and be unique within its directory; note that a different extension will make duplicate filenames unique. (For instance, PRICES.XLS and PRICES.BAK qualify as unique filenames.)

The extension is comprised of the three characters after the period in the filename. *Excel* recognizes a number of extensions, including the ones listed in the following table.

Extension	Description
XLS, .XLC, .XLM, .XLW	*Excel*'s default formats for its spreadsheet, chart, macro, and extended workspace files. If you choose the Normal option on the Save As dialog box, *Excel* saves your current file in one of these formats, as appropriate.
.TXT	Text for transferring data to a word processor as text files. Only the text and values displayed are saved. Columns are separated by tabs, and rows are separated by carriage returns.
.CSV	Comma Separated Values format. This is like Text format, except that the columns are separated by commas. Some people find that it's easier to transmit files in this format than in others.
.SLK	Shown on the menu as SYLK. Used for transferring data to other Microsoft worksheets, such as Microsoft *Excel* for the Apple Macintosh, or Microsoft *Multiplan*.
.WKS	Used for transferring data to *Lotus 1-2-3* version 1A, or to *Symphony* on the IBM-PC.
.WK1	Used for transferring data to *Lotus 1-2-3* version 2.
.DIF	Used for transferring data to an application that requires Data Interchange Format, such as *VisiCalc*. DIF format saves values, but not formulas.
.DBF	DBF 2 is for transferring data to *dBASE II* files; DBF 3 is for transferring data to *dBASE III* files.

Files are stored in directories, much as you might store file folders in different drawers. Each file drawer, or directory, presumably contains files that are somehow related. So it is with your computer: Under DOS 3.3, you can create as many directories as you need to hold the various files you'll be working with, including those created with *Excel*.

If you're running *Excel* under Microsoft *Windows* version 2.0 or higher, you can use all the *Windows* and non-*Windows* applications, files, and directories from the *Windows* environment.

Under MS-DOS 3.3, directories are organized something like an upside-down tree. At the very top of the tree is the root directory, which is the main directory. There is one root directory for each of your computer's disk drives: A:, B:, C:, and so forth, to however many disk drives your computer has.

Figure 4-1 is an example of a "tree" consisting of a root directory, some main directories, and some files.

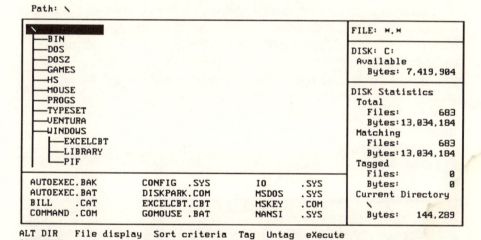

Figure 4-1. "Tree" Directory Organization

Within the root directory are other directories, each with a name. These represent the main branches of a tree. Each directory may contain subdirectories and files. A subdirectory is a directory within a directory.

To get to a file within a directory, you must specify the pathname, which tells MS-DOS how to get to the file you want. A complete pathname might look like this:

C:\WINDOWS\EXCEL\FINANCE\SALES87.XLS

Chapter 4

This pathname tells MS-DOS to look on drive C for the root directory, indicated by the backslash (\). Once there, it is to look for the directory WINDOWS. Another backslash tells it to look for the subdirectory EXCEL, and yet another backslash tells it to look within the EXCEL subdirectory for the subdirectory FINANCE. Finally, within the FINANCE subdirectory, it is to look for the file named SALES87.XLS. (There may also be files named SALES87.XLC and SALES87.XLW, representing associated chart and workspace files, but *Excel* retrieves only the file named SALES87.XLS.)

Normally, when you're working on a spreadsheet, related files are in the same directory where you will be saving the spreadsheet. This usually winds up being the one in which your *Excel* program files are also located, and it is considered the current directory. (It's the default *Excel* uses when you store a file without specifying a complete pathname.) You can use other directories with *Excel*, but you'll have to either type the pathname each time you work with it or change the current directory so that it more nearly specifies the one you want to use. The Microsoft *Excel Reference Manual* gives a fairly thorough discussion of how to change the current directory, under the "Directories" heading.

When you open a file, you see something like the dialog box in Figure 4-2.

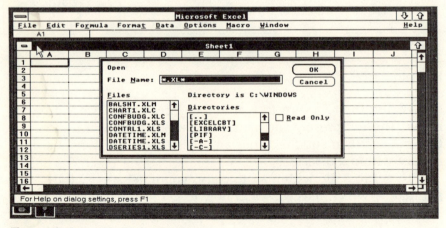

Figure 4-2. Open File Dialog Box

Files in the current directory are listed on the left, and the current directory is shown after the words *Directory is*. In the Directories box are the directories available on this path; in Figure 4-2, (..) is the root directory, and under WINDOWS there are the EXCELCBT and LIBRARY directories. The dialog box also shows you the other disk drives that you can use; in this case, the floppy disk drive (A:) and the hard disk (C:).

If, when you retrieve or save a file, you wish to use another directory, specify as much of its pathname as is necessary. For instance, if you'll be using another directory on drive C:, you can leave off the drive indicator. If you're changing subdirectories within the same directory, you don't have to use a pathname that tells *Excel* to go all the way back up the tree to the root directory, then back down through the same main directory.

Consider the backslash a command that tells MS-DOS to change directory levels. The first backslash refers to the root directory. When it's followed by the name of a main directory, MS-DOS looks there. When that directory name is followed by a backslash, MS-DOS knows that it is to look for a subdirectory, whose name follows the backslash. It's a bit like climbing up and down a tree in order to get from branch to branch.

Saving Your Work

Excel makes it easy to save your work. If you're willing to accept the defaults for drive, directory, and filename and extension, then the keystrokes Alt + F + S or double-clicking on File Save with your mouse automatically turns your current work into a file tucked away safely on disk. If you want to specify something different, it will take a few more keystrokes, but it still isn't much trouble.

Why so easy? Because the programmers at Microsoft have probably experienced (in their very early programming years, no doubt) the penalties for not periodically saving work in progress.

Periodically saving your work is important. We have all had variations on one of the following situations, which should convince you to save your work every now and then, rather than waiting until you've finished working.

You're working late one night, and you've made one last run to the coffee machine. While you're away from your desk, the new facilities assistant comes by and, in the interest of saving electricity, turns off your computer.

Chapter 4

You've brought a disk home so you can work on a project after dinner. You've spent about an hour of analysis on the data, and while your attention is diverted to answer the phone, your toddler comes in. In playing with your keyboard behind your back, he locks up the keyboard, forcing you to reboot the computer.

You have an important presentation tomorrow. Your boss just handed you some new figures to use in updating your data and redoing your charts. You're halfway through making the changes when the building lights flicker, then go out. Your computer also goes down, taking your revisions with it.

Frustration is hardly the word for what you feel!

While you may never have experienced precisely the situations described above, you've probably at least come close to losing some important segment of work because you failed to back it up. To make that process easier, the developers of *Excel* made it very simple to periodically save your current work as you go along.

The File menu, shown in Figure 4-1, has four commands—Save, Save As. . ., Close, and Exit—that are concerned with saving your files.

When you save your file with Save or Save As. . ., *Excel* takes a snapshot of the current worksheet and saves that, leaving the worksheet on your screen and allowing you to continue to work on it. With the Close and Exit commands, however, *Excel* removes the file from the screen and from active working status.

When *Excel* saves a file, it saves not only the values, text, and formulas, but also all the worksheet settings such as formats, fonts, styles, window size, and type and display settings. When the file is next retrieved, all those settings are in place, ready to use.

When you use Save to save a file which previously existed in another form, normally *Excel* removes the older version from the disk, then writes the current version in memory to disk under the same filename and extension.

With the Save As. . . command, *Excel* presents the Save As. . . dialog box. The shaded bar shows you the filename and extension last used to save the file. You can use this or type another filename, complete with pathname, if you want. If you accept the current name as the new filename, simply press the Enter key to choose OK or click the OK bar with your mouse. If you want to change anything, start typing. The presence of just one new character causes *Excel* to clear the shaded bar so you can type your new filename (or pathname).

However, if you choose Options, *Excel* gives you a number of other choices. Among them are the nine file formats, which correspond to the extensions discussed earlier. If you want to save your file in a format other than one of the *Excel* default formats, choose the appropriate button.

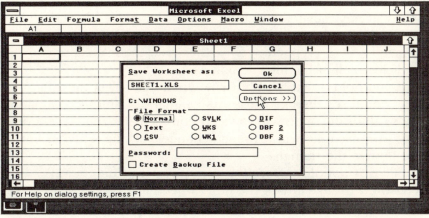

Figure 4-3. Save As... Dialog Box with Options

You can specify a password of as many as 16 characters for your file. Once you've specified a password, the file can be opened only by typing the password correctly. This differs from the password protection you specify when you want to protect your spreadsheet from changes (under Protect Document). If you want to protect your file with a password, be sure you write it down and store it somewhere safe. This lets you open the file in case you forget the password.

The first time you save a new file, you may want to turn on the Make Backup check box. This creates a backup copy of the document every time you save it in the future. The next time you open the file, *Excel* renames the old version using the same filename, but with a .BAK extension. Then when the file is saved under any of *Excel*'s commands, the new version will have the name with the default *Excel* extension, and the old version will remain. This may take up some disk space, but it's useful if one of the situations discussed earlier happens—in effect, erasing your most recent work.

The File Close command does just what its name indicates: It closes the currently active file and, if there are any unsaved changes, asks you if you want to save them. If you answer *yes*, *Excel* saves the file on disk just as if you had issued the File Save command. The difference is that the file is also removed from your screen. File Close is particularly useful if you're working with several files open at once and you want to put one or more of them away.

If you have several windows open for a single file and you want to close only one of those windows, use the Control Close command (Alt + Hyphen + C). Otherwise, the File Close command closes all of the file's windows.

If you hold down the Shift key when you select the File menu, you'll see the File Close All command. Use this command to close all of the open windows on your screen. You'll see a dialog box for each file with unsaved changes, asking whether you want to save the changes.

File Exit not only closes the currently active file, but also asks if you want to save any of the other open files, one by one, and then leaves *Excel* and returns to the operating system. This is the command you use when you need to use another program that's not accessible with the version of *Windows* you're using. Like File Close, File Exit asks you whether you want to save the changes you've made to any open files, and then it closes them one by one, saving the current versions if you indicate you want to save the changes.

Save Workspace is a command you may find useful once you get comfortable with the concept of having several files open at once and working with all of them at the same time. A workspace file differs from a normal data file in that it contains a list of the names of documents that were open in your workspace when you issued the Save Workspace command.

Using the Save Workspace command allows you to stop safely in the middle of a complex project to attend a meeting or go to lunch or even go home for the evening and later reopen all the files you were working on—with just one command. However, each of the files must have been saved on disk at least once before. If you haven't saved a file earlier, you won't be able to reopen it.

Note: You can work on any individual file that's saved in a workspace file. When it is saved, the updated version is what's retrieved in the workspace file. Also, any changes you make to its window size and position are reflected the next time you open the file as part of a workspace.

To save your work as a workspace file, choose File Save Workspace. You'll see a small dialog box like the one in Figure 4-4, asking for the filename you want to give the workspace file.

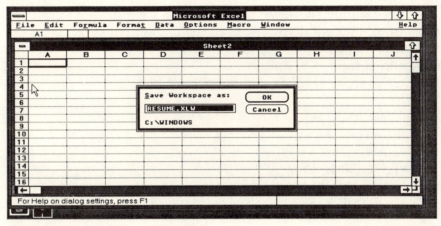

Figure 4-4. Save Workspace Dialog Box

While *Excel* normally suggests the filename RESUME, you can choose anything you like as a filename. The normal extension for a workspace file is .XLW, but you can change that, too, if the change is appropriate to what you're doing.

Once you get used to the idea of using a workspace to hold several open files simultaneously, you may decide to do that regularly.

You can set up a special autoexec.bat file that automatically opens a workspace whenever you open a certain worksheet or macro file.

You can use the concept of a workspace to set up related files while you work on a budget, inventory control, or accounting problem.

You can even modify the file used when you first start up *Excel*—the WIN.INI file—which contains all your default settings such as currency and time formats, column size, and other settings.

Chapter 4

Using Workspaces

To give you an example of how workspaces look and function (and also to give you a preview of how *Excel* lets you link separate worksheets into a consolidated report), let's use a set of sample files that Microsoft provides with your *Excel* disks. If you're working with a hard disk, note that these files are included in the LIBRARY directory and are installed during the Setup process. If you're working with floppy disks, you'll want to use the Library disk.

This example shows you how you can use separate sales reports from different divisions, even using different currencies, and combine them into a single consolidated report with amounts shown in current U.S. dollars.

This exercise requires you to open six files:

AUSTRAL.XLS
GREATBRT.XLS
JAPAN.XLS
WESTGERM.XLS
CONSTANT.XLM
QUARTMP.XLS

The first four are the divisional sales reports. CONSTANT.XLM is a macro file that you use to update currency conversion rates. QUARTMP.XLS is the quarterly report template.

With *Excel* open and a blank worksheet on your screen (make sure all your other files have been closed, since you'll have several open by the time we finish this exercise):

- Choose the File Open command to change directories.
- With the File Open dialog box on your screen, use the Tab key and down-arrow key to highlight the [LIBRARY] directory.
- Press the Enter key to choose the [LIBRARY] directory or use your mouse to double-click the [LIBRARY] directory entry. (When you've finished this project, return to the normal WINDOWS directory by choosing the [..] directory.)
- Once you're in the LIBRARY directory, open the four divisional sales reports, one at a time. Each appears in its own window, occupying one quarter of the screen. When all four have been opened, your screen looks like the one in Figure 4-5.

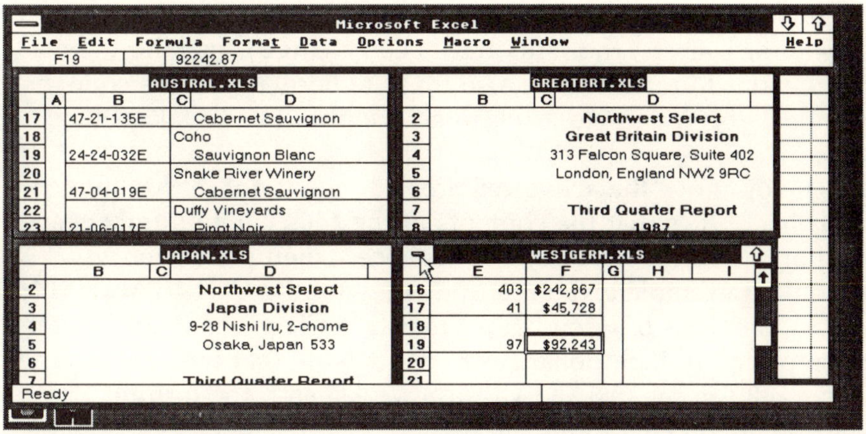

Figure 4-5. Four Sales Reports

Since each is a window, you can move from report to report by selecting it on the Window menu. If you want the window to be larger, use the Control menu (press Ctrl + Hyphen or click the hyphen in the upper left corner of the window you want to enlarge, choose the Size command, and move the arrows in the direction(s) along which you want to make the enlargement).

When you've finished working in that window and are ready to return the report to the original size, simply use the same Size command on the Control menu and reduce the report to fit in its corner of your screen. This isn't necessary, however, since you can have each of the individual reports be whatever size is most comfortable for you to work with.

If you want to accept the currency rates in effect when the developers at Microsoft wrote the example, you don't have to open CONSTANT.XLM. If you'd like to update the currency rates, open this macro file and be sure you have up-to-date currency rates on hand. (You can get them from the Foreign Exchange rates table in the business section of your newspaper. Use the most current value in the columns headed "Foreign Currency in Dollars.")

To run the macro, press Ctrl + C, and enter the appropriate values in response to the questions.

When the currency values are the way you want them, open the quarterly report template. You may be asked if you want to update the values; choose Yes if this question appears. The template overlays the four divisional reports on your screen.

Note: There are several nondefault values present in this worksheet. For starters, the fonts have been changed, making the material easier to read. Notice also that the Format Borders command has been used to leave some gridlines in and take others out.

If you move the active cell around, you'll notice that the formula bar shows that the contents of the cells where numbers appear are actually formulas. For instance, when the currency values in the example given are updated with the CONSTANT.XLM macro, the sales of Friendship Vineyards Chardonnay in Australia are reported in U.S. dollars as $780.16. Note that with D14 as the active cell (on the QUARTMP.XLS worksheet), the formula bar shows the contents to be

=AUSTRAL.XLS!F14*DOLLAR

This is the way *Excel* refers to the contents of cells in other currently active worksheets. In this case, the formula refers to the worksheet file (AUSTRAL.XLS!) and a cell within that file (F14) and multiplies that value by the dollar conversion value for Australia, which is stored as the named variable DOLLAR. (In the case of Great Britain, the equivalent conversion value is stored as POUND.)

If you move the active cell around the consolidated report, you'll find that most of the values shown are taken from the component divisional sales reports, and that the only calculations that are done on the summary sheets are the totals in columns K and L. This is a simple example of how you can use separate worksheets to do calculations and bring the results together in a composite worksheet.

The entire environment you're seeing—all the separate divisional worksheets, the currency conversion macro file, and the consolidated report—constitutes a workspace. You can add and delete files from your worksheet by opening and closing them individually. Or you can save the entire set of files as a workspace, perhaps calling it QUARTER. (*Excel* will add the extension .XLW for you.) However, you'll also have to save or close the individual files. Once they're saved or closed, you can open the whole set of files again by opening the workspace file.

This concept of saving associated files as a workspace is one of *Excel*'s unique features. It makes it far easier for you to work on linked files, saving them on an interim basis as your work gets interrupted, and later retrieving them all as they were when you had to leave.

A word about saving the consolidated report, however. The Microsoft *Excel* Sampler, where these reports are briefly discussed, suggests using a file-naming convention to keep templates separate from the working files they produce. The convention suggested is to use the letters *TMP* as part of the filename of a template.

That's one good approach. However, the letters *TMP* frequently mean *temporary* to other people, and if anyone else has access to your directory, they may regard a filename with the letters *TMP* as a file that can be permanently modified. While you can protect against that with *Excel*'s password or cell-locking options, you may wish to devise your own criteria for filenames—such as starting a template filename with a special character other than a letter or number.

In any case, once you have loaded the template with data, save it with a name other than QUARTMP.XLS.

As you get used to the concept of being able to save and retrieve groups of associated files in addition to being able to work on them individually, you'll find it easy, for instance, to save as a workspace all of the spreadsheet and database files associated with a list of accounts receivable or payable, or a spreadsheet and its associated charts showing sales by region and product.

Retrieving Your Files

Three of the top four items in the File menu are associated with opening files:

New. . .   Presents a dialog box asking you what kind of file you want to open.

Open. . .   Presents a different dialog box, asking you to identify the drive, directory, filename, and mode of the existing file you want to open.

Links. . .   Allows you to open files that are linked to the currently active file. Linked files can be files that are used together in a workspace, or they can be independent files that only sometimes need to be together in the same workspace.

The Links... command presents you with a dialog box showing you the names of supporting files in the current directory, or complete pathnames if necessary.

We'll look at each of these forms of opening a file in this section.

The New File

The New... command creates an empty document in a new window. This can be a worksheet, a chart, or a macro sheet. As mentioned above, you specify which one you want in the dialog box when you choose the File New command.

However, there are shortcut keys which allow you to open a new file without using the menu; a few are shown in the following table.

Keys	Description
Shift + F11	Opens a new worksheet.
F11	Opens a new chart.
Ctrl + F11	Opens a new macro sheet.

If you want to create an additional window for a file that is already open, use the Window New Window command.

If you're creating a new worksheet, it will operate under the settings you've chosen in the Options Workspace dialog box, or under the default settings if you haven't modified them.

If you're creating a new chart from data stored in cells on an already-open worksheet, the data is automatically plotted according to some *best fit* rules that *Excel* uses. You can change the appearance of your chart with any of the Chart commands.

If you create a new chart while there is data on the Clipboard (you've cut or copied data), *Excel* displays a blank chart. You then must use the Edit Paste or Edit Paste Special commands to fetch the data and plot it on the chart.

If you create a new macro sheet, you're presented with a blank macro sheet.

When you turn on Macro Record, you also create a new macro sheet.

This new macro sheet also operates under the settings you've chosen in the Options Workspace dialog box, or under the default settings if you haven't modified them.

The Already-Existing File

Use the File Open command to open an already-existing file. This includes any *Excel* worksheet, chart, macro, or workspace files, as well as files from any other program.

Excel can open any file that is in one of the formats shown in the following table.

File Type	Extension
Excel	.XLS, .XLC, .XLM, .XLW
An ASCII text file	Any extension
A CSV file	If it has the .CSV extension
Lotus 1-2-3, Symphony, or compatible	.WKS, .WK1
SLK	Any extension
DIF	Any extension
DBF2 or DBF3	Appropriate extensions

When you choose the File Open. . . command, the dialog box assumes you're interested only in *Excel* files and displays a list of the files in the current directory that have the characters .XL and another character as their extension. That's what is shown in the File Name box. This allows you to choose from a list of files that includes all the .XLS, .XLC, .XLM, and .XLW files.

If the file you want to open doesn't fit that description, you can type in the filename and extension, or use some combination of characters and asterisks to indicate the set of files you'd like to inspect. For instance, if your current directory includes some *Lotus 1-2-3* files that you'd like to use under *Excel*, type the file specification

.WK

in the File Name box to see a list of all the *Lotus 1-2-3* files in the current directory. *Excel* will show you a list naming each file in the current directory that has the letters *WK* as the first two letters of its extension.

However, this assumes that the file you're after is in the current directory, which is shown in the following phrase

Directory is C:\WINDOWS

Below that line, in the Directories box, is a list showing all the other disk drives installed under *Excel's* setup program, and the names of any other subdirectories on drive C that use the WINDOWS directory. If you choose another drive, *Excel* shows you the directories available on that drive. The directory immediately above the one you're using is referred to by two periods: [..]. Choose it in the Directories list and press the OK bar if you want to change directories on the current drive. *Excel* then shows you the list of files from that directory.

The Read Only check box is particularly useful if you're using *Excel* on a network, where access to your files is not controlled. If you open a file with the Read Only box turned on, others on the network can also open your file at the same time. They may change the file that you're looking at, and you may be unaware of the changes until the next time you open it. You, however, can't change the file if you've opened it with the Read Only box turned on.

If, however, you leave the Read Only box turned off, you can change the file, and others on the network opening the file will only be able to open it—not change it.

Password Protection

If the file has been saved with a password, you're asked for it when you issue the File Open command. Type the password in the *Password:* box in the dialog box and press the OK bar. If you type an incorrect password, *Excel* warns you.

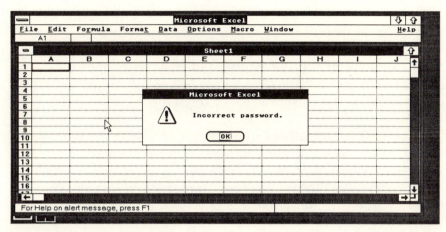

Figure 4-6. Password Warning

Excel then clears the screen of the Open File dialog box. When you type the password correctly, the file opens as normal.

Opening Linked Files

Use the File Links command to open files that are linked to the currently active file.

You saw a demonstration of how linked files work with the earlier discussion of workspace files. Each of the supporting individual sales reports, along with the macro file, was linked to the consolidated report. Formulas in the consolidated report that referred to values in another worksheet used the *Excel* convention of the exclamation mark.

Let's take a closer look at this kind of formula.

The way worksheets are linked in *Excel* is through formulas in which the current worksheet makes an external reference to a value found in another worksheet. The exclamation mark tells *Excel* that the formula is to be found in an *Excel* file other than the current one. To make an external reference, the formula in your current file should look something like one of the formulas found in the composite sales report:

AUSTRAL.XLS!F14*DOLLAR

The first part of the formula, AUSTRAL.XLS, tells *Excel* to look to another file in the current directory and names it. The part of the formula after the exclamation mark tells *Excel* which

Chapter 4

cells or values in the external file are involved and what to do with them. In this case, the external reference formula tells *Excel* to multiply the contents of F14 in AUSTRAL.XLS by the named value DOLLAR. (DOLLAR happens to be a value that's set by another external file—the CONSTANT.XLM macro file that we used to update the current value of foreign currencies in U.S. dollars.)

The Link. . . command comes into use when you're opening several linked files and don't know exactly what should be open. When you choose the Link. . . command, *Excel* displays a dialog box showing you the names of the supporting files in the current directory. If one of those files is still closed, the entire pathname is shown (Figure 4-7).

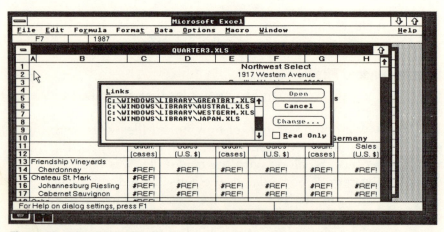

Figure 4-7. File Link Dialog Box

Notice in the illustration that the reference for WESTGERM.XLS is different from the others. That's because this file was still closed when the File Link command was issued. Notice that the filename for WESTGERM.XLS contains the complete pathname, including drive and directory.

If you want to open a listed file that's still closed, you can do it through this dialog box. Make sure the pathname is highlighted and choose the Open bar. If you want to open more than one of the linked files shown, select as many as you want. Use the arrow keys to select a single file, the Shift and arrow keys to select several that are together, or the Ctrl and arrow keys plus the

Working With Files

space bar to select several files that aren't together. When the Links box displays what you want to open, choose the Open bar.

The difference between using the Links command to open multiple linked files and using the File Save Workspace command to create a file listing a group of files that will be opened all at once has to do with choice:

- If you'll be using the same group of files again and again, it makes sense to save them as a workspace and open them all at once.
- If you'll be selecting from a group of linked files, not always needing to have the same files opened, use the Link command to open only those you need at the time.

The Links dialog box also shows you another option: the Change... bar. This lets you change the list of supporting files used by external references in the currently active file. To change a link, select the new supporting files in the Links list and choose the Change... bar. For each link you want to change, *Excel* shows a new dialog box (Figure 4-8).

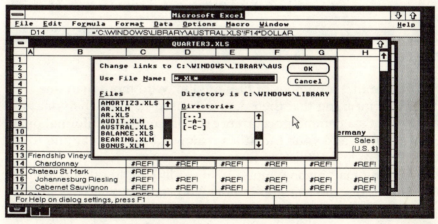

Figure 4-8. Links Change Dialog Box

The Use File Name bar shows the type of files displayed in the Files list box by extension. As you move the highlight bar down the list of files shown, the name of each file appears here. You can also type the name of a file you want to use as a new

Chapter 4

supporting file. If you want to change the drive or directory, select what you want in the Directories box and choose the OK bar. Then you can come back and use the Links command again to choose the file you want.

Some Basic Concepts Behind Linking

If you're familiar with programming and using a link editor to link separately compiled subroutines into a main program, you can understand how linking works within *Excel*. If not, look at the diagram in Figure 4-9.

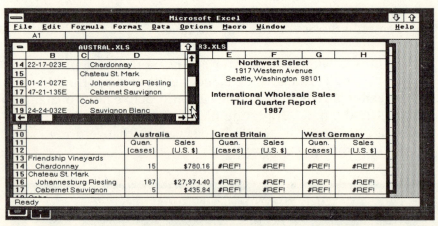

Figure 4-9. Example of Linked Files

Notice that a number of files are linked to more than one other file, meaning that their data gets used in more than one place. That's a common occurrence in Management Information Systems files, and your *Excel* files may wind up contributing to a large system in a similar manner.

Linking may involve more than just linking to other files in the current directory or application. You can also specify a link to a file in a different application—such as other worksheet or database programs. We'll look at that process shortly.

Once you get started linking a lot of files, however, you may have trouble keeping the links established if you move or change references in one file. You may also lose the link if you move a file from one directory to another and have to re-create the link with the Links command.

If you follow some basic rules, you'll keep problems to a minimum:

- If you're going to use a value or a formula in more than one file, name it. That way, if you move the cell's contents or change them in any way, the name will let *Excel* keep track of it.

    Excel adjusts external references differently from the way it does normal references. When you move supporting cells, external references in dependent formulas are not adjusted to reflect the new location of the supporting cells. However, the names used for these supporting cells are updated to reflect their new locations. Hence, any link from the dependent file to the supporting file will be through the list of names, and location of the supporting cells won't matter.
- Keep external reference formulas simple. *Excel* can update values for simple external references without opening the supporting worksheets. More complex ones require that the supporting files be open, thus requiring more memory and slowing performance.
- Name the results of calculation in a supporting file; then use the name when you need to make an external reference. For instance,

    NORTH.XLS!TotSales

is simpler to reference than

    =SUM(NORTH.XLS!$F$3:$F$15)

Creating a Link Between Worksheets

You create a link between worksheets when you use a value from a previously created worksheet in the current worksheet. To do that:

- Open the worksheets you want to link, and activate the supporting worksheet window. Be sure the supporting file is open, or *Excel* will display an error message later on, when you're trying to copy the cell reference over to the dependent file.
- Select the cell or range you want to use in the dependent worksheet.

Chapter 4

- Choose Edit Copy. A dotted line appears around the cell or cells you've selected.
- Activate the dependent worksheet window.
- Position the active cell where you want the supporting cell, or the upper left corner of the supporting range, to go.
- Choose Edit Paste Link. You'll see the external reference formula appear in the formula bar, and the appropriate value will show in the active cell and any other cells involved.

Note: *Excel* automatically creates external reference formulas using absolute cell references unless names have already been given. If you want to type the formula, you can.

When you open a worksheet that is linked to dependent files, or if you decide to leave some dependent files closed in order to save memory, you may see a message asking whether you want to update references to unopened documents. These refer to external reference formulas. If you want *Excel* to update the simple external reference formulas, choose the Yes bar. If you want to use the last values in them, choose the No bar.

If the external reference formulas are more complex and you choose the Yes bar, the values in cells containing more complex external reference formulas will be replaced by the error value #REF!, which will stay there until the supporting files are opened. If you choose the No bar, the last values will be used.

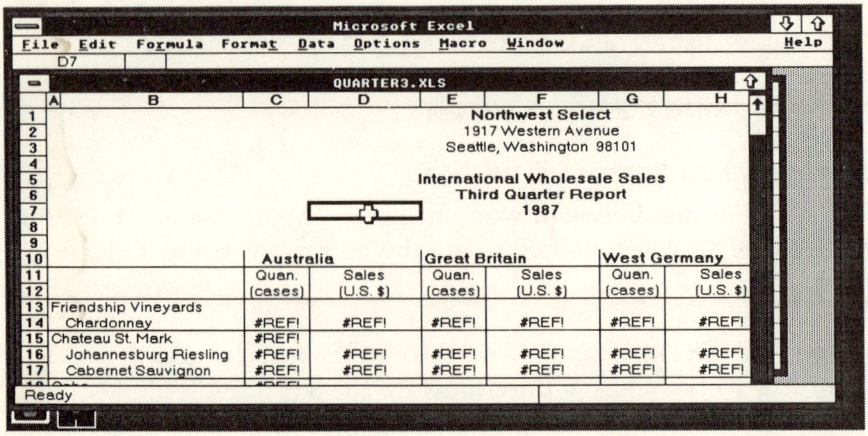

Figure 4-10. Linked Worksheet with Unopened Supporting Files

In Figure 4-10, the Australia and Great Britain supporting files have not been opened, but the QUARTER3.XLS file has been opened. The message about unopened documents was answered with *No.* Notice that the cells that require data from all the unopened supporting files now contain the error value #REF!. As soon as these files are opened, these error values automatically change to the corresponding values. (If you do this in the sequence described here, the Australia, Great Britain, and West Germany windows overlay the Consolidated Report window, hiding the columns of supporting figures. To see these figures and put the supporting windows behind the window containing the consolidated figures, choose the QUARTER3 window on the Window menu.)

The formulas in cells containing references to values in unopened files look different in the formula bar. When the active cell is moved to a cell containing a reference to a value in the unopened file, the formula bar shows the full pathname.

Cell references to values in opened files use the filename convention described earlier (that is, AUSTRAL.XLS!D14).

Using Files from Other Programs

You can use files from other programs with *Excel*, either completely or as individual cell values. If your other program operates under *Windows*, you can establish automatic links from files created with that program to your current worksheet. However, you can also use data from another program even if it doesn't operate under *Windows*.

Using Data from Another File Under *Windows*

You can link a current worksheet to a file created by another program running under Microsoft *Windows* provided that both applications are running under version 2.0 or higher. The program doesn't necessarily have to be from Microsoft, but it must meet the *Windows* environment requirements; most programs that do so will usually have some words to this effect somewhere early in a user's guide or other documentation.

Installing other programs under *Windows* 2.0 won't be described in detail here. The basic concepts of windowing are covered in the *Excel Reference Manual* under the topic "Windows." The purpose of having the other programs installed under *Win-*

Chapter 4

dows is so that they can share the Clipboard and other utilities, and so that the file-access method is one that *Excel* can share.

One method by which *Windows* applications share data is called Dynamic Data Exchange (DDE). It's covered in detail in the *Excel* Reference Manual.

The other method involves using the Clipboard, an electronic facility in *Windows* where data is temporarily stored while it's being moved or copied from one application to another. The Clipboard utility program is examined in Appendix D, but several Clipboard commands are often mentioned in this book:

Edit Copy
Edit Copy Picture
Edit Cut
Edit Paste

In order to use data from another program running under *Windows*, you must be sure that it ultimately becomes data that can be stored meaningfully in a cell. Numeric data has to be in a form that can become data that *Excel* can work with. This may require that you use one or more of *Excel*'s functions or the Data Parse command to manipulate it.

For instance, if there is a date buried in a text string in your incoming data, you may want to use the text-processing functions to strip the other data away, leaving just the date, and if necessary use one of the date functions to store the date in a format *Excel* can use.

Generally, however, most numeric data is likely to be stored in a cell-like format that *Excel* can use so that you can directly link to the location of the supporting data.

When you're linking to a file created with a non-*Excel* program but running under *Windows*, the procedure you use is similar to linking to another *Excel* file:

- Open both the dependent worksheet and the non-*Excel* file to which you wish to link.
- Activate the supporting-document window.
- Select the cell, range, value, or field of the data you want to use, and choose Edit Copy.
- Activate the dependent-worksheet window.

- Position the active cell where you want the incoming data to go.
- Choose Edit Paste Link.

Excel establishes the link with a formula that follows specific conventions, in the form

='APPLICATION_NAME'|'DOCUMENT_NAME'!reference

Each portion of the formula tells Excel how to find the data you want, as the following table explains.

APPLICATION NAME	Must be immediately preceded by an equal sign and immediately followed by a vertical bar (|). The application name must either be a legal *Excel* name or one enclosed in single quotation marks. In the example above, APPLICATION_NAME is enclosed in quotation marks to make it acceptable to *Excel*.
| (vertical bar)	Must separate the application name and the document name. It's used to tell *Excel* that what follows is not just a different *Excel* directory.
'DOCUMENT_NAME'	Must be the name of the file in the other application. (Some applications, particularly some network servers, consider documents to be "topics;" use the "topic" name here, in that case.) This name can be as many as 255 characters long and may include the full pathname, the name of a terminal, and any opening parameters necessary for *Excel* to use to get to the document you want. If you have any questions about *Excel* being able to understand the document name (perhaps because of the presence of some characters required at the other end but considered illegal by *Excel*), enclose the document name in single quotation marks.
!	Separates the document name from the cell reference or value.
reference	The cell, range, name, value, or field of data you want to use. What goes here can be a cell or range address, the name of the cell or range, the value you want to use, or the reference to the data field (in a database, for instance) containing the information you want to use. Cell-referencing methods are discussed in an earlier chapter, and greater detail about getting data from a database is found in Chapters 8 and 11. If the name of the data looks like a cell reference (such as AT50, which could be taken to be the cell on row 50 in column AT, or which may be the name of a value derived when some condition reaches 50), enclose it in single quotation marks.

The procedure for opening and updating a worksheet linked to another application is very similar to that used in opening and updating another linked *Excel* worksheet. When you open a worksheet containing remote references to another application, *Excel* asks you if you want to reestablish links to that other application. Answer *yes* if you want the links; answer *no* if you want to use the last values received from that application.

If *Excel* tries to establish a link and fails (the supporting application isn't running or can't be accessed), *Excel* asks whether you want to start the application. If you agree, *Excel* tries to start the application; if it can't, the cells with external references to this application display the #REF! error value.

Summary

This chapter has shown you how to open and save files within *Excel* and how you can use some built-in capabilities to back up your files.

Chapter 5
Editing What You Have

Once your data has been entered, you may discover that you've made some mistakes or that you want to move data around or even change something about the way your worksheet looks. This is where you'll find the Edit commands useful.

The Edit menu contains a number of commands which help you manipulate existing data.

Undo	Lets you reverse the effects of the just-prior command.
Repeat	Lets you repeat the last command you chose, if possible, including the options you selected in the dialog box.
Cut	Specifies that selected cells will be moved when you choose the Edit Paste command.
Copy	Specifies that selected cells will be copied when you choose the Edit Paste or the Edit Paste Special command.
Paste	Moves or copies the selection of cells you've identified with the Cut or Copy command.
Clear	Removes data, formulas, or both from the current document.
Paste Special...	Copies selected parts of the copy area into cells you choose and lets you specify how these parts are to be manipulated.
Paste Link	Copies data into the current worksheet and establishes a link to the copied cells.
Delete...	Removes the selected cells from the worksheet and shifts other cells to close up the space.
Insert...	Inserts a blank cell or range of cells into the worksheet and shifts selected cells to make room for the new cells.
Fill Right	Copies the contents and formats of the cells in the leftmost column of selected cells into the rest of the columns in the selected cells, overwriting anything that's there.
Fill Left	Appears on the Edit menu if you hold down the Shift key while selecting the Edit menu. It works the same as the Fill Right command, except that it fills from the rightmost column into columns to the left.
Fill Down	Copies the contents and formats of the cells in the top row of selected cells into the rest of the rows in the selection, overwriting anything that's there.

Chapter 5

Fill Up	Appears on the Edit menu if you hold down the Shift key while selecting the Edit menu. It works the same as the Fill Down command, except that it fills from the bottom rows into rows above it.
Copy Picture	Appears on the Edit menu only if you hold down Shift when you select the Edit menu. It copies a pictorial representation of the current selection onto the Clipboard, where it can be pasted into another application.

The Edit commands work with some of the commands on the Formula menu to allow you not only to edit the contents of a cell, but also to perform editing within complex formulas, to search for specific cells or data, and to replace specific information.

The Formula menu's commands let you edit formulas and use previously named blocks of data, functions, or formulas within formulas you're constructing. These commands are outlined in the following table.

Paste Name...	Pastes a predefined name into the Formula bar.
Paste Function...	Pastes a built-in function you specify into the Formula bar.
Reference	Converts selected references in the Formula bar from relative to absolute, from absolute to mixed, or from mixed to relative.
Define Name...	Creates, deletes, or changes a name for a cell or cell range, value, or formula.
Create Names...	Lets you name several rows of data by using the text at one edge of the data.
Apply Names...	Lets you replace cell addresses with predefined names.
Note...	Lets you attach explanatory information to a cell and add, delete, or edit it.
Goto...	Scrolls the worksheet to a named area or cell address.
Find...	Locates text or numbers in a cell.
Replace...	Lets you find and replace characters in all cells or in a cell range you specify.
Select Special...	Selects cells having the characteristics you specify.

Most of the menu items listed above can be used with shortcut keys. These will be mentioned as each of the commands in this chapter is discussed.

Selecting

When you want to change an item, you usually need to select the cells involved first. You select one or more cells by highlighting.

The way you select depends on how many cells you want to select.

Selecting on a Worksheet

To select a single cell on a worksheet:

- Press the arrow key to move to the cell you want to select.
  Or
- Use the mouse to click the cell you want to select. The currently active cell is always assumed to be the cell selected.

To select a range of cells on a worksheet (a range is a rectangular block of cells):

- Use the arrow keys to move to the upper left cell of the range you want.
- Hold down the Shift key while you use the arrow keys to extend the highlighting to include the cells you want.
    Or, with a mouse, click and drag through the cells you want.

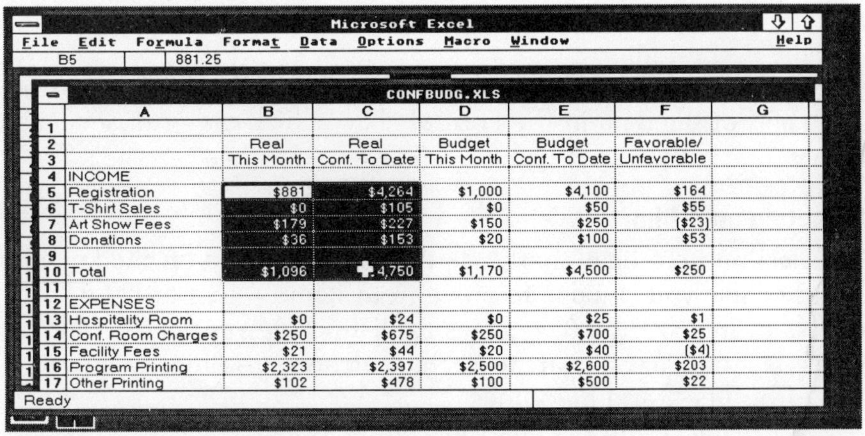

Figure 5-1. Selected Range on a Worksheet

To select multiple unconnected cells or cell ranges:

- Select the first cell.
- Press F8 (which turns on the Extend key) and use the arrow keys to extend the selection.

Chapter 5

- Then press Shift and F8 to keep that selection, and use the arrow keys to move to the next cell you want to select.
- Repeat the process.

If you have a mouse, click and drag through the first selection. Then hold down the Ctrl key as you click and drag through each of the next selections.

Selecting Within the Formula Bar

You can also select within the Formula bar. If you're constructing a fairly elaborate formula and have not yet pressed the Enter key, you can perform fairly large-scale editing on the formula by selecting portions of what is already on the Formula bar:

- If you press Shift and the arrow keys, you'll extend the selection from the current character one character to the right or left, or one line up or down.
- If you press Ctrl + Shift and the arrow keys, you'll extend the selection one word to the right or left, or one line up or down.
- If you press Ctrl + Shift + Home you'll extend the selection to the start of the Formula bar data.
- If you press Shift + End you'll extend the selection to the end of the current line.
- If you press Ctrl + Shift + End you'll extend the selection to the end of the data in the Formula bar (which may run several lines).

Selecting on a Chart

To select an item on a chart, use the direction keys on the keyboard or use your mouse to move from item to item or between classes of items. *Excel* recognizes as distinct classes charts, plot areas, legends, axes, chart text, chart arrows, gridlines, data series, drop lines, and hi/lo lines.

For instance, on the chart in Figure 5-2, a bar has been selected as indicated by the boxes at the top and bottom and on the sides of the bar.

Editing What You Have

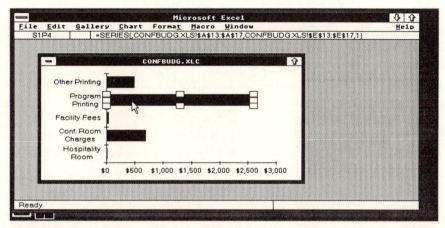

Figure 5-2. Selected Item, Bar Chart

The way a selection appears varies with the type of chart. In the sample pie-chart shown below, the segment that has been selected is indicated both by highlighting and by the presence of the boxes.

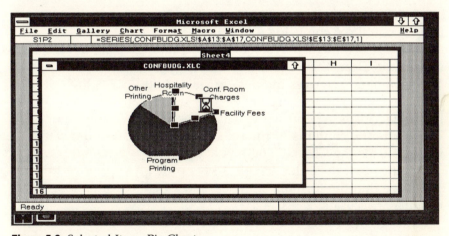

Figure 5-3. Selected Item, Pie Chart

Highlighting means that this is the version you'll be working with next. The boxes, however, can be black or white to indicate what may be done with the selected item.

Black boxes mean that the selection can be formatted with commands and moved or sized with the keyboard or mouse. White boxes mean that the selection cannot be moved or sized

Chapter 5

directly. However, some items, such as the legend or axis labels, can be formatted or realigned with commands.

Removing Data: Clearing and Deleting

Like most worksheet programs, *Excel* makes a distinction between deleting something and erasing or clearing it.

When you delete something, *Excel* removes the contents of the cell or cells, as well as the cell itself. When you clear something, only the contents of the cell are removed. Let's use a simple example to demonstrate the difference.

On a blank worksheet, make the entries shown in the table below.

In this cell:	Enter this:
A1	2
A2	2
A3	=A1+A2

When you press the Enter key after you've typed the formula for A3, you'll see the value 4 in cell A3.

Now move the active cell to cell A2, and choose the command Edit Clear; then choose OK when the dialog box appears. This command removes the data in cell A2 but leaves the cell otherwise intact. (You can use either of two alternate methods. With the active cell as A2, press the backspace key, then the Enter key. This clears the contents of the selected cell. Or, press the Del key, which causes the Clear dialog box to appear.)

Notice that the value in cell A3 is now 2. If you move to A3, you'll see that the formula is intact, and that the evaluation of the formula is accurate: 2 + 0 = 2.

Move back to cell A2, and retype the 2. Now your worksheet looks like the original example.

With the active cell as A2, this time choose the Edit Delete command. Choose the Shift Cells Up option in the dialog box. Notice that when you choose the OK bar, the 2 disappears from cell A2, and the error message #REF! appears.

What has happened is that cell A2 has been deleted, and the rows below it have been moved up to close the space. This means that the formula which used to be in A3 is now in A2.

Since the formula refers to what used to be A2, there is now an error in the formula.

(To restore the just-prior condition of your example, choose the Edit Undo command. If you have not pressed any other keys, the Undo command puts A2 and its contents back where they were. If anything else has been typed, however, you'll see a *Can't Undo* message.)

As a general rule, the Clear command is better for removing data from cells when there's any suspicion that the addresses of those cells might be used as part of formulas in other cells. The Clear command dialog box for a worksheet gives you several options for clearing only part of a cell's contents (Figure 5-4).

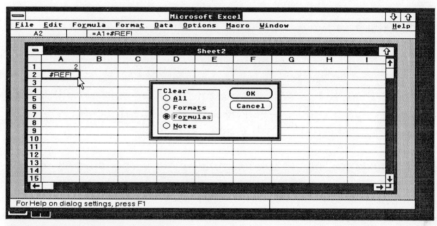

Figure 5-4. Edit Clear Dialog Box

The options are slightly different for the Clear command when it's used with a chart. If the entire chart has been selected with the Chart Select Chart command, the Clear command erases the chart's data series, format, or both. If the Formula bar is active, Clear erases only the part of the formula that has been selected.

The Delete command is better for completely wiping out whole rows or columns or for removing one or more cells so that *Excel* can shift other cells around to fill in the space.

To delete a row or column, select the row or column and choose Edit Delete. *Excel* automatically moves the remaining rows or columns to fill in the space.

To delete one or more cells, select the cell or cell range, and choose the Edit Delete command. A dialog box appears, asking how you want the remaining cells moved—to the left or up. Choose the option you want, and then choose the OK bar.

Inserting

Excel has two different concepts of inserting.

The *insertion point* is the point within a cell or a formula where the next character will appear. The default within *Excel* is that you can always insert at the point of the blinking vertical line.

The Edit Insert command lets you insert one or more blank cells, columns, or rows into an existing worksheet.

To insert a blank cell:

- Select the area where you want the new cells inserted.
- Choose the Edit Insert command, and when the dialog box appears, specify the direction in which you want existing cells moved.
- Choose the OK bar, and the existing cells—complete with data, formats, and formulas—will be moved in the direction you specify to make room for the new blank cells.

For instance, one of the examples in an earlier chapter uses the projected income statement in Figure 5-5, showing monthly assumptions about income and expenses.

	A	B	C	D	E	F
1	Balance Sheet for Year 87-88					
2						
3		January	February	March	April	May
4						
5	Assets					
6						
7	Cash	$345,639	$323,856	$301,345	$303,546	$307,4
8	Accounts Receivable: Trade	$5,645,547	$4,692,125	$4,891,235	$4,964,235	$5,008,7
9	Accounts Receivable: Other	$185,037	$221,691	$179,234	$191,290	$186,4
10	Inventory	$457,924	$652,334	$589,134	$593,751	$455,2
11	Other Current Assets	$23,675	$11,546	$14,763	$15,017	$14,0
12						
13	Total Current Assets	$6,657,822	$5,901,552	$5,975,711	$6,067,839	$5,971,8
14						
15	Plant and Equipment	$3,456,672	$4,012,565	$4,014,643	$4,019,533	$4,020,6

Figure 5-5. Income Statement, Monthly Figures

Suppose we want to change this to add three-month summaries. What will happen to the rest of the spreadsheet?

Before starting, it should be understood that the Undo command works with Insert as well as with Delete. So if we make a mistake and want to undo the Insert command, it can easily be changed.

With that said, let's insert a new column after the March figures, one which can hold the quarterly summary figures. We'll look at the new column's impact after it's in place.

To insert the new column:

- Position the active cell anywhere in column E and press Ctrl + space bar. If you're using a mouse, click the column heading, Apr-88. This selects all of column E.
- With the column highlighted, choose the Edit Insert command.

Since you selected the entire column, *Excel* doesn't ask you how you want the remaining cells adjusted, and it moves everything to the right.

If you want to take out the newly inserted column, choose the Edit Undo command before you type anything else. The blank column disappears and the rest of the worksheet shifts back to the left.

However, you're probably interested in adding quarterly summary figures. You'll see how to do that quickly in the section where copying is explained, later in this chapter. Before that, however, you need to know one of the effects of inserting blank cells, whether they are single cells, ranges, or whole columns or rows.

Suppose that the spreadsheet in Figure 5-5 had year-end summary figures in the column following the December figures. Chances are the formula used to add up those figures would have been a SUM function, perhaps

=SUM(B6:M6)

By inserting a column, *Excel* would automatically adjust any such formulas to the right of the inserted column to allow for the new locations. However, *Excel* would assume that the newly inserted column contained data that should be added in, and hence would modify the function to read:

=SUM(B6:N6)

Unfortunately, that's not what you mean. You'd be adding the monthly figures for January, February, and March to produce the quarterly summary figures in Column E, and then adding those same three sets of monthly data, along with the first-quarter summary figures, to the data in the remaining nine columns to get an annual total.

Corrective action would involve modifying the year-end formulas to add only the monthly figures or to add four quarterly summary figures (if you added columns for summaries for the second, third, and fourth quarters).

Cut and Paste: Moving and Copying

You can move cells around on your worksheet, transferring entire blocks of calculations to other locations. You can also copy cells containing formulas or values to other locations. In both cases, the cell references automatically adjust to reflect the new locations.

Moving is done by first selecting the cells involved and then using the Cut and Paste commands; copying is done by sometimes selecting the cells, then using the Copy command. However, there are other kinds of copying that involve the special forms of the Paste command. We'll look at both kinds of operations in this section.

When you move a set of cells, you remove them from one location and put them in another. This is as if you were literally cutting out the block of cells, moving them to a new location and pasting them in place there. Because this analogy is so easy for most people to grasp, the designers of *Excel* chose the Cut and Paste commands to accomplish the tasks involved in moving cells.

To illustrate how you can move cells, let's move some around a small sample worksheet. Figure 5-6 is an example of a worksheet on which we can practice.

Editing What You Have

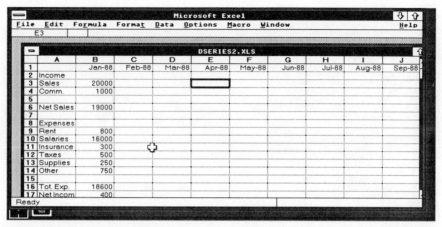

Figure 5-6. Sample Worksheet

The Net Sales, Total Expenses, and Net Income cells contain formulas as follows.:

These Cells:	Contain These Formulas:
Net Sales (B6)	=B3-B4
Total Expenses (B16)	=SUM(B9:B14)
Net Income (B17)	=B6-B16

(You can devise your own worksheet to follow this exercise; be sure to put in a few formulas so that you can see how the move and copy operations handle the references.)

Whatever cells are involved in a move or copy operation must first be selected. Let's use the expense figures just to illustrate how this works. Select all of the Expenses cells, from B9 to B16.

- Position the active cell on B9.
- Press F8.
- Use the down-arrow key to highlight the range.
  Or, use your mouse to click and drag so that the range is highlighted.

With the cells selected, choose the Edit Cut command. (You can also use the shortcut keys, Shift + Del.) Notice that a dotted marquee appears around the selected cells.

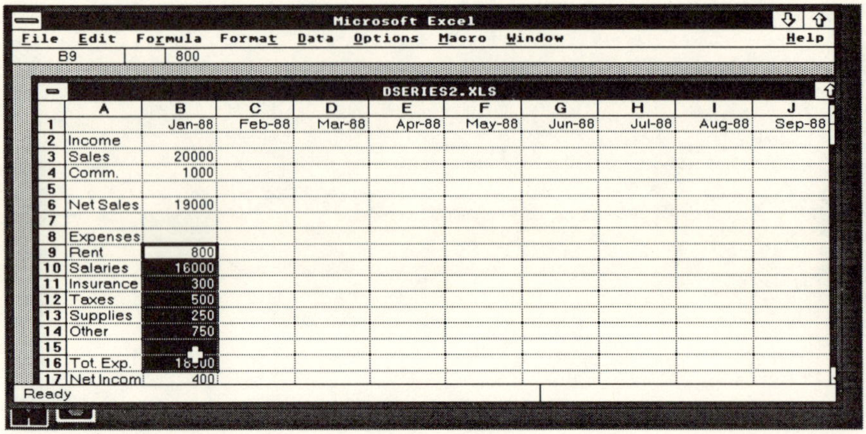

Chapter 5

Figure 5-7. Selected Cells, Sample Worksheet

Now move the active cell to some other location in the worksheet—for instance, one column to the right. Notice that the dotted line continues to outline the cells you're going to move. When the active cell is where you want to put the new cells, either press the Enter key or choose the Edit Paste command. (You can also use the shortcut keys, Shift + Ins).

Notice several things about the cells in their new locations:

The SUM formula at the bottom of the range now reflects the new location of the cells. If you position the active cell in C16, you find that the formula now reads:

=SUM(C9:C14)

The formula in B17 now reflects the new location, too; it now reads:

=B6-C16

Excel automatically adjusts references to the moved cells. Any references within the moved area to other cells within the moved area still designate the same cells, although the cell addresses will be different. References to cells outside the moved area will be the same.

However, references to cells in the area where the moved area was pasted now produce the error value #REF!, since the move operation in essence deleted whatever had been there before.

You can also move cells from one worksheet to another with the same Cut and Paste commands. The only thing to be careful of is that references to the area that is moved to another worksheet will produce the error value #REF! once the cells are moved.

What to Do When Things Go Wrong

If you find error values in the moved cells or in other cells referencing the moved cells, immediately choose the Undo command before pressing any other key. This restores everything to its prior value.

If you don't want to undo the entire move operation, use the Formula Find command to locate the cells with error values, and correct them so that they refer to the cells you want.

Just to assure yourself that everything works as described, move the same block back to its original location. You can double-check yourself by looking at the formulas in B14 and B16; after the move, they'll reflect values in column B instead of those in column C.

So how is copying different? Copying lets you duplicate cells in another location without moving the original cells.

Excel, however, broadens the definition of copying to allow you to:

- Selectively copy specific cell or data attributes.
- Copy only nonblank cells.
- Transpose cells.
- Combine the contents of the copied cells with those already there.
- Copy all or part of a formula bar or another cell entry into the Formula bar.
- Copy names or functions into a formula.
- Copy data and formats from one chart to another.

Let's start with something simple, however.

A Simple Copying Exercise

With the sample worksheet on your screen:

- Select the Expenses cells again (B9:B14).
- Instead of choosing the Edit Cut command, choose Edit Copy.

Chapter 5

(You can use the shortcut keys, Ctrl + Ins to do the same thing.)
   Notice the message in the Status Bar.
- Move the active cell to a new location—cell C9, for instance.
- When you have the active cell in the top position of the area where you want the cells copied, you can either choose the Edit Paste command or press the Enter key.

Either action results in the selected cells being duplicated in the new location, as the example in Figure 5-8 shows.

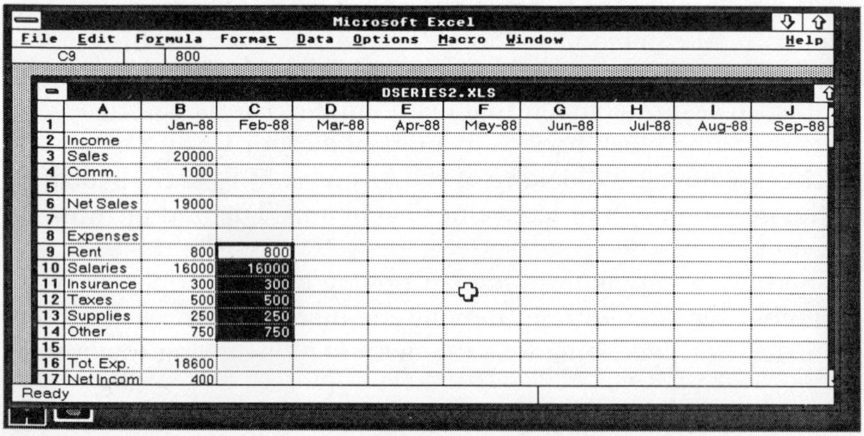

Figure 5-8. Sample Worksheet, Copied Cells

There are differences between the results of the move and the copy operations. While a move operation results in adjustment of relative cell references, any references within the copied area to cells outside the copied area will not be to the same cells, but rather to cells in the equivalent position relative to the copied formula.

For instance, suppose the figure in B13 were not a number, but a formula reflecting a percentage of commissions:

   =200+0.15*B4

When the Expenses figures, but not the Income figures, are moved, this formula remains the same, still referencing B4. When the Expenses figures are copied to a new location, however, such as was done with the figures in the illustration above, the formula refers to the equivalent location above and becomes:

=200+0.15*C4

Notice also that, once the cells have been copied, the copied cells remain highlighted until you move the active cell. This means that you can copy the same set of cells anywhere else on the worksheet—or even to another worksheet—with the same procedure. (If you copy to another worksheet, use the Edit Paste command.)

If you want to put the same formula or values in several adjacent cells (for instance, using the same formulas to compute total income, total expenses, and net income when you're doing a 12-month income statement), use the Edit Fill command. It and the Edit Copy command work a bit differently.

Instead of selecting just the cell or cells you want to copy, select both the source and destination cells. Now we're going to copy the formula for Net Sales into the 11 columns to the right so that as data gets entered for sales and commissions for each month, the same formula can be used to compute Net Sales. In row 6, select columns B through J.

To copy the formula in B6 into the cells to the right, simply select the Edit Fill Right command. The formula is copied, and each of the destination cells shows a value of 0. If you check on the contents of these cells, you'll see that the formula is there; because there are no values in the rows above it, its current evalution is 0.

Edit Fill Left and Edit Fill Down and Up work the same way. Select the source and destination cells (destination cells must be adjacent to the source cell) and choose the appropriate command.

Copying Specific Cell or Data Attributes

The Edit Paste Special menu lets you be selective about what you want to copy. With it you can also manipulate copied data. The area you select for pasting must have the same size and shape as the area from which you're copying. However, as with the other Paste command, you can use the source cells as often as you like.

Edit Paste Special works only with the Edit Copy command—not with the Edit Cut command.

When you choose this command, after selecting the cells and

Chapter 5

using the Edit Copy command, you'll see a dialog box like the one in Figure 5-9.

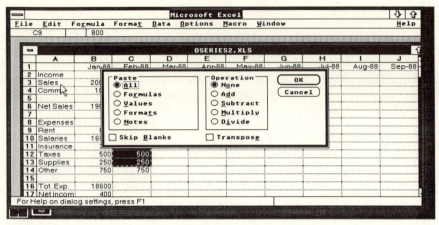

Figure 5-9. Edit Paste Special Dialog Box

The selections work as described in the table below.

Selection	Definition
All	Pastes all properties of the selected cells.
Formulas	Pastes whatever has been entered in the Formula bar for the source cells; this can include values as well as formulas.
Values	Pastes only the values as displayed in the source cells.
Formats	Pastes only the formats of the selected cells.
Notes	Pastes only the notes attached to the cells.

Notice that these are mutually exclusive options: you can't choose Formats *and* Values, for instance. However, these are the options you'll want when you're interested in using only part of the current contents of a source block of cells.

The same dialog box lets you specify how to manipulate and combine data from the source cells into the paste area. The Operation box specifies what you can do, and the table below describes what happens when you perform various actions.

Action	Definition
None	Has the same effect as that of the Edit Paste command.
Add	Adds the specified parts of the source cells to the paste-area cells and puts the results in the paste area.
Subtract	Subtracts the specified parts of the source cells from the paste-area cells and puts the results in the paste area.
Multiply	Multiplies the contents of the paste-area cells by the contents of the source cells.
Divide	Divides the contents of the paste-area cells by the contents of the source cells.

Copying Only Nonblank Cells

Normally *Excel* copies both blank and nonblank cells when you select a cell range to copy. The Edit Paste dialog box lets you specify that only the nonblank cells are to be copied.

Transposing Cells

This option on the Edit Paste Special dialog box lets you change the orientation of your data when you paste it somewhere else. Data that has been in adjacent rows in a column will be in the same row but adjacent columns, and data that has been in columns will be in rows. However, *Excel* also fills in the other cells in the rectangle, as shown in Figure 5-10.

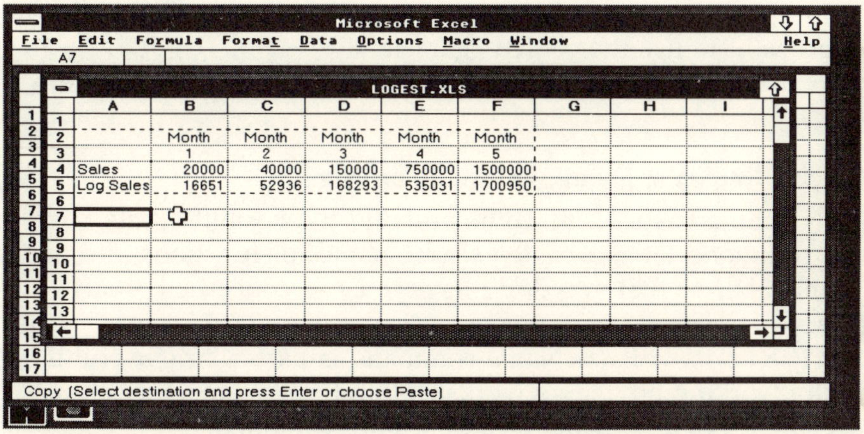

Figure 5-10. Data Before Transposing with Edit Copy Special

Chapter 5

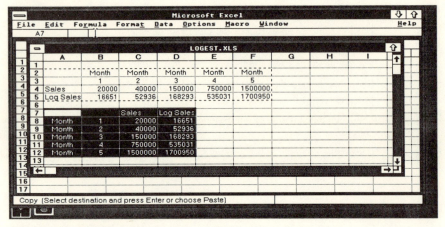

Figure 5-11. Data After Transposing with Edit Copy Special

Copying into the Formula Bar

Use the Edit Paste command to save time when you're constructing long formulas or labels.

You may need to duplicate a label or a particularly intricate set of characters within a formula (for example, if you're constructing a set of nested IF statements). When typing something like this in the Formula bar:

- Select the characters you want to copy.
- Choose the Edit Copy command.
- Move the insertion point in the Formula bar to the point where you want to use the copied characters.
- Choose Edit Paste. The characters now also appear at the new location.

Copying Names or Functions into a Formula

The Formula Paste Name command and the Formula Paste Function command let you paste existing names or functions into the Formula bar so that you don't have to be as concerned about accuracy or spelling.

The Formula Paste Name command is particularly useful if you're working on a large worksheet and can't remember either the address of a particular cell or what it is named.

When you choose the Formula Paste Name command and there are names already defined, a dialog box appears showing all the currently defined names in use for this worksheet. (If no

108

names have been defined, the Formula Paste Name command is grayed.)

To use one of the names in a formula:

- Make the Formula bar active, with the insertion point placed where you want the name to go.
- Choose the Formula Paste Name command.
- When you see the list of existing names, choose the name you want to use. The name is pasted at the insertion point.

The Formula Paste Function command works pretty much the same way. A dialog box appears, showing the names of all the functions, followed by any function macros defined on open macro sheets. (A function macro is preceded by the name of its macro sheet and an exclamation point.) Use the arrow keys (and PgDn or PgUp keys) or scroll through the list until you find the name of the function you want, and then choose it.

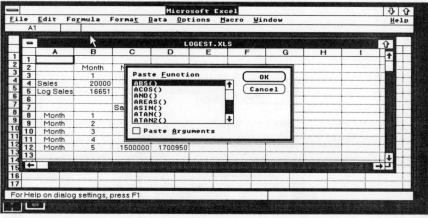

Figure 5-12. Formula Paste Function Dialog Box

However, here's where Formula Paste Name and Formula Paste Function are different. There's a check box below the list of functions. If this Paste Arguments box is turned on, when you paste the function name into your formula, you'll also paste into place text descriptions of the function's arguments as prompts.

For instance, if you can't remember the arguments for a Net Present Value function but you want to use it in a formula with the Formula bar active:

Chapter 5

- Scroll through the Paste Function box until NPV( ) is highlighted and be sure the Paste Argument box is turned on.
- Press the Enter key.
    The NPV function appears at the insertion point in the Formula bar, followed by text describing the arguments:

    NPV(rate,value1,value2,. . .)

- Move the insertion point to the first letter in *rate* and type the rate. (Notice that the word *rate* disappears).
- Leave the comma in place and move the insertion point to the next word that describes an argument—in this case, *value1*—and type the number or reference that belongs here, and so on.
- Delete any arguments or other characters that you don't need, and leave the right parenthesis in place. When you press the Enter key, *Excel* will either accept what you've done with the function or tell you that there is an error.

Copying Data and Formats from One Chart to Another

Use the Edit Paste Special command to copy data series, formats, or both from one chart to another. You'll be asked which elements to copy with the dialog box that appears.

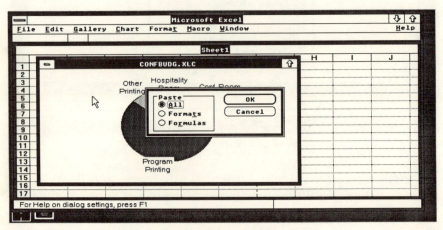

Figure 5-13. Edit Paste Special Dialog Box for Charts

Copying Data from a Worksheet into a Chart

You can copy data from a worksheet to a chart with the Edit Paste Special command. When a chart is an active document, the dialog box looks different, however.

The Values in the dialog box tell *Excel* where to look for the data series for the chart: If you leave the Rows button on, the contents of each row in the selected cells become a data series; if you turn on the Columns button, each set of column data becomes a data series.

The two lower check boxes let you tell *Excel* where to look for the name of the data series and the categories of data. If you have turned on the Rows button, the check boxes below ask you whether the series names are in the first column and the categories are in the first row. If they are, turn these boxes on, and *Excel* uses the contents in the first column of each row as the name of that data series, and the contents of the first row as the categories for the chart.

If the Series Name in First Column box is turned off, *Excel* uses the contents of the cell in the first column of each row as the first data point of the series. If the Categories in First Row box is turned off, *Excel* uses the contents of the first row as the first data series in the chart.

If you turn on the Columns button, the check boxes read Series Names in First Row and Categories in First Column; they work in the reverse manner of what was just described above.

The Replace Existing Categories check box lets you use the categories from the selected cells for the data series already in the chart as well as for the data series you're pasting into the chart. If you turn on this check box, the existing categories are replaced.

Formatting Your Work

Formatting your spreadsheet or chart lets you change the appearance of your work—the way your data is displayed (as numbers, currency, percentages, or dates, for instance, or how it's aligned or what typeface and size it uses). You are also able to define how borders, headings, and gridlines are handled, how data is displayed within a window, and how the worksheet is printed. Chart-formatting techniques allow you to add or change chart objects or text.

Default Values

Within *Excel*, numbers and text have certain default formats. Numbers are assigned the General format (*Excel* uses the number format that seems most appropriate) and are right-aligned, while text is left-aligned and error and logical values are centered. Columns are eight characters wide, the font is ten-point

Helvetica, and the same-size characters are available in bold, italic, and bold-italic, as well as normal, typefaces. There are no special borders or shading.

Within a window, cell values are displayed (rather than formulas), gridlines and headings are shown, and text is displayed in black against a white background.

As you might guess, you can change any of these values, and more, to tailor the appearance of your work both on the screen and as printed.

Assigning Formats as You Work

As you're constructing your worksheet or chart, you can assign formats and have them stay in place as you work, even if you clear the contents of a cell or range.

If you want to use different formats within the same worksheet (dates in one column, dollar amounts in another, percentages in yet another) you may find it best to format the cells involved before you enter the data. That way, no matter how you type the data, it appears in the format you want, provided it doesn't overflow the cell width.

To preset a format for a range of cells:

- Select the cells in which you will enter your data.
- Choose the Format Number command.
- When the menu appears, choose the format you want to apply to the selected range. This can include number, date, and time formats, as well as alignments, fonts, and column width. However, if you use nondefault formats, once you move beyond the selected range, the default formats will be in effect.

Alignment and Justification

Text is normally aligned on a left border. You can select cells where you want text right-aligned or centered. Use the Format Alignment command.

You can also use this command to override *Excel*'s defaults for alignment of numbers or logical or error values.

You use a different command to justify text in charts. Use the Format Text command to align unattached text and attached text labels for chart objects (such as a label for a category).

With the Format Text command in a chart window, you can align horizontal text left, right, or centered, and you can align vertical text to the top, bottom or center.

The Format Justify command is especially useful if you're trying to make text fit within a particular block of cells on a worksheet. If you're typing full paragraphs, try the approach described below.

Type your text as you would any paragraph, starting with the upper left cell of the area where you want the text to go. Remember that an individual line can hold a maximum of 255 characters. You'll see the characters scroll through the active cell as you type, but the full line will appear in the Formula bar. You'll have to insert a carriage return at the end of each line.

Since each line will be entered as the contents of the leftmost column, whatever formatting applies to the leftmost cells will be in effect for the line.

When you've finished typing the text, select the block of cells where you want the text to fit. Make sure you include the cell you began entering text into. (It doesn't matter whether the text you typed is wider or narrower than the block you specify, but it may matter if there is data underneath the specified block. When *Excel* justifies text within a selected block, it asks whether it's OK that the text doesn't fit. If you answer *OK*, it fills cells below the selected block with any excess text, and if data is there, the text overwrites the data.)

Figure 5-14 shows an example of text that has been entered to fit within columns.

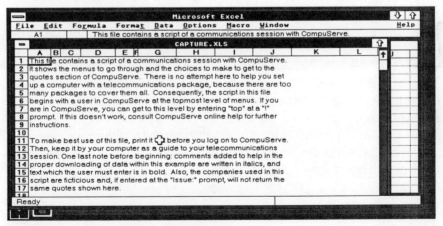

Figure 5-14. Text Entered in a Worksheet

Once your paragraph is entered, you may also want to reformat it using one of the Alignment options, or you may want to reposition it within other cell limits, using the Format Justify command. For instance, the text from Figure 5-14 is justified so it will fit within column A in Figure 5-15.

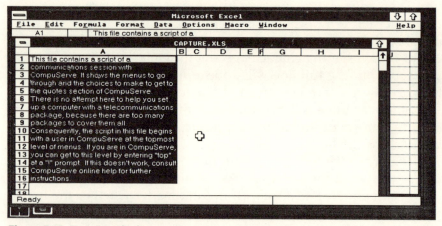

Figure 5-15. Text Justified

How do you do that? With the text as shown in Figure 5-14, select a column and then use the Format Justify command. *Excel* warns you that the text will extend beyond the range of cells selected, but since that's OK, just let it happen. *Excel* goes ahead and justifies the text so that the lines fit within column A.

This technique is very handy when you want to append worksheet comments that should always be present—not hidden from immediate view the way notes are.

Borders, Headings, and Gridlines

You can add borders to data or text so that it stands out, and you can add shading to distinguish it even further. Borders are straight lines and can be added at any combination of the left, right, top, and bottom edges of a selected cell or block of cells.

When you choose the Format Border command, you see a list of choices in a dialog box like the one in Figure 5-16.

Editing What You Have

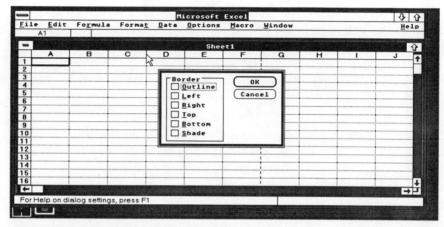

Figure 5-16. Format Border Dialog Box

These choices apply to the cell or cells that are currently selected. Turn on the check boxes for the kind of border you want.

For instance, suppose you decide to outline the text inserted above. After you've used the Format Border command, your worksheet will look like the one in Figure 5-17.

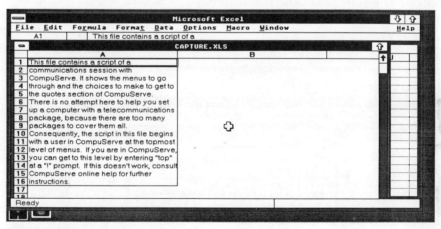

Figure 5-17. Border Around Text

You can make the text stand out even more by choosing the Shade option, which will shade the entire block.

There are some other tricks that can add interest to your worksheet. You can create double underlines by using a narrow row height for one row:

Chapter 5

- With a mouse, drag the horizontal gridline in the row heading below the row you want to reduce.
- With the keyboard, use Format Row Height and pick a number less than the standard height of 13.
- If you'll be turning off gridlines, select the narrow row and turn on the Top and Bottom border check boxes to outline it.

Use the same technique to make double column lines. (With a mouse, drag the vertical gridline in the column heading. With the keyboard, select Format Column Width and use 1 as the number. If you'll be turning off gridlines, select the narrow column and use the Left- and Right-border check boxes to outline it.)

You can remove the column and row identifiers from your worksheet with the Options Display command. This leaves only your text and data on the screen—a close approximation of what your printed worksheet will look like (unless you specifically ask that row and column headings be printed).

When you turn off gridlines, all that's left on your worksheet is text and data (and row and column headings, unless you've turned them off). You turn off the gridlines with the same Options Display command, which lists several things you can do (Figure 5-18).

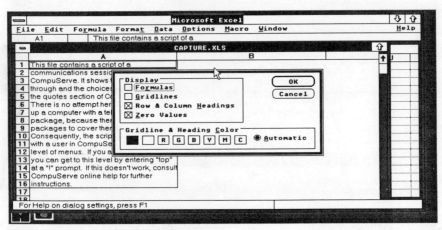

Figure 5-18. Options Display Dialog Box

Turning off the gridlines still leaves your data in columns and rows but makes it look less like a spreadsheet. Figure 5-19 is an example of what the sample worksheet, complete with text, looks like with no gridlines.

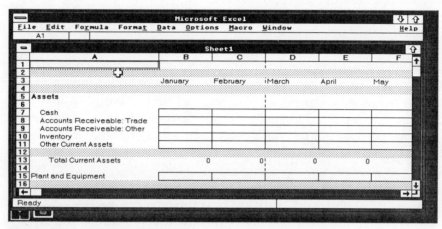

Figure 5-19. Gridlines Turned Off

You can see other examples of worksheets with the gridlines off in some of the files in the EXCELCBT and LIBRARY directories. In the EXCELCBT directory, the ACCOUNT.XLS and COMPARE.XLS files, for example, show worksheets without gridlines. In the LIBRARY directory, the files AMORT123.XLS and AR.XLS also show worksheets without gridlines. (The file AMORT123.XLS also shows columns outlined with borders.)

Print Formats

You can greatly modify the version of your worksheet that gets printed by using some of the options available with the File Print and the Options Set commands. These are discussed in detail in Chapter 7, "Printing."

However, it may be of interest to you here to realize that you can make use of all the fonts that your printer employs, simply by first using *Excel*'s install process and then specifying the printer you'll be using when you get ready to print the worksheet or chart. You can even use the Preview option to see exactly how the printed pages will appear and to make further adjustments before printing.

Formatting a chart is discussed in detail in Chapter 9, "Graphs and Charts." The chapter shows you how to customize your chart with a variety of formatting tricks.

Adding Notes to Your Worksheet

A *note* is a comment attached to a particular cell in a worksheet or macro. It doesn't appear on the regular worksheet or macro screen unless you select the Formula Note command or you're displaying the Info Window. You can also specifically choose to print the note with or without the attached worksheet.

Notes are particularly useful when you're constructing a fairly elaborate worksheet and need reminders about why a particular formula was used or what assumptions have been made. They're also very helpful when more than one person is developing a worksheet, and a trail needs to be left as to what variables are being utilized for specific purposes and what names are being used.

You create notes with the Formula Note command. When you use this command, a dialog box appears.

The Cell box indicates the currently selected cell or the cell note currently selected in the Notes in Sheet box. The Notes in Sheet box lists all the notes in the current document by cell address and first words of each corresponding note.

The Note box shows the text of the note associated with the cell displayed in the Cell box. This is where you type a new note when you're creating it.

To create a new note, select the cell you want to annotate, choose the Formula Note command, and type the text of the note in the Note box. Don't press Enter to create a new line—your text automatically wraps around to the next line. If you want to insert a blank line or paragraph break, press Ctrl + Enter. When your note is as you want it, choose the OK bar.

Here's an example of a note that accompanies a not-so-obvious calculation in a worksheet (Figure 5-20).

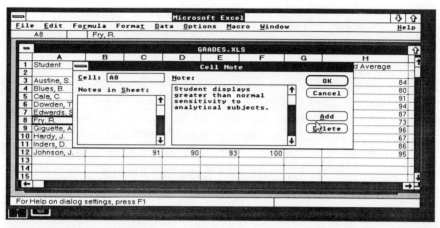

Figure 5-20. Sample Note

You can quickly duplicate the same note in other cells. Type the new note as described above, but instead of choosing the OK bar, choose the Add bar. *Excel* attaches the note to the current cell but returns to the Cell box. Use the arrow keys or the mouse to select the next cell to which you want to attach this note, or type the cell reference. Then press Alt + N to move to the Note box. As long as you don't type anything new, *Excel* adds the same text as a new note for the additional cell.

Interestingly enough, you can use most of this procedure to add many different notes to your worksheet. When you've finished typing the first note, choose the Add bar and specify the new cell reference. The note you've typed is attached to its cell, and *Excel* moves to the new cell reference. Anything you type replaces the old text in the Note box, so you can create a completely different note without ever leaving the dialog box. Continue this process—choosing the Add bar, moving on to a new cell, and typing the new note—for as many cells as you wish to annotate. When you've typed the last note, choose the OK bar.

You can reposition the dialog box the same way you would any other window, with the Formula Note Control menu. Use the Control Move command or drag the dialog box with your mouse to see cells that may be under the dialog box.

A note can be deleted by selecting the cell involved, choosing the Formula Note command, and choosing the Delete bar when the dialog box appears.

You edit notes the same way you edit formulas except that you need the Formula Note command to display the note.

The Info Window, when used with the Formula Select Special command, lets you scroll through existing notes. Choose the Window Show Info command to display the Info window, and set the Info parameters to display notes if they aren't yet indicated. Move and size the windows so that you can see both the worksheet window and the Info window; then activate the worksheet window. If you want to work within a certain range, select it. Otherwise, selecting a single cell lets you view all notes in the worksheet.

Now choose the Formula Select Special command, and, in the dialog box, select Notes. When you choose OK, *Excel* selects all cells that have notes attached to them. Press the Tab key to move through the selected cells and see the notes attached to them, or use Ctrl + Tab to move between ranges of selected cells.

To print notes, choose the File Page Setup command and select the options you want from the dialog box. If you want to have the cell references printed with each note, turn on the Row and Headings check box. Then choose the OK bar. Next choose the File Print command and select the options you want. If you want to print only the notes, select Notes. If you want both the worksheet and associated notes, select Both. Then choose the OK bar. The notes will start printing.

Using Windows

If you've been working with the program throughout the book as examples have been presented, you're aware that windowing is an important concept in *Excel*. Indeed, the environment under which *Excel* normally runs is called *Windows* because it allows more complex passing of data back and forth between programs. On a more limited basis, you can do this with windows within *Excel*.

What a window does in *Excel* is let you have more than one document active and accessible on your screen. One of the more obvious examples is that you can have both a worksheet and a related set of charts accessible on your screen. Another example is that you can have several related worksheets on your screen so that you can accurately pass data from one to another. A third example is that you can open multiple windows into a single very large worksheet.

There are two basic types of windows in *Excel*:

- An *application window* displays menus and provides the workspace for any documents used within the application.
- A *document window* displays an individual document (spreadsheet, chart, macro sheet) within the application window.

The application window you'll see most often is one containing a menu bar. Which menu bar you see depends on which type of document window is currently active. Figure 5-21 shows what the application window looks like with no document open.

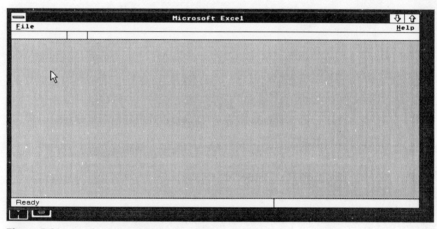

Figure 5-21. Application Window, No Document

A worksheet window is one of several kinds of document windows. You see one when you open a new file in *Excel* (Figure 5-22).

Chapter 5

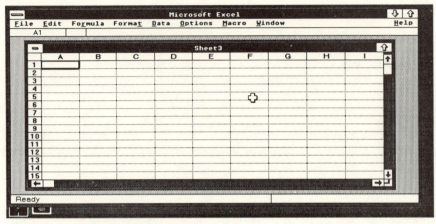

Figure 5-22. Worksheet Window

When a worksheet window is active, the application window displays worksheet menus.

A chart window is another kind of document window (Figure 5-23).

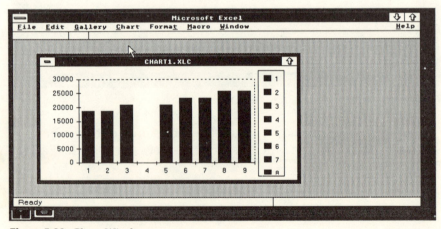

Figure 5-23. Chart Window

When a chart window is active, you can create 44 different types of predesigned charts and a number of customized charts. The application window displays chart menus.

A macro sheet window is where you create and store macros (Figure 5-24).

Editing What You Have

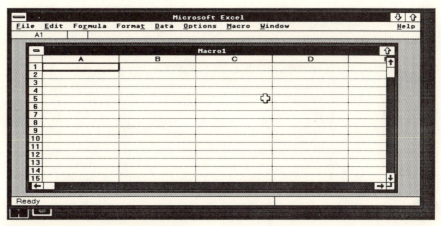

Figure 5-24. Macro Sheet Window

When a macro sheet is active, the application window displays the same menus that are displayed for a worksheet.

There are several special types of application windows. The Info window lets you look at a variety of information about a particular cell on a worksheet or a macro sheet.

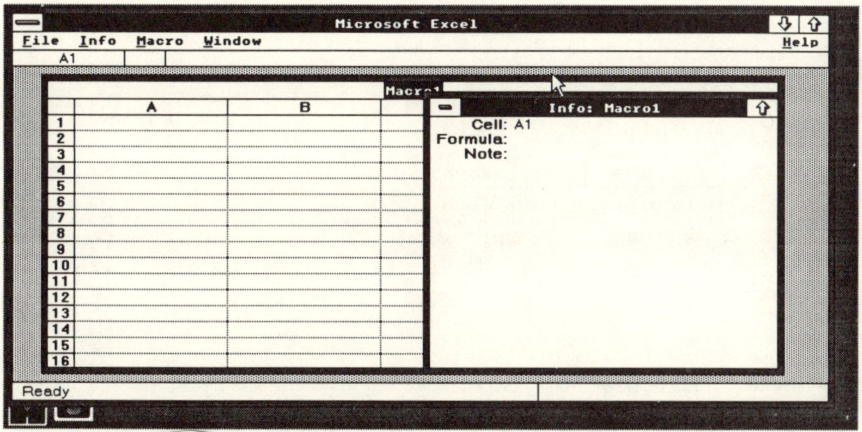

Figure 5-25. Info Window

The Help window gives you quick information about commands, dialog boxes, concepts, basic tasks, worksheet functions, and *Excel* equivalents for *Lotus 1-2-3* and *Multiplan* commands. The Help application window has its own set of commands across the top of the Help window.

Chapter 5

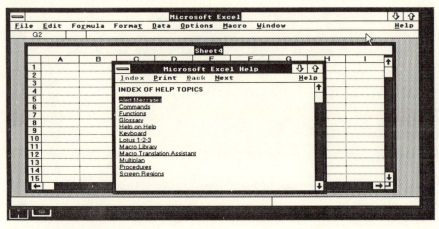

Figure 5-26. Help Window

The Control Panel window lets you adjust system settings such as screen colors, date and time, printer assignments, mouse settings, and communications port assignments. The Control Panel is a separate application, started with the Control Run command on the Control menu.

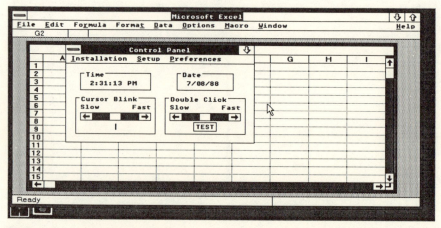

Figure 5-27. Control Panel Window

The Clipboard window lets you see what you have on the Clipboard, a utility program that runs under Microsoft *Windows* version 2.0 or higher.

Editing What You Have

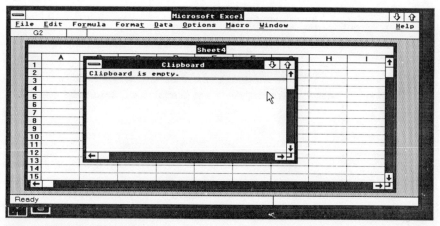

Figure 5-28. Clipboard Window

The Macro Translation Assistant window lets you convert *Lotus 1-2-3* macros into *Excel* macros. The Macro Translation Assistant is a utility program started with the Control Run command on the Control menu. Translating macros and other files into *Excel* files is discussed in Chapter 11.

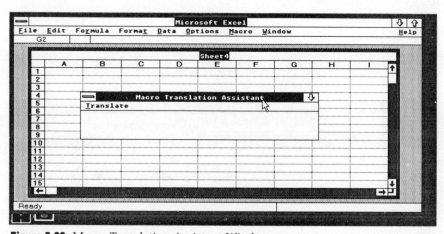

Figure 5-29. Macro Translation Assistant Window

The Spooler window lets you control the process of printing documents while you're doing other tasks. The Spooler is a utility program that can store several documents in a print queue and handle the interface to a printer while you go back to a worksheet, chart, or macro sheet. The Spooler is discussed in Chapter 7.

Chapter 5

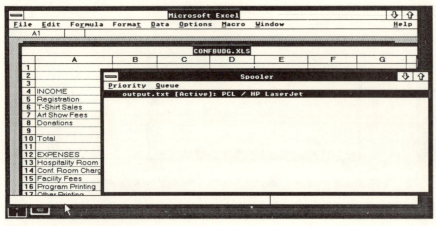

Figure 5-30. Spooler Window

Window Commands

In Chapter 2 you saw how to use the Control menu to manipulate the size and placement of a window. The Control commands let you adjust the size of each window, move it around on the screen, restore it to its original size, close it, and run applications from within the window.

The Window menu lets you rearrange which window is active and displays the Info window for the active cell. What you see as commands depends on which windows are active. Figure 5-31 represents the sort of Window menu you'll normally see.

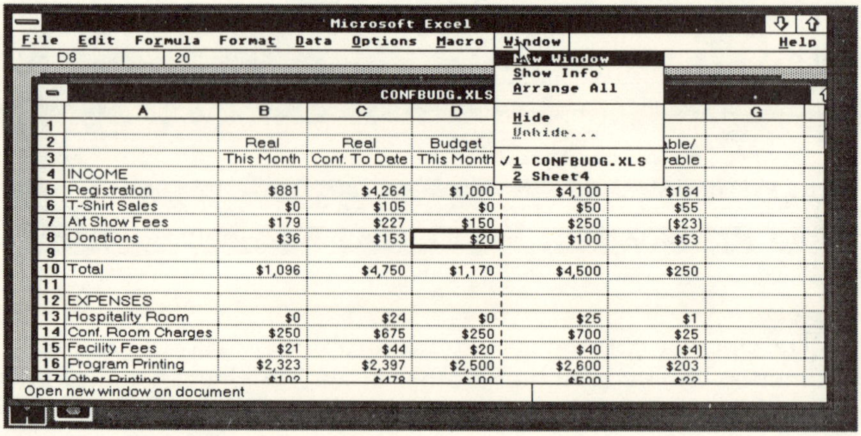

Figure 5-31. Window Menu

126

Editing What You Have

The three sections of the Window menu have to do with different aspects of windowing. The top group, which includes the New Window, Show Info, and Arrange All commands, deals with presenting windows on your screen. The second group, Hide and Unhide, has to do with making a window visible on your screen. The third group, generally called the Activate Window command, lists the currently active files that are available as windows. If more than nine files are open in *Excel* at once, the bottom line shows the More Windows command.

The New Window command creates an additional window for the currently active document. This lets you look at two or more sections of the same document at once, a useful tool when you're working on a large spreadsheet and can't remember how certain cells or cell ranges are arranged. The New Window command differs from the Control Split command in that scrolling in the windows created with it occurs independently, while scrolling in windows created with Control Split can be synchronized.

A new window created with the New Window command simply overlays the previous window, but with the same data showing. Unless there are many windows, the filename for each of the windows thus created is visible as a line above the one in front of it. Each new window of the same file has the same filename, but the extension is followed by a colon and the number of the window. Note in Figure 5-32 that the currently active window is window 2 of the same file and that the filenames of previous windows are visible.

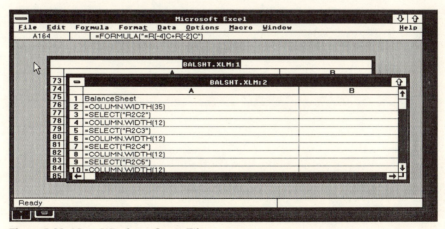

Figure 5-32. New Window, Same File

Chapter 5

The Show Info command shows the Info window for the current cell. This window was discussed earlier. If you want to return to the worksheet and put the Info window away, choose the Show Document command, which appears in the same place on the Window menu when the Info window is active. (The shortcut key for these two commands is a toggle: Press Ctrl + F2, and the current version of the command is implemented.)

The Arrange All command rearranges the windows currently open in *Excel* so that the available space is used effectively. For instance, when two windows are open, *Excel* rearranges them as shown in Figure 5-33.

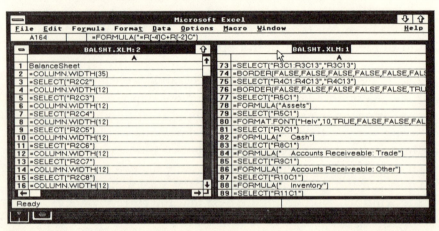

Figure 5-33. Two Windows after Arranging

When three windows are open, *Excel* arranges them as shown in Figure 5-34.

Editing What You Have

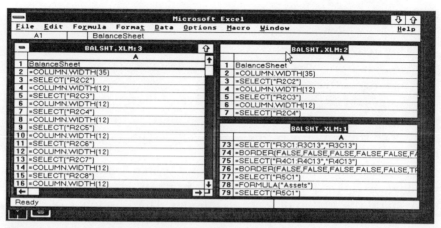

Figure 5-34. Three Windows after Arranging

And when four windows are open, *Excel* arranges them as shown in Figure 5-35.

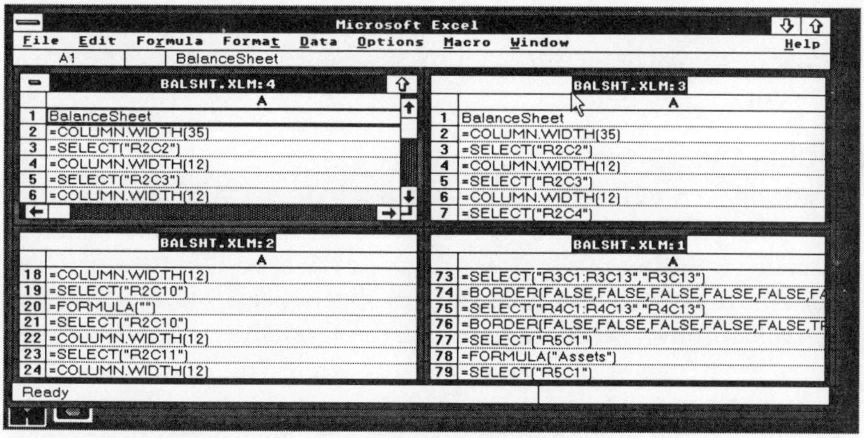

Figure 5-35. Four Windows after Arranging

The Hide and Unhide commands are particularly useful for managing your screen efficiently when you have several documents open (because of external references or because they contain macros you need to use). When you use the Hide command on a worksheet, it disappears from your screen but stays in your electronic workspace, allowing you to use the screen for documents that need to be seen. The Unhide command lets you reverse this, listing all hidden windows and giving you the option of choosing which ones to unhide.

The Activate command, as mentioned above, is actually a list of open files from which you choose the one you want to use as the currently active window.

When you open a window into one of these files, it fills the screen, overlaying the previous arrangement of the screen. However, once the window is open, you can use the Arrange All command to reposition the open windows.

You use the Window Control menu to manipulate data in a window. Chapter 2 includes some information about this menu in the general discussion of Control menus. The Window Control menu appears when you press Alt + Hyphen.

The shortcut keys shown to the right of each command give you alternate ways of using the commands.

Once you have opened several windows on your screen, select the one in which you want to work by using the Activate Window command. If this changes the arrangement of visible windows, use the Arrange All command, and perhaps the Hide command, to rearrange the windows so that you can see the ones you need.

Splitting the Screen

In addition to dividing the screen into windows, you can split the screen into panes with the Split command on the Window Control menu. Splitting the screen into panes is especially useful when you're working with large worksheets because you can see and scroll through separate panes of the worksheet simultaneously or freeze portions of one pane while you scroll through cells in another pane.

You can split any open worksheet vertically, horizontally, or in both directions. The panes scroll synchronously along the direction of the split.

To split a worksheet into panes:

- On the Window Control menu, choose the Split command (click the hyphen in the upper left corner of the worksheet or press Alt + Hyphen).

    A four-headed arrow appears in the upper left corner, just under the hyphen. Two gray split bars extend, one horizontally and one vertically, from this arrow, indicating the initial position of the split.

Editing What You Have

- To split the screen vertically, use the right and left arrows, or drag the vertical bar with your mouse, to position the split bar where you want it.
- To split the screen horizontally, use the up and down arrows, or drag the horizontal bar with your mouse, to position the split bar.

When you press the Enter key, you'll have created a figure similar to that in Figure 5-36.

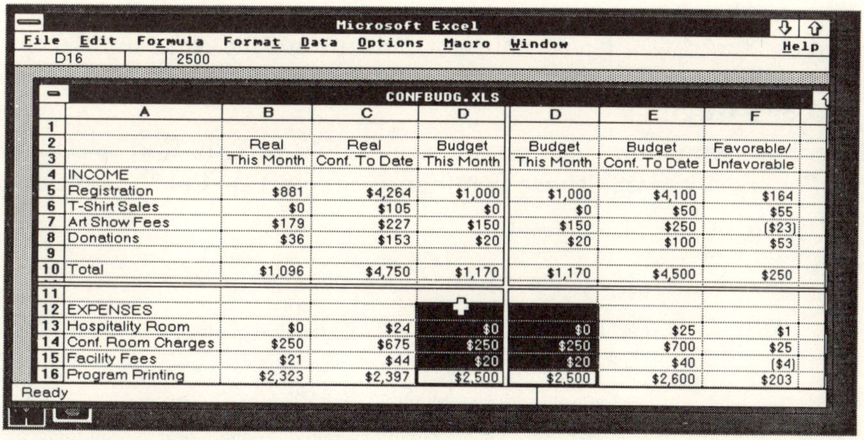

Figure 5-36. Split Screen

You can further split the panes using the same procedure.

Move the active cell around one of the panes and you'll see that the cells in the other pane scroll synchronously. To jump from pane to pane, press F6 or click with the mouse on the pane you want.

To restore the panes to a single worksheet, follow the split procedure described above but move the bars back to their original positions along the left edge and top border of the worksheet; then press Enter. Be sure that the gray bars go all the way to their original positions above the letter labels for the columns and to the left of the row numbers.

If you don't want everything in the panes to move synchronously, you can freeze a pane with the Freeze Pane command on the Options menu. When you choose this command, the pane where the active cell is located freezes, allowing you to jump to the next pane and scroll through that one as you need. To unfreeze a pane, position the active cell in that pane and choose the

Chapter 5

same command. (Freeze Pane is a toggle; when a pane is frozen, the command you see is Unfreeze Pane; when no panes are frozen, the command you see is Freeze Pane.)

When Freeze Pane is in effect, the line between panes changes from the double line normally in effect for splits to a single dark line. It may not be as obvious from a cursory look at the screen.

One useful application of Freeze Pane is to keep the titles of columns and/or rows visible on your worksheet while you work on remote parts of it. For instance, if you're working on a two-year monthly Income Statement projection, you may find it useful to freeze the row titles as you work on the second-year figures.

Find and Replace

Excel has some built-in commands to let you quickly find specific cells or specific data. These commands are grouped at the bottom of the Formula menu.

Command	Description
Goto...	Lets you select a specific cell, cell range, or named area of the worksheet.
Find...	Lets you find a cell containing data you specify.
Replace...	Lets you find cells containing certain data and automatically replace the contents with data you specify.
Select Special...	Lets you select one or more cells that contain a specific type of contents, are different, or refer to each other.

The Goto... Command

When you choose the Goto... command, *Excel* displays a dialog box with the list of names currently in use in your worksheet (Figure 5-37).

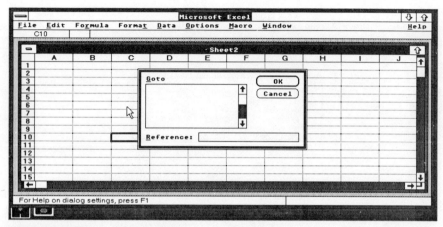

Figure 5-37. Goto. . . Dialog Box

You can choose one of the names listed or type the cell or range reference of your destination in the Reference box. When you choose OK, the active cell jumps to that location.

You can use the Goto. . . command to select a range of cells, too. If you hold down the Shift key when you choose the OK bar, or if you press F8 before you choose the Goto. . . command, all cells between the active cell and the cell you jump to will be selected.

Once you've used the Goto. . . command, you can return easily to the point from which you came. The next time you choose the Goto. . . command, *Excel* suggests (in the Reference box) the address of the cell from which you jumped.

When the Formula bar is active, you can use the Goto. . . command to include a name or reference in the formula. When you choose the OK bar, your worksheet scrolls to that reference.

The Find Command

Find lets you locate cells containing specific formulas, values, or a particular character sequence. The search area depends on whether you have a single cell or a range selected when you choose the command.

If you have a single cell selected, *Excel* starts with that cell and looks to the end of the worksheet. If you have a range selected, *Excel* looks only within that range.

When you choose the command, a dialog box appears on your screen (Figure 5-38).

Chapter 5

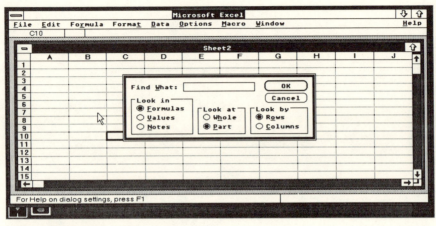

Figure 5-38. The Find Dialog Box

In the Find What box, type the characters you want to find. Next, tell *Excel* where to look for the characters by specifying one of the selections in the Look In box. If the characters are in a formula as displayed in the Formula bar, select Formula. If the characters are values as displayed in the cells, select Values. If the characters are in notes attached to the cells for this worksheet, select Notes.

Next, in the Look At box, select Whole if you want *Excel* to match the entire formula, value, or note, or Part to match only part of it.

Under the Look By box, tell *Excel* which is the most efficient way to search: by Rows, if the cell likely to contain your character string is probably to the left or right of the active cell, or by Columns, if the cell is likely to be above or below the active cell.

When your search parameters have been correctly specified, choose OK. If you want to search backward through your worksheet (from the active cell toward cell A1), press the Shift key when you choose the OK bar.

The Replace Command

Replace works much the same way Find does except that the characters you specify are used to replace the characters found. You can repeat this in any number of cells in your worksheet.

As with the Find command, if you select one cell, *Excel* searches the entire worksheet; if you select a range, *Excel* limits its search to that range.

When you choose the Replace command, you'll see a dialog box (Figure 5-39).

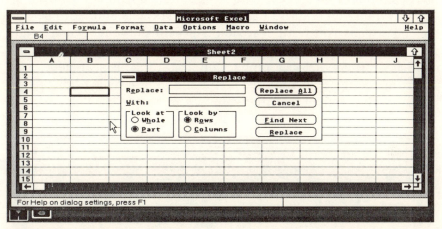

Figure 5-39. The Replace Dialog Box

In the Replace box, type the characters you want *Excel* to find and replace. Be sure you don't press the Enter key after this, or *Excel* will replace your characters with a set of blank spaces. In the With box, type the characters you want *Excel* to use to replace what you typed in the Replace box.

In the Look At box, choose Whole to match the entire formula or value, or Part to match only part of the formula or value. In the Look By box, select Rows to search by rows, or Columns to search by columns.

To replace all occurrences of a set of characters, choose the Replace All bar. *Excel* replaces all instances of these characters from the active cell to the end of the worksheet. If you want *Excel* to search backward, hold down the Shift key when you choose Replace All.

To replace data in the first cell found and then find the next occurrence, choose the Find Next bar. Again, use the Shift key if you want *Excel* to search backward.

To replace only the first occurrence of the search characters, choose the Replace bar.

When there are no more occurrences of the search string, *Excel* displays a message indicating so.

Chapter 5

The Select Special... Command

The Select Special command lets you search for and find cells with particular types of contents without specifying a character string. When you want to use the Select Special command, select the cell or cells you want searched. As with the other search command, if you select only the active cell, *Excel* searches the entire worksheet; if you select a range, only that range is searched. Then choose the Select Special command, and a dialog box appears on your screen (Figure 5-40).

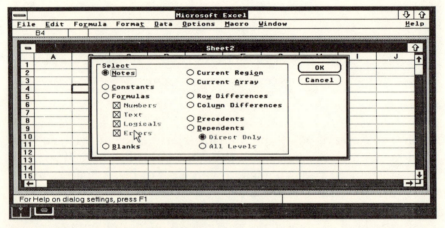

Figure 5-40. Select Special Dialog Box

Choose the appropriate combination of selection criteria and press the OK bar.

If you select Notes, *Excel* selects all of the cells in the search area containing notes. If you select Constants, *Excel* selects cells in the search area that contain numbers, text, logical values, error values, or any combination thereof. If you select Formulas, you can also narrow the search further by specifying formulas that produce number values, text, logical values, error values, or any combination of these results. If you specify Blanks, *Excel* selects cells that contain blanks.

When the selection process is finished, *Excel* displays a multiple selection of cells in the search area containing the type of contents you selected. You can then move through the cells by using the Tab key and the Shift + Tab combination, and you can move between selected blocks with Ctrl + Tab.

The Select Special command can also be used to select cells that differ in content from the ones you specify, or to find cells that refer to each other.

When *Excel* looks for cells with differences, it looks through rows and/or columns, depending on what you've chosen on the dialog box.

If you've chosen Row Differences with one of the Formula options, with only one cell selected, *Excel* reports cells in the same row as the selected cell that contain formula configurations different from that of the selected cell. The same process applies to finding column differences.

The same selection process also can be applied to a situation where a range is used as the basis for comparison. If you have chosen Row Differences, *Excel* uses the cells in the same column as the active cell as the basis for comparison; if you have chosen Column Differences, *Excel* uses the cells in the same row.

The Select Special command also lets you find cells containing precedents (cells that the formulas in the selected cell or range refer to) or dependents (cells with formulas that refer to the selected cell or range). When specifying your search parameters, turn on the dialog box buttons for Precedents or Dependents.

Excel searches the entire worksheet for precedents and dependents. If you select a range before searching, *Excel* selects all cells in the worksheet that are precedents or dependents for any cell in that range.

You can further narrow your search for precedents and dependents by turning on the Direct Only or the All Levels button. If you select Direct Only, *Excel* reports only those cells with precedents that are specifically referred to by the selected cell or cells, or with dependents that specifically refer to the selected cell or cells. If you select All Levels, you'll see the entire network of references to or from the selected cell or cells.

Recalculation

Two commands on the Options menu let you determine when *Excel* is to recalculate values on your worksheet.

Ordinarily, *Excel* saves processing time by calculating cells only when a value is changed, and then only those cells directly affected by the change. This happens automatically. It also normally calculates on the basis of the underlying stored values in the cells, not on the basis of their display formats.

Chapter 5

The Calculation and the Calculate Now command allow you to change these calculation parameters.

When you choose the Calculation command, a dialog box appears:

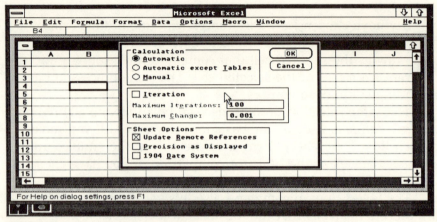

Figure 5-41. The Calculation Dialog Box

The first set of options lets you specify how recalculation is to occur: automatically (as described above), automatically except for tables, or manually. Under automatic recalculation, *Excel* redraws any open charts linked to the active worksheet every time you make changes on the worksheet. This may prove tedious if you have several charts open. If you choose the Manual button, *Excel* waits to recalculate until you either choose the Calculate Now command or press F9.

However, when you're using manual recalculation, you need to specify whether you want *Excel* to calculate only the active worksheet, or all documents currently open. Normally, *Excel* recalculates all the open worksheets. If you want to recalculate only the active worksheet, hold down the Shift key when you choose the Options menu. The command you'll see will be Calculate Document (rather than Calculate Now). You can achieve the same thing with the shortcut key: Shift + F9.

The Iteration box in the dialog box lets you determine how to handle circular references. A circular reference involves formulas that depend upon each other for calculated results. Iteration lets *Excel* try to find solutions for formulas that would otherwise cause a circular reference message to appear on your screen.

138

When *Excel* goes through an iteration, it recalculates the worksheet, using the results of the previous calculations. In the Iteration box, you can control the degree to which iteration takes place and set limits on the maximum amount of change in a value from one iteration to the next.

If you want to specify a maximum number of iterations, type the number in the Maximum Iterations box. If you want to set a maximum change value, type it in the appropriate box. When *Excel* recalculates circular references, it either calculates the maximum number of times or until all cells change by less than the amount in the Maximum Change box, whichever occurs first. Note that *Excel* suggests default values when the dialog box appears.

The Sheet Options box gives you some other options that can affect recalculation. If you want to update formulas with references to data in other applications, turn on the Update Remote References check box. Otherwise, *Excel* will use the most recent values received from these remote references. (This applies only to the active sheet.)

You may want to adjust dates to take into account data you intend to use with *Excel* for the Macintosh, which uses a 1904 date system. If you want your dates and related calculations adjusted, turn on the 1904 Date System check box.

Protecting Your Work

There are several ways to protect your work from accidental or unauthorized changes, a safeguard that becomes far more important if you're working with sensitive data, or with files that must be shared by several users.

You can protect a file on disk by assigning a password to it, which means only those users being able to enter the password are able to open it. This also applies to linked documents: if a password-protected file must be opened to read data, the user working on that file has to enter the password.

To put password protection on a file, choose the File Save As command and select the Options button. In the text box, type the password. (Write it down separately, and keep that memo in a different, safe place so you can find it later.) Then choose OK. Next time anyone tries to open the file, *Excel* asks for the password—which must be typed correctly for the file to be opened.

Chapter 5

If you want to remove password protection, go through the File Save As procedure again, but in the password box, select the password and press Del to remove it. Then choose the OK bar.

However, you can selectively protect the contents of a document. Locking a cell means that its contents can't be changed until the cell is unlocked. Hiding a cell means the cell's formula is not displayed in the formula bar when the cell is selected. Only the results of the formula appear.

Locking or hiding a cell is accomplished in two steps. First, select the cell or cells you want protected, then choose the Format Cell Protection command. Turn on the Locked and Hidden check boxes as appropriate. Repeat the process until you get the protection you want. Then use the Options Protect Document command, and turn on the Contents check box and choose OK. Figure 5-42 illustrates the dialog box.

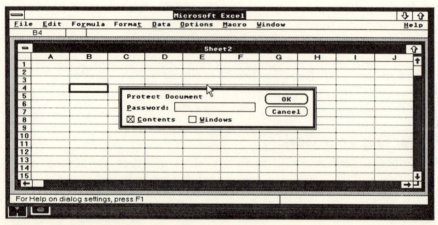

Figure 5-42. Options Protect Document Dialog Box

If you want to prevent others from turning off the cell protection, type a password before you choose OK.

If you want to turn off cell protection, use the same procedure, but choose the Options Unprotect Document command.

Excel's default is that all cells are locked, but the Protect Document option isn't turned on. This means after you have entered data, if you wish to protect what you've entered from your own mistakes, all you have to do is use the Options Protect Document command. However, that will protect all the cells available to you. (You won't even be able to enter data in blank cells.) You may want to select the cell area where you want to work next, and turn off the protection for that area.

As you noticed on the dialog box, you can also use this procedure to protect an entire window. Protection of a window means that the window can't be resized or moved, new windows for that document can't be opened, and windows for that document can't be closed individually.

To protect a window, if the active document is a worksheet or macro sheet, choose the Options Protect Document command; if the active document is a chart, choose Chart Protect Document. In the dialog box, turn on the Windows check box, and choose OK. If you want password protection, type a password before you choose OK.

Protecting a chart works the same way as protecting a document. The Chart Protect Document command appears on the Options menu when a chart is the active document. To protect a chart, choose the Chart Protect Document command, and turn on the Contents check box. If you want to use a password, type one. Then choose OK.

Summary

This chapter has shown you a number of editing commands and techniques, and has given you some practice examples so you could see how these commands and techniques work. *Excel*'s editing capabilities let you fine-tune your worksheet. You can move and change data, insert and delete cells as needed, search for and selectively replace character strings, use windows and panes within windows, and use several techniques for protecting data while you work.

Chapter 6
Formulas and Functions

The most beloved feature of a spreadsheet, for dedicated users, is its ability to use formulas to manipulate and reference values by location or name. This feature alone made many of the users of early spreadsheets evangelists who devoutly tout the labor-saving power of personal computers.

Adding and subtracting values from each other is nothing new to anyone who does checkbook math. The power of a spreadsheet becomes obvious when you realize that you can set up a formula to reference these values by specific cell references (A35+B36) or by name (INCOME-EXPENSES), and have the spreadsheet perform the calculation every time, regardless of what values you've put in A35 or INCOME or any of the other references.

This chapter will show you how to use formulas and functions within your spreadsheet.

Entering Formulas

A *formula* is recognized by *Excel* as a string of characters starting with an equal sign (=). Once you put = as the first character in a cell, *Excel* tries to evaluate the remainder of that entry as a mathematical expression that may include values, operators, cell references, names, and/or functions. If *Excel* can evaluate these characters successfully, the result of the calculation appears in the cell. Otherwise, you see an error message.

Existing values can be constants that are entered with the formula or values that have been linked to previously defined cells. For instance, if you want to determine a monthly payment but you're working with an annual interest rate that's already in cell C5, you can get the monthly interest rate by dividing that value by 12:

C5/12

In this example, both C5 and 12 are considered constants, since both have been previously defined.

Chapter 6

In another example, if you type the formula $=B32-G45$ while the active cell is cell H48, *Excel* subtracts whatever is currently in cell G45 from whatever is in cell B32 and stores the results in cell H48.

Operators come in four types: arithmetic, text, comparison, and reference.

- Arithmetic:

+	Addition
−	Subtraction or negation
*	Multiplication
/	Division
%	Percentage
^	Exponentiation

- Text:

    &   The ampersand is the only text operator. It joins two or more text values, creating a new text value. For instance, if you want to join a first name and a last name as a new text value, use the ampersand: The formula ="Prof. "&"Kennedy" produces the new text value "Prof. Kennedy."

- Comparison:

=	Equals
<	Less than
<=	Less than or equal to
>	Greater than
>=	Greater than or equal to
<>	Not equal to

A comparison operator compares values on either side of the operator and produces a logical value of either TRUE or FALSE. For example, the formula $=Netincome>5000$ evaluates whatever is currently in the cell named *Netincome* and compares it with 5000. If the value in Netincome is greater than 5000, the formula produces the value TRUE; if not, it produces the value FALSE.

Note: Don't try to use comparison operators in the Find What text box—they're not recognized as comparison operators there.

- Reference:

  :   Range—results in one reference to all the cells from the cell to the left of : to the cell to the right of it.

  space   Intersection—results in one reference to the cells common to the two references, or results in the #NULL error value when the two references have no cells in common.

  ,   Union—results in one reference that includes the two references.

Reference operators allow you to combine absolute references, relative references, and named areas.

Tip: The range reference operator lets you refer to entire columns (B:B refers to all cells in column B), entire rows (3:3 refers to all cells in row 3), all rows in a range (5:9 refers to all cells in rows 5–9), or the entire spreadsheet (A:IV).

Excel evaluates the operators in a formula according to the following priorities:

Operator	Definition
–	Negation
%	Percent
^	Exponentiation
* and /	Multiplication and division
+ and –	Addition and subtraction
&	Text operator
= < > <= => <>	Comparison operators

To change this order, group values in parentheses. *Excel* evaluates what's in the parentheses first and then uses those values to calculate the rest of the formula.

Cell references were discussed earlier, in Chapter 3. You can use an absolute or relative cell reference ($D$5 is an absolute reference to cell D5; G11 is a relative reference, which is allowed to shift if move, insert, or delete operations change its current location).

What's a Function?

Functions are formula shortcuts. Microsoft *Excel* comes with 129 different built-in formulas, or functions, which you can use if you also supply the necessary data in the required format. Each of them is discussed later in this chapter.

A word of warning about functions: Since they start with a text string, such as DATE or GROWTH, be careful not to use the name of a function as the name of a cell or cell range.

Some of the functions supplied with *Excel*, such as SUM, AVERAGE, and PMT, are standard forms of a mathematical formula you could type. However, there are other functions—such as IF, CHOOSE, and LOOKUP—that would be difficult, if not impossible, to type in a single cell since they involve some programming or multiple steps. Some, such as IRR, involve many iterations of a test calculation, something that's impossible to do in a single cell.

Functions have a particular syntax, which means you have to enter the name of the function and the data that goes with it in a particular order and with proper punctuation. Most of *Excel*'s functions enclose the associated data in parentheses, like this:

=SUM(C5:D11)

The left parenthesis must immediately follow the function name. If you put a space—or, for that matter, any inappropriate character—between the function name and the left parenthesis, *Excel* displays an error message. There must be a corresponding right parenthesis at the end of the arguments or *Excel* will display another error message.

The information inside the parentheses is called an *argument*. Most of the functions have one or more of these arguments. They tell *Excel* which cells or values the function is to act upon. In the sample function above, *Excel* is being told to total the values it finds in all the cells from C5 through D11.

Suppose your worksheet looks like Figure 6-1.

Formulas and Functions

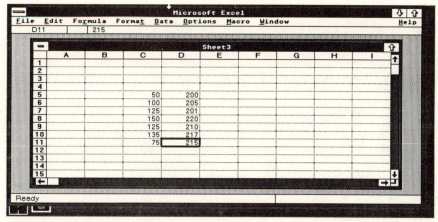

Figure 6-1. Worksheet Sample

Excel adds the values in the range like this—

50+100+125+150+125+135+75+200+205+201+220+210+217+215

—and comes up with a total of 2228. The values C5:D11 are considered an argument. If you were to specify more than one cell range, you'd need to separate the ranges with commas: =SUM(C5:D11,E5:F11). When using arguments with *Excel* functions, use a comma to separate the arguments.

Some functions let you use more than one kind of value as arguments. The SUM function lets you also use numbers or even text as arguments. Here's an example using numbers:

=SUM(5,10,15,20,25)

Excel adds the numbers indicated and displays the result, 75, in the cell where you typed the function. In this particular function, you can combine cell addresses and numbers as well as other values and get a numeric total. Later in this chapter, there is more detail about what kind of arguments are used with each function.

When typing the functions and their arguments, you can use upper- or lowercase letters, or you can mix them. *Excel* doesn't distinguish case in functions.

It's important to type the correct number of arguments for any function you use. If a function requires three arguments, for example, and you only supply two, *Excel* either substitutes what it thinks is an appropriate value (usually 0, FALSE, or " ", the empty text value) or returns an error message.

If, in the explanations later in this chapter, you see an argument followed by three dots (. . .), it means that you can have more than one argument of the previous data type. For example,

=MIN(number1,number2,. . .)

means that you can have several numbers as arguments, like this:

=MIN(100,520,C25,E48)

Note: You may need to use as an argument a reference that uses a comma to indicate union. For example, =AREAS(B5,D4) might appear legitimate to you as another way of indicating a range, but *Excel* interprets B5 and D4 as separate arguments and, since AREAS requires only one reference, returns an error message. In such a case, use parentheses to enclose the values on either side of the comma: =AREAS((B5,D4)).

Pasting Functions

Unlike many other spreadsheet programs, *Excel* makes typing a function name easier by giving you a Formula Paste function. When you select the cell or cells where you want a particular formula to go, and you choose the Formula Paste function from the Formula menu, *Excel* shows you a list of all the built-in functions, along with any others you may have created with function macros. Select the one you want. If you want *Excel* to remind you which arguments are needed for the function, turn on the Paste Arguments check box.

Next, choose the OK button and type or edit the arguments, separating them with commas. When the formula appears as it should, complete with arguments, press the Enter key. The formula is then stored in the cell or cells you have selected.

Function Definitions

In each of the function explanations in the remainder of this chapter, you'll find the function name along with the arguments it needs, a brief definition, and an explanation that includes some examples of how to use the function.

Date and Time Functions

Excel stores date and time values as numbers. *Date* is stored as an integer in the range 1–65380, representing the dates in sequence from January 1, 1900, through December 31, 2078. *Time* is stored as a decimal fraction in the range 0–0.9999, representing each second from 0:00:00 (midnight) to 23:59:59 (one second before midnight). Date and time calculations are performed on this serial number much as if it were any other integer or decimal number. What you see in a cell, however, depends on which function you used and how the cell is formatted. (See "Formatting Options," in Chapter 3, for date and time format options.)

DATE(year,month,day)
Serial number of date specified

When you specify the date in the format shown, *Excel* stores the serial number corresponding to that date in the cell. For example, if you specify =DATE(88,1,1) *Excel* returns the serial number 32143. What you see in the cell, however, depends on the format of the cell. You may see 01/01/88, or 01-Jan-1988, or the serial number, depending on the format.

Year, month, and *day* must be numeric values: *Year* must be in the range 0–1999, *month* must be in the range 1–12, and *day* must be in the range 1–31.

Example:	Returns:
=DATE(88,06,01)	32295
=DATE(100,01,01)	36526

DATEVALUE ("datetext")
Serial number of *datetext*

DATEVALUE differs from DATE in that you enter text rather than numbers as the argument. Like DATE, DATEVALUE needs a date from January 1, 1900, to December 31, 2078. You can use any of *Excel*'s date formats, such as *12/31/87* or *31-Dec-87*.

If you omit the year portion of the argument for DATEVALUE, *Excel* uses the current year from your computer's built-in clock. Time information entered as part of the argument is ignored.

Note: Be sure that the 1904 Date System check box in the Options Calculation box has been turned off unless you want

Chapter 6

to have the date serial number begin with January 2, 1904. If you've imported a file from Microsoft *Excel* for the Macintosh, the 1904 Date System box has been turned on automatically.

Example:	Returns:
=DATEVALUE("01/01/88")	32143
=DATEVALUE("Apr-04")	32237

DAY(serialnumber)
The day of the month equivalent to *serialnumber*

    DAY converts the serial number you give into a date, paring off the month and year information and returning only the number representing the day.

    You can also enter *serialnumber* as a text value such as *4-15-1988* or *15-Apr-1988*. With this function, *Excel* converts a date entered in recognizable text form to a serial number.

    As with DATEVALUE, the description assumes that the 1904 Date System check box in the Options Calculation dialog box has been turned off.

Example:	Returns:
=DAY(5)	5
=DAY(32237)	4
=DAY("15-Apr")	15

HOUR(serialnumber)
The hour of the day equivalent to *serialnumber*

    HOUR converts the time serial number you give into the hour of the day, paring off any information about minutes and seconds. The hour is in a 24-hour clock, ranging from 0 (midnight) to 23 (11 p.m.).

    You can also enter the argument as text, such as *15:45:00* or *3:45:00 PM* or one of the other acceptable time formats.

    You may also wish to use TIMEVALUE within the HOUR function to get the hour portion of a string that is in one of the time formats.

Example:	Returns:
=HOUR(.5)	12
=HOUR(1357.13579)	3
=HOUR(TIMEVALUE("9:15"))	9

MINUTE(serialnumber)

The minute of the hour equivalent to *serialnumber*

MINUTE converts the time serial number you give into the minute of the hour involved, paring off any information about hours and seconds.

You can also enter the argument as text, such as *20:15:00* or *8:15:00 PM* or one of the other acceptable time formats.

Example:	Returns:
=MINUTE(1.5)	0
=MINUTE(0.01)	14
=MINUTE("2:35:52 PM")	35

MONTH(serialnumber)

The month of the year equivalent to *serialnumber*

MONTH converts the serial number you give into the number corresponding to the equivalent month of the year (1–12). As with the previous date and time functions, *Excel* assumes that the 1904 Date System check box has been turned off.

You can also enter the argument as text, such as *4-15-1988* or *15-Apr-1988*.

Example:	Returns:
=MONTH(12345)	10
=MONTH(.7531)	1
=MONTH("01-Jan-1988")	1

NOW( )

Serial number of the current date and time

NOW lets you insert the current date and time into your worksheet. What *Excel* reports is the serial number for both date and time, in the form 11111.11111. To use the serial number in one of the time or date formats, format the cell appropriately.

If you want just the current date, use the INT function with NOW; if you want just the current time, use the MOD function (see the examples below).

Note that the parentheses are required even though they contain no arguments.

Chapter 6

Example: Returns:
=NOW( )   32203.59
=INT(NOW( ))   32203
=MOD(NOW( ),1)   0.59

SECOND(serialnumber)
The equivalent in seconds of *serialnumber*

SECOND converts the time serial number you give into the second of the hour involved, paring off any information about hours and minutes.

You can also enter the argument as text, such as *20:15:00* or *8:15:00 PM* or one of the other acceptable time formats.

Example: Returns:
=SECOND(.007)   5
=SECOND(32445.007)   5
=SECOND("1:52:27 PM")   27

TIME(hour,minute,second)
The serial number of the time specified

The TIME function translates the time you enter into the corresponding time serial number. The time entered can be positive or negative as long as the resulting serial number is positive. You can also enter time as text, provided that it's surrounded by quotation marks.

Example: Returns:
=TIME(12,0,0)   0.5
=TIME(19,45,15)   0.82309
=TIME(16,48,0)-TIME(12,0,0)   0.2

TIMEVALUE(timetext)
The serial number of *timetext*

Like DATEVALUE, TIMEVALUE translates the value specified in *timetext* into an equivalent time serial number. The value in *timetext* can be in any of the *Excel* time formats.

Example: Returns:
=TIMEVALUE("2:24 AM")   0.1
=TIMEVALUE("7:15:45 PM")   0.80213

WEEKDAY(serialnumber)
The day of the week equivalent to *serialnumber*

WEEKDAY translates the serial number given into an integer corresponding to the equivalent day of the week. The integer ranges from 1 (Sunday) to 7 (Saturday).

You can also enter the argument as text in an acceptable date format.

Example:	Returns:
=WEEKDAY("6/1/88")	4
=WEEKDAY(32143)	6

YEAR(serialnumber)
The year equivalent to *serialnumber*

YEAR converts the serial number you give into the number corresponding to the equivalent year, from 1900 to 2078. As with the previous date and time functions, *Excel* assumes that the 1904 Date System check box has been turned off.

You can also enter the argument as text, such as *4-15-1988* or *15-Apr-1988*.

Example:	Returns:
=YEAR(29747)	1981
=YEAR("15-Apr-1988")	1988

Logical Functions
AND(logical1,logical2,. . .)
Returns the value TRUE if every argument is true; otherwise returns false.

AND can have as many as 14 arguments, which can be logical values or arrays or references containing logical values. If any array or reference argument contains text or empty cells, those values are ignored. If any argument contains a numeric value of 0 or 1, it is evaluated as logical false or logical true, respectively.

If there are no logical values in the range specified, the error message #VALUE is returned.

Example: Returns:
=AND(TRUE,FALSE)   FALSE
=AND(TRUE,TRUE)   TRUE
=AND(C4,D6,E8,F10)   TRUE if each of the cells
                                  mentioned can be evaluated
                                  as TRUE

FALSE( )

Returns logical value FALSE

FALSE is frequently used in IF or conditional formulas, where it's important to recognize that a false condition is one of the potential results. The logical 0 it returns is the same as a numeric 0.

Note that the parentheses are required even if they contain no argument.

Example: Returns:
=FALSE( )   FALSE or 0

IF(logicaltest,truevalue,falsevalue)

Tests *logicaltest;* returns TRUE if *logicaltest* is true, FALSE if it is false

IF is used to make conditional tests of cell values and formulas. If *logicaltest* is evaluated as true, the next argument is used; if *logicaltest* is evaluated as false, *falsevalue* is used.

Truevalue and *falsevalue* can be numbers, text, more tests or other formulas, or even macro instructions dictating where the cursor is to be positioned next.

As many as seven IF functions can be nested as *truevalue* and *falsevalue* arguments, permitting you to construct some fairly elaborate conditional tests.

If any of the arguments are arrays, every argument is evaluated when the IF statement is executed. If some of the arguments are action-taking functions, all of the actions are taken.

Example: Returns:
=IF(B5>C8,"Over   "Over Limit" if B5 is greater
Limit","OK")   than C8

NOT(logical)

Returns TRUE if *logical* is false, FALSE if *logical* is true

NOT reverses the value of whatever is given in the argument. If the argument can be evaluated as TRUE, then the NOT function is evaluated as FALSE.

Example:	Returns:
=NOT(TRUE)	FALSE
=NOT(2+2=4)	FALSE

OR(logical1,logical2,. . .)

Returns TRUE if any of the arguments are true; otherwise returns FALSE

OR can have as many as 14 arguments. Each one is evaluated, and if any of them are TRUE, the result is TRUE. Arguments can be logical values, numbers, or text versions of logical values. Arguments that are empty cells, error values, or text that can't be translated into logical values will result in an error message. If any of the arguments are arrays or references, only the logical values within them are evaluated.

Example:	Returns:
=OR(TRUE,FALSE)	TRUE
=OR(2+2=4,5*2=9)	TRUE
=OR(A25,C47,F35)	FALSE if each of the cells mentioned contains conditional expressions that are evaluated as FALSE

TRUE( )

Returns logical value TRUE

TRUE, like FALSE, is frequently used in IF or conditional formulas, where it's important to recognize that a true condition is one of the potential results. The logical 1 it returns is the same as a numeric 1.

Note that the parentheses are required, even if they contain no argument.

Example:	Returns:
=TRUE( )	TRUE

Mathematical Functions

ABS(number)
Absolute value of *number*

The absolute value of *number* is the value of a number without its sign.

Example:	Returns:
=ABS(4)	4
=ABS(−4)	4

EXP(number)
The constant *e* (*e* = 2.718. . .) to the power of *number*

The constant *e*, 2.71828182845904, is the base of the natural logarithm. The EXP function calculates *e* raised to the power of the number you specify. (To calculate powers of other bases, use the ^ to indicate exponentiation.)

EXP is the inverse of LN, the natural log of number.

Example:	Returns:
=EXP(1)	2.71828182845904
=EXP(LN(2))	2

FACT(number)
Factorial of *number*

The factorial of a number is equivalent to

(number)*(number-1)*(number-2)*. . .*(number-n)

where (*number-n*) = 1. *Number* should be an integer, or the non-integer part is truncated.

Example:	Returns:
=FACT(1)	1
=FACT(2.5)	2
=FACT(4)	24 (4*3*2*1=24)

INT(number)
Number rounded down to the nearest integer

INT shaves off the decimal or fractional part of *number* and leaves the integer part. It rounds the number to the nearest integer.

Example:	Returns:
=INT(3.14159)	3
=INT(4*B55)	The integer portion of the result of multiplying the contents of B55 by 4

LN(number)
Natural logarithm of *number*

LN returns the natural logarithm of the number you specify, using the mathematical constant *e* as a base. The number you give as an argument must be positive.

LN is the inverse of the EXP function.

Example:	Returns:
=LN(100)	4.60517
=LN(2.7182818)	1
=LN(EXP(4))	4

LOG(number,base)
Returns the logarithm of *number*

LOG10(number)
Returns the base 10 logarithm of *number*

Both LOG and LOG10 return the logarithm of the number you specify. If you omit *base* with the LOG function, Excel assumes it to be 10, and the result is the same as if you had used the LOG10 function.

Example:	Returns:
=LOG(10)	1
=LOG10(10)	1
=LOG(86,2.7182828)	4.45

MOD(number,divisor)
Remainder of *number* divided by *divisor*

MOD evaluates the formula *number/divisor*, where *divisor* is any number other than zero and returns the remainder (modulus). The result has the same sign as that of the divisor. If the divisor is 0, *Excel* displays an error message (#DIV/0!).

Example: Returns:
=MOD(8,2)   0 (8/2 has no remainder)
=MOD(7,2)   1
=MOD(3,−2)   −1
=MOD(−3,2)   1

PI( )
Value of pi.

Returns the number 3.14159265358979 rounded to the format used in that cell. The parentheses are required.

Example: Returns:
=PI( )   3.14159
=PI( )/2   1.57079
=PI( )*diameter   The circumference of a circle

Trigonometric Functions
ACOS(number)
Arc cosine of *number*

The arc cosine of a number is the angle in radians whose cosine is the number. The number you specify must be between −1 and 1. If you want to convert from radians to degrees, multiply the result by 180/PI( ).

Example: Returns:
=ACOS(−0.5)   2.094
=ACOS(1)   0
=ACOS(0)   1.570796

ASIN(number)
Arc sine of *number*

The arc sine of a number is the angle in radians whose sine is the number. The number you specify must be between −1 and 1. If you want to convert from radians to degrees, multiply the result by 180/PI( ).

Example: Returns:
=ASIN(0)   0
=ASIN(1)   1.570796
=ASIN(−.05)*180/PI( )   30 (degrees)

ATAN(number)

Arc tangent of *number*

The arc tangent of an angle is the angle in radians whose tangent is the number given.

Example:	Returns:
=ATAN(1)	0.785398
=ATAN(1)*180/PI( )	45 degrees

ATAN2(xnumber,ynumber)

Arc tangent of point defined by *xnumber* and *ynumber*

ATAN2 determines the arc tangent of the angle represented by the angle represented by the *x*-axis and a line drawn from the point of coordinates *xnumber* and *ynumber* to the 0 point on both axes. The result is an angle in radians. A positive result is a counterclockwise angle from the *x*-axis; a negative result is a clockwise angle.

Example:	Returns:
=ATAN2(1,2)	1.107149
=ATAN2(−5,10)	2.034444
=ATAN2(−1,−1)*180/PI( )	135 degrees

COS(radians)

Cosine of *radians*

Returns the cosine of the value you specify in *radians*, where *radians* is an angle.

Example:	Returns:
=COS(1)	0.540302
=COS(0)	1
=COS(60*PI( )/180)	.5

SIN(radians)

Sine of *radians*

Returns the sine of the value you specify in *radians*, where *radians* is an angle.

Example:	Returns:
=SIN(0.5)	0.47942554
=SIN(1)	0.84147098
=SIN(PI( )/2)	1

TAN(radians)
  Tangent of *radians*
  Returns the tangent of the value you specify in *radians*, where *radians* is an angle.

Example:	Returns:
=TAN(4)	1.157821
=TAN(0)	0
=TAN(45*PI( )/180)	1 (the tangent of 45 degrees)

Statistical Functions

AVERAGE(number1,number2,. . .)
  Average of numbers given as arguments
  Calculates the average of the values specified as *number1, number2,* and so on. You can have as many as 14 arguments, each of which can be numbers or arrays or references that contain numbers. Arguments containing text, logical values, or empty cells result in those values being ignored.

Example:	Returns:
=AVERAGE(2,6,10)	6
=AVERAGE(A4:A8)	15 if cells A4–A8 contain the values 11, 13, 15, 17, and 19.

COUNT(value1,value2,. . .)
  Counts the numbers in *value1,value2,. . .*
  COUNT determines how many numbers are in cells referenced by *value1, value2,* and so on. You can specify as many as 14 arguments. Arguments can be arrays, references, numbers, empty cells, logical values, or text representation of numbers. However, if an array or reference contains empty cells, logical values, text, or error messages, those values are ignored.

Example:	Returns:
=COUNT(D5:D6)	2 (assuming D5 and D6 contain numbers)
=COUNT(D1,D5:D7)	4 (assuming all four cells contain acceptable values)
=COUNT(0.5,FALSE, "SIX",25,3,3.141593,#DIV/0!)	4

COUNTA(value1,value2,. . .)
Counts the values in *value1,value2,. . .*

COUNTA determines how many values there are in the list of arguments. If an argument is an array or reference, empty cells within the array or reference are ignored.

Note: COUNTA determines values, but COUNT determines numbers. Like COUNT, COUNTA can have as many as 14 arguments.

Example:	Returns:
=COUNTA(E48:E49)	2 if E48 and E49 contain values
=COUNTA(4,,8)	3
=COUNTA(E48:E49,TRUE,25)	4

GROWTH(knowny's,knownx's,newx's)
Values on an exponential trend line

GROWTH fits an exponential curve to the data *knownx's* and *knowny's*. It then returns the *y* values along that curve for the *newx's* array you specify.

The array *knownx's* can include one or more sets of variables. If only one variable is used, *knowny's* and *knownx's* can be ranges of any shape as long as they have the same dimension. If more than one variable is used, *knowny's* must be a range with a height or width of 1.

If the array *knowny's* is in a single row, then each row of *knownx's* is considered to be a separate variable.

If you include *newx's*, one dimension of that array must be the same as *knownx's*. If the *knowny's* array is in a single column or a single row, then *knownx's* and *newx's* must each have the same number of columns or rows.

If you omit *newx's*, that array is assumed to be the same as *knownx's*. If you omit both *knownx's* and *newx's*, each is assumed to be the array [1,2,3,. . .] and the same size as *knowny's*. If any of the numbers in *knowny's* are negative, you'll get the error message #NUM!.

Formulas that return arrays must be entered as array formulas, with the Ctrl + Shift + Enter keys. This is a complex operation, and you're advised to look at the section on Arrays in the Microsoft *Excel* Reference Manual.

An example of GROWTH's operation is given in Figure 6-2.

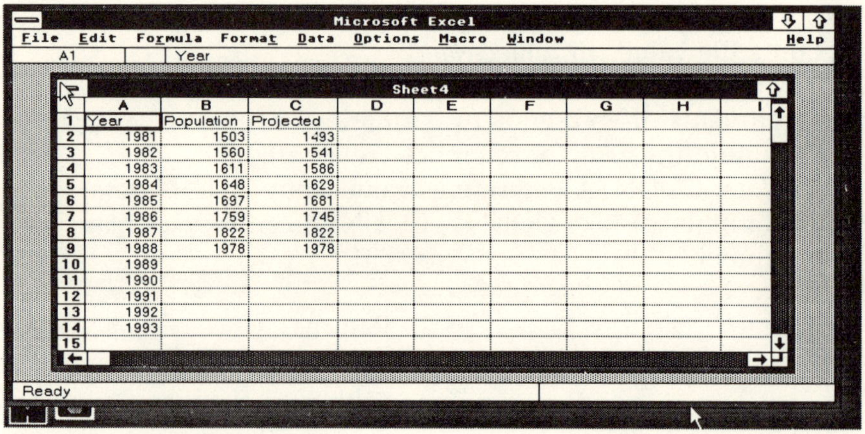

	A	B	C	D	E	F	G	H	I
1	Year	Population	Projected						
2	1981	1503	1493						
3	1982	1560	1541						
4	1983	1611	1586						
5	1984	1648	1629						
6	1985	1697	1681						
7	1986	1759	1745						
8	1987	1822	1822						
9	1988	1978	1978						
10	1989								
11	1990								
12	1991								
13	1992								
14	1993								
15									

Figure 6-2. Sample Spreadsheet

In the example, you can calculate the growth in population for the subsequent five years based on data for the previous eight. In the formula

=GROWTH(B2:B9,A2:A9,A10:A14)

values in C10:C15 are projected values. You can also get values along the calculated exponential curve for the known eight years with the formula

=GROWTH(B2:B9)

which shows those values in C2:C9.

LINEST(knowny's,knownx's)

Parameters of linear trend

LINEST calculates a straight line that fits your data, and it produces an array that describes that line.

A linear projection with a single variable is usually written as a series of data points solving the equation

$$y = ax + b$$

where a is the slope of the line and b is value of y at the point at which the line crosses the y-axis. Once you know the values of a and b, you can calculate any point on the line by inserting x or y values.

Formulas and Functions

Not all data fits a smoothly sloping line, however. LINEST makes an estimate of what this smooth slope would be, allowing for each data point to have the smallest possible deviations from the line. Figure 6-3 is an example of some property values over a period of years.

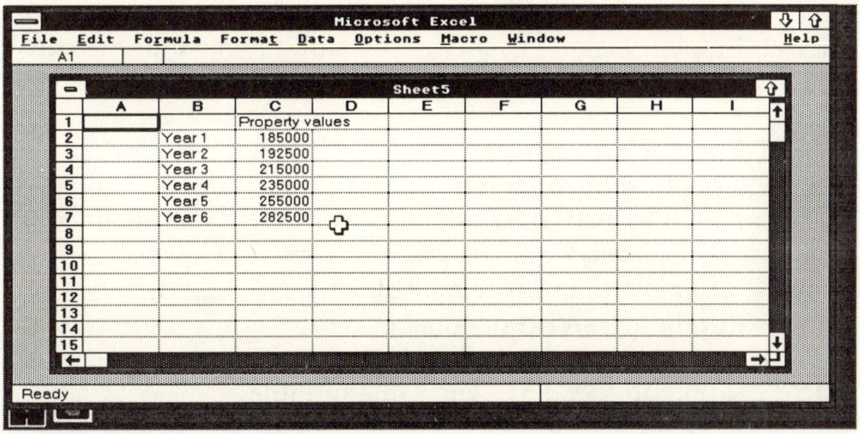

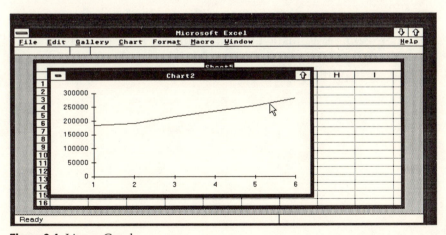

Figure 6-3. Sample Spreadsheet

Figure 6-4 illustrates one attempt to make that data fit a smooth line.

Figure 6-4. Linear Graph

The LINEST function to find *a* and *b* in this case is

=LINEST(C2:C7)

In this case, they're *x* and *y*. Because the *x*-axis is a sequential progression (Year1, Year2, Year3,. . ., which is equivalent to the array [1,2,3,. . .]) you can omit the *knownx's*.

Other factors being equal, you could use this set of data and the linear formula it produces to project where property values will go in the next few years. A word of warning, however: Other factors are rarely equal. While linear projections are a useful tool in making estimates, be sure to take into account the "other factors" that could influence results.

LOGEST(knowny's,knownx's)
Parameters of exponential trend

Like LINEST, LOGEST attempts to fit the data contained in the arrays in *knowny's* and *knownx's* to a curve. However, while LINEST attempts to produce a linear projection, LOGEST attempts to produce an exponential curve.

The same conventions about data that were described in LINEST apply to LOGEST. The same formula,

$y = ax + b$

applies to exponential curves.

Example:
Business school students frequently run into case studies where some optimistic entrepreneur has forecast growth with a "hockey stick" curve. The projected growth curve looks like that shown in Figure 6-5.

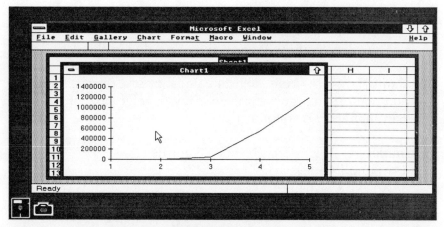

Figure 6-5. Hockey Stick Growth Curve

Assuming some of the assumptions about sales and marketing and product development and support are correct, it's still more reasonable to assume that growth won't be along straight lines, but, rather, along a curve.

If we were to go along with our entrepreneur's optimism, we'd be more likely to get projected sales data using the LOGEST function as shown in Figure 6-6.

	A	B	C	D	E	F
1	Annual Cash Flow Projection					
2		Month	Month	Month	Month	Month
3		1	2	3	4	5
4	Sales	20000	40000	150000	750000	1500000
5	Log Sales	16651	52936	168293	535031	1700950
6						
7	Op. Exp.	3000	5000	30000	45000	60000
8	Marketing	1250	15000	30000	50000	80000
9	Mfrg.	1100	3000	12500	40000	65000
10	R & D	10000	12000	30000	60000	90000
11						
12	Tot. Exp.	15350	35000	102500	195000	295000
13						

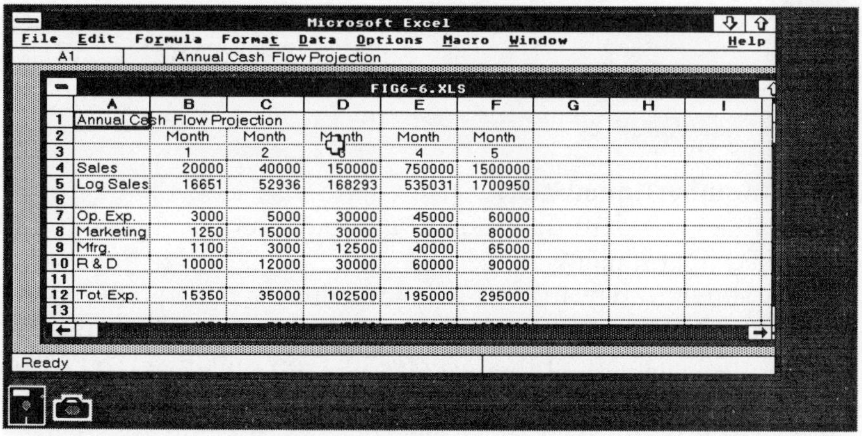

Figure 6-6. Sample Spreadsheet

MAX(number1,number2,...)

Largest number in series given

MAX gives you the largest numeric value in the list of arguments. You can specify as many as 14 arguments, which can be numbers, empty cells, logical values, or text representations of numbers. If an argument is an array or reference, only numbers in that array or reference are used.

Example:
=MAX(15,2,19,8,11)
=MAX(C5:C9,22,B4:B8)

Returns:
19
35 if B4:B8 contains the series 31, 31, 33, 34, and 35 and C5:C9 contains the series 5, 10, 15, 20, and 25.

MIN(number1,number2,...)

Smallest number in series given

MIN gives you the smallest numeric value in the list of arguments. The same limitations about arguments that are true for MAX apply to MIN.

Example:
=MIN(15,2,19,8,11)
=MIN(C5:C9,22,B4:B8)

Returns:
2
5 if B4:B8 contains the series 31, 31, 33, 34, and 35 and C5:C9 contains the series 5, 10, 15, 20, and 25.

STDEV(number1,number2,...)

Estimate of standard deviation of a population, given sample specified in arguments

A standard deviation of a list of values is the square root of the variance of all those values from the average. STD is used to test the reliability of that average as representative: The more the individual values vary from that average, the higher the value STDEV returns. Conversely, the less the individual values vary from that average, the lower the STDEV value and hence the more reliable the mean is likely to be.

In a normally distributed population, 68 percent of all data points fall within one standard deviation of the mean (+/−1 standard deviation, where the single largest number of values is assumed to be at the mean). Normal distribution also assumes that about 95 percent of the data points fall within two standard deviations.

The values given in the arguments should be numbers; text, logical values, or empty cell values cause errors.

Note: Use STDEV if the numbers you're using as arguments represent a sample of the population. STDEV uses the *nonbiased*, or *n1*, method. If the numbers represent the entire population, use STDEVP. STDEVP uses the *biased*, or *n2*, method.

Example:
Suppose you have cell values as shown below.

	A	B	C	D	E
Row 47	241	198	203	247	225

The function =STDEV(A47:E47) equals 21.95905.

STDEVP(number1,number2,. . .)

Standard deviation of a population based on the entire population given in arguments

STDEVP calculates the standard deviation of a population, given the entire population as arguments.

Like STDEV, STDEVP can have as many as 14 arguments, and text, logical, or empty cell values cause errors.

Example:
Assume you have the data below, which represents a complete *population* or all the data points there are for this calculation.

	A	B	C	D	E
Row 32	141	150	137	153	145

The function =STDEVP(A32:E32)= 5.810336

SUM(number1,number2,. . .)

Sum of *number*s

SUM adds up all the values either shown or referenced. You can have a maximum of 14 arguments with SUM, and ar-

Chapter 6

guments that are numbers, empty cells, logical values, or text representations of numbers are considered. If an argument is an array or a reference, only numbers in that array or reference are used; empty cells, logical values, text, or error values in the array or reference are ignored.

Example:	Returns:
=SUM(A5:A15)	The total of all values in cells A5 through A15.
=SUM(25,B9:D11)	The total of 25 plus the contents of B9 through D11.

TREND(knowny's,knownx's,newx's)
   Values on linear trend
   TREND, like LINEST, calculates a straight line that fits your data. It then returns the *y* values along that line for the array of *newx*'s you supply.
   A linear projection with a single variable is usually written as a series of data points solving the equation

$$y = ax + b$$

where *a* is the slope of the line and *b* is value of *y* at the point at which the line crosses the *y*-axis. Given the known *x* and *y* values, *Excel* calculates the *a* and *b* values and then uses the resulting formula to determine further points on the line described by the values you give as *newx*'s.
   TREND, like LINEST, is useful in making linear estimates of growth but is subject to the same limitations.
   You can use TREND for polynomial curve fitting by using the same variable raised to different powers (x^2, x^3, x^4, and so on) and declaring the range containing the values of the different powers as the *knownx's*. See the discussion on TREND in the Microsoft *Excel* Functions and Macros Manual for an example involving polynomials.

Example:
   Suppose you had the data shown in Figure 6-7 as sales data for the first four months of the year, and you wanted to project what the next four would be like.

Formulas and Functions

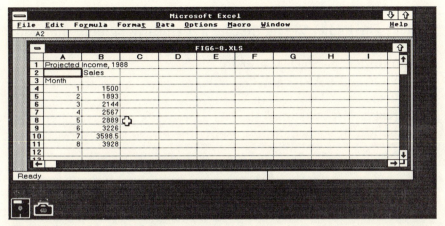

Figure 6-7. Sample Spreadsheet

The function =TREND(B4:B7,A4:A7,A8:A11) = 2889 for month five and produces a trend line as shown in Figure 6-8.

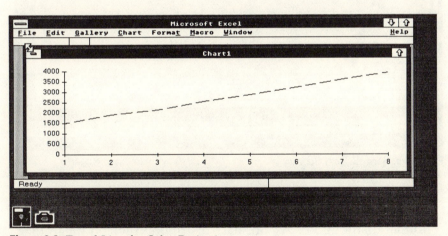

Figure 6-8. Trend Line for Sales Projection

VAR(number1,number2,. . .)
   Estimate of variance of a population based on sample given in arguments

VARP(number1,number2,. . .)
   Variance of a population based on the entire population
   Variance is another of the standard measures of reliability of a set of data. The square of the standard deviation from the

169

Chapter 6

mean, it measures how much data points vary from the mean value. The higher the figure, the more nearly random the sample is likely to be. (See the discussion about deviation from the mean under the STDEV entry.)

VAR and VARP can each have as many as 14 arguments. Any text, logical values, or empty cell values cause errors.

Note: VAR assumes that its arguments are a sample of the population. If your data represents the entire population, use VARP.

Example:

Suppose you have student test scores as shown in Figure 6-9.

	A	B	C	D	E	F	G	H
1	Student		Test A	Test B	Test C	Final Exam		Weighted Average
2			20%	20%	20%	40%		
3	Austine, S.		78	86	82	88		84
4	Blues, B.		68	77	84	85		80
5	Cala, C.		98	90	91	87		91
6	Dowden, T.		90	100	91	94		94
7	Edwards, S.		83	87	89	88		87
8	Fry, B.		69	76	78	72		73
9	Giguette, A.		93	92	97	99		96
10	Hardy, J.		57	68	67	72		67
11	Inders, D.		86	81	84	89		86
12	Johnson, J.			90	93	100		95

Figure 6-9. Sample Test Scores

You'd like to know if the test was reasonable, and you're willing to say that it was reasonable if the test scores follow a normal distribution. A "normal" distribution would mean that about ⅔ of the test scores were +/−1 standard deviation from the mean.

A large standard deviation—and hence, a large variance—means that scores are widely scattered. A smaller standard deviation and a smaller variance means that scores are closer together. This is what you want if the test is to be considered a reasonable test of what students have learned, other things being equal.

The function =VAR(D3:D12) lets you determine whether the test scores for Period 3 fall into a normal pattern. VAR, remember, works on a sample of the population, not the population as a whole. The result, 86.45555556 indicates the test might not have been so reasonable.

The function =VARP(C3:F12) gives you a look at the distribution for the entire population. The answer, 100.2875, indicates that your tests may not have been appropriate for this class.

Financial Functions
DDB(cost,salvage,life,period)
Calculates the depreciation of an asset using the double-declining–balance method

Double-declining balance is a method of determining the depreciation of an asset. It's most often used when you want to depreciate an item quickly in its early years of useful life, and not so quickly in its later years.

DDB uses the formula

$$((\text{cost} - \text{total previous depreciation})*2) / \text{life}$$

to determine the amount of depreciation for a period. You need to supply as arguments the original *cost* of the item, its *salvage* value at the end of its useful life, a number representing its useful *life*, and the *period* for which you want to know DDB depreciation. The numbers specified for life and period must be in the same unit: years, months, weeks, and so on. All four arguments must be positive numbers.

Example:
You've bought a new copier for your business. You paid $1,800, and you expect it to last for four years, at the end of which time you think you might be able to get $150 for it. The double-declining–balance method produces the following depreciation figures for it:

=DDB(1800,150,4,1)	900 depreciation for the first year
=DDB(1800,150,4,2)	450 depreciation for the second year
=DDB(1800,150,4,3)	225 depreciation for the third year
=DDB(1800,150,4,4)	75 depreciation for the fourth year
=DDB(1800,150,48,1)	75 depreciation for the first month
=DDB(1800,150,48,2)	71.87 depreciation for the second month
=DDB(1800,150,208,1)	17.31 depreciation for the first week

FV(rate,#periods,pmt,pv,type)
Future value of an investment

FV is one of the five *Excel* functions that are concerned with annuities. *Annuity* is a term referring to a series of constant cashflows made over a continuous period of time.

FV lets you determine the net amount you'll get at the end of a specified number of periods if you make regular payments into an account which gains a fixed rate of interest.

The arguments *rate*, *#periods*, and *pmt* are required; *pv* (present value) and *type* are optional.

Rate is the interest rate per period. It is entered as a number and a decimal fraction (if any) with a percent sign. (Eight percent is entered as 8%; six-and-a-half percent is entered as 6.5%.)

#periods is the total number of payment periods. In a 30-year loan with monthly payments, *#periods* would be 360.

Pmt is the amount of the payment each period. It doesn't change from period to period and, in a fully amortized loan, contains principal and interest payments. However, though the amount stays the same, the percentage of each payment that reflects principal and interest changes from period to period. *Excel*'s convention is that if you pay it out, *pmt* is a negative number; if you receive it, *pmt* is a positive number.

Pv is present value, or the net amount you could get for the projected series of cashflow.

Type indicates when payments are due: 0 if they come at the end of each period, and 1 if they come at the beginning of each period. If omitted, *type* is assumed to be 0.

Example:
Suppose you are trying to save enough money to take time off and go to Fiji for several months. You can't plunk down several thousand dollars right now, but you figure you can squirrel away $200 a month for three years in an investment that will safely pay 11 percent per year. How much will your nest egg be worth at the end of three years?

The FV function to tell you what you'll have to work with is

=FV(11%/12,36,−200)

which gives you a return of 8484.62. You can get quite a suntan with that.

IPMT(rate,per,#periods,pv,fv,type)
Interest payment for an investment

IPMT returns the interest payment for a given series of cashflows over a specified period of time and at a constant interest rate.

IPMT is useful for calculating how much of any given payment on a loan is interest. If you know the full payment amount, you can then also determine how much of the payment is principal.

Rate, *#periods*, *pv*, *fv*, and *type* were discussed in the description of the FV function. (*FV* and *type* are optional; if omitted, they're assumed to be 0.) *Per* is the number of the period for which you want to determine the amount of interest. If you start making monthly payments in January, the September payment will be payment 9.

Example:
You have a four-year, $5,000 loan, gotten at 10-percent interest, on which you began making payments in December. You know you can deduct the interest portion of that month's payment on your tax return, so you use the IPMT function to figure it out:

=IPMT(10%/12,1,48,5000)   Returns −41.67

The PPMT function works in a similar way, but it determines the amount of principal in a payment.

IRR(values,guess)
Internal rate of return for series of cashflows in *values*

IRR gives you an investment rate for a series of cashflows you specify as arrays or references. Unlike an annuity, which would require equal cashflows, IRR can handle unequal amounts and both income (positive) and payments (negative). If the payments are monthly, the rate you get is a monthly rate.

Guess is optional and represents your estimate of what the IRR will be. Since IRR is an iterative calculation, *guess* narrows the field by giving *Excel* a place to start. *Excel* tries a number of

Chapter 6

values until it gets a result that is accurate to within .00001 percent, but gives up (with a #NUM! error message) if it hasn't found an accurate answer within 20 tries. If you omit *guess*, it is assumed to be 0.1 (10 percent). If the answer seems odd, or if you get the #NUM! error message, try a different value for *guess*.

What IRR computes is the discount rate that equates the present value of future cashflows to the cost of the investment. In other words, at what interest rate could the cost of this investment be placed in order to generate the present value of the cashflows you specify?

The cells you specify in *values* must contain numbers, and at least one must be negative and at least one must be positive.

Example:

You want to purchase a small fourplex and fix it up, and you plan to sell it after 18 months. Your projected cashflows are shown in Figure 6-10.

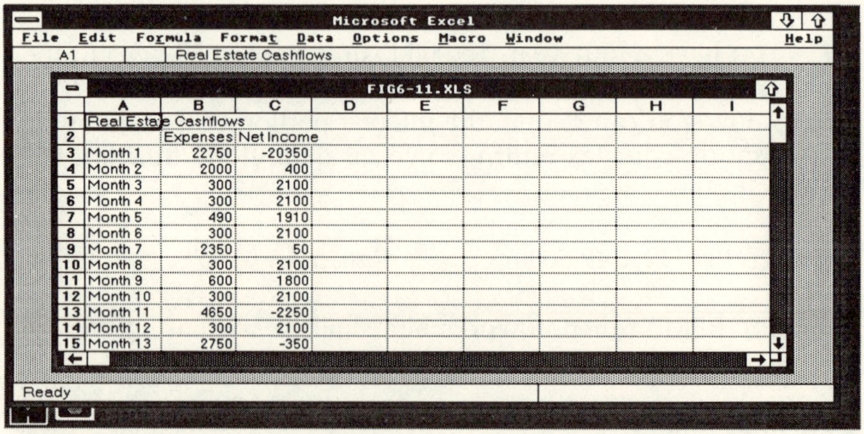

	A	B	C
1	Real Estate Cashflows		
2		Expenses	Net Income
3	Month 1	22750	-20350
4	Month 2	2000	400
5	Month 3	300	2100
6	Month 4	300	2100
7	Month 5	490	1910
8	Month 6	300	2100
9	Month 7	2350	50
10	Month 8	300	2100
11	Month 9	600	1800
12	Month 10	300	2100
13	Month 11	4650	-2250
14	Month 12	300	2100
15	Month 13	2750	-350

Figure 6-10. Real Estate Cashflows

To calculate the rate of return at the end of the investment period, the IRR function is

=IRR(C1:C7)=8.94%

MIRR(values,financerate,reinvestrate)
Modified internal rate of return

Formulas and Functions

A modified internal rate of return takes into account both the cost of the investment, in *financerate*, and the interest received in reinvestment of cash, in *reinvestrate*. As with IRR, the cashflows are in the array or range specified in *values*. *Financerate* applies to the first value, which ordinarily would be the purchase cost of the investment, and *reinvestrate* applies to any subsequent cashflows.

Example:
Take the example shown above for IRR. When you purchased the fourplex, you had to get the money from some other place, where we could reasonably assume that it was earning interest. The rate at which that down payment was earning interest is what you specify as *financerate*.

The cashflows are assumed to go directly into some account that also earns interest, such as a money market fund, and the rate at which those cashflows earn interest is what you specify as *reinvestrate*.

Since you've already specified a reinvestment rate, along with a rate at which your down payment was also earning interest, it's not necessary to give a guess as to the internal rate of return.

If your down payment had been earning 9.5 percent, and the reinvestment rate of your cashflows is 9 percent, the MIRR function looks like this:

=MIRR(C1:C7,9.5%,9%)=8.95%

NPER(rate,pmt,pv,fv,type)
Number of payments of investment
NPER is useful for determining how long it will take you to pay off a loan. It assumes that payments will be regular and that the interest rate is constant. The values *rate*, *pmt*, and *pv* must be specified; *fv* and *type* are optional.

Example:
You've loaned a cousin $1,000, at 7 percent interest, to be repaid in $75 monthly installments. How long will it take for the loan to be paid off? The NPER function shows you:

=NPER(7%/12,=75,1000)=14

NPV(rate,value1,value2,. . .)
  Net present value of the amounts you specify in *values*
    NPV (Net Present Value) calculates the current worth of a series of future payments (negative values) and income (positive values), discounted at a rate you specify.
    The net present value of an investment is today's value of a series of future cashflows, both positive and negative. It assumes that the rate you specify is what you might have received for a competing investment or for the rate of inflation. This is not the same as an interest rate, which compounds growth on a regular basis.
    NPV lets you compare dissimilar investments that provide future cashflows, taking into account factors that could influence what you might otherwise earn over equivalent periods.
    In the computation of NPV, the interest is removed from a future amount to arrive at the initial amount invested. The process of reducing future values to present values is called *discounting*, so net present value is sometimes called a *discounted* value. The interest to be subtracted is called the *discount*, and the rate of interest is called the *discount rate*. It is this discount rate that you specify in an NPV function.

  Example:
    You have an investment that requires a $10,000 investment in a year but will pay annual cashflows to you over the subsequent three years in the amounts of $3,000, $4,200, and $6,800. Assume that, between the rate of inflation and the rate you can get for the money used for your down payment, you will use a discount rate of 10 percent. What will be the net present value of this investment?

    =NPV(10%,-10000,3000,4200,6800)   Returns $1188

  The way this works is that the cashflows are discounted at the rate indicated to come up with a current value for the income stream. Then the down payment is subtracted from this to produce the NPV for the entire investment.

PMT(rate,#periods,pv,fv,type)
  Periodic payment on investment
    PMT calculates the periodic, regular payment for an investment at a constant interest rate.

Rate is the periodic interest rate. If you use an annual interest rate but want monthly payments, specify the annual rate divided by 12: 8%/12.

Specify the *number of periods* for the life of the investment. If you will be making monthly payments, multiply the number of years by 12 to get the number of monthly payments.

The value given for *pv* represents the amount of the investment, or the principal.

The *fv* (future value) and *type* arguments are optional and assumed to be 0 if omitted. They were discussed in the description of the FV function.

Example:
You're buying a car, with an $8,500 loan gotten at 12.5-percent interest, over a period of five years. What will your monthly payments be? Using the PMT function:

=PMT(12.5%/12,60,−8500)   Returns 191.23

PV(rate,#periods,pmt,fv,type)
Present value of investment

PV determines the present value of an annuity, or regular series of cashflows, at a constant rate of interest over a specified number of periods. The values *rate*, *#periods*, and *pmt* are required; *fv* and *type* are optional.

Example:
You're approached by a broker who is offering you a limited partnership interest that will pay you $500 a month for five years. You can invest these payments and get 8 percent on your money. The cost of the partnership interest is $20,000. Should you buy an interest?

The PV function tells you:

=PV(.08/12,5*12,500)   Returns −24659.22

The negative result signifies the amount of money you'd pay out now in order to get the annuity specified. Since the broker is asking $20,000 as the price, it sounds like a good deal.

RATE(#periods,pmt,pv,fv,type,guess)
Rate returned on an investment

RATE is similar to IRR and MIRR in that it returns an interest rate. Where it differs is that IRR and MIRR can work with uneven cashflows, but RATE needs the constant payments of an annuity.

The values *#periods*, *pmt*, and *pv* are required for RATE; *fv*, *type*, and *guess* are optional.

Like IRR, RATE is an iterative calculation. *Excel* tries a maximum of 20 guesses at a solution; if they haven't converged to within 0.0000001 after you've made 20 tries, you'll get a #NUM! error message.

Example:
You've borrowed $15,000 from your parents to complete the down payment for a house. You've promised to pay it back at $200 a month for ten years. What implicit rate of interest have you agreed to? The RATE function tells you:

=RATE(10*12,−200,15000)   Returns 0.008511, the monthly interest rate

Convert this to an annual rate by multiplying it by 12, for an effective annual interest rate of 10.21 percent.

SLN(cost,salvage,life)
Straight-line depreciation for an asset

Straight-line depreciation is the simplest and most commonly used form of depreciation. It assumes that an item depreciates in linear fashion, with equal amounts of value lost each year of its useful life.

Example:
Suppose you own a rental property, and you've purchased a new washer and dryer for it. Because they're considered "business equipment" for tax purposes, you can depreciate them and deduct the depreciation when you compute your taxes. To make things easier, you decide to use straight-line depreciation. The appliances cost you $780, and you expect them to last five years, after which time you can probably get $100 for them when you trade them in on newer models.

The SLN function to tell you how much you'll be able to deduct for them each year is

=SLN(780,100,5)

which returns 136

SYD(cost,salvage,life,period)
Sum-of-the-years'-digits depreciation for an asset

SYD is a form of depreciation that results in more depreciation in the earlier years of an item's useful life and less toward the end.

Each period's depreciation will differ, so SYD has you specify the period for which you want to determine the amount of depreciation. If you're looking for an annual amount, specify the year number of the item's life. (Be sure to use the same unit for both *life* and *period*.)

Example:
You've bought a truck for $15,000 that has a useful life of ten years, and you estimate a salvage value of $1,000. Using the SYD method, how much depreciation can you take in the first year?

=SYD(15000,1000,10,1)   Returns 2545.45

Note: When you're preparing to calculate tax deductions that involve depreciation, it's wise to compare what the different methods will produce for you. For instance, compare the depreciation amounts for the same truck if you use the double-declining–balance method and the straight-line method:

=DDB(15000,1000,10,1)   Returns 3000
=SLN(15000,1000,10)   Returns 1400

In this case, you'll get more depreciation the first year using the double-declining–balance method. However, you may want to weigh your decision in terms of how much depreciation you'll get in subsequent years.

Chapter 6

Information Functions
AREAS(reference)
Number of areas in *reference*

AREAS counts the number of separate groupings of cells in the range specified in *reference*. It's an especially useful function in a macro where you want to test whether a reference is a multiple selection.

Example:	Returns:
=AREAS(C2:C20)	1
=AREAS(POPULATION)	3 if the range named POPULATION refers to C2:C20, D2:D16, and D17:D20

CELL(infotype,reference)
Information about formatting, location, or contents of *reference*

CELL returns data about the upper left cell in the range identified in *reference*. If *reference* is omitted, *Excel* assumes it's the current cell. If *reference* is a multiple reference (such as POPULATION in the AREAS example above), *Excel* returns the error value #VALUE!.

Infotype must be a text value that specifies the type of cell information you want, and it should be one of the values in the table below:

Infotype	Result
"width"	Column width of cell, as an integer
"row"	Equals the row number in *reference*
"col"	Equals the column number in *reference*
"protect"	Lock status: 0 if cell is not locked, 1 if it is
"address"	Coordinates of the first cell in *reference*, as text
"contents"	The value currently in *reference*
"prefix"	A text value corresponding to the label prefix of the cell: "'"　　Left-aligned "''"　　Right-aligned "^"　　Centered " "　　Anything else
"type"	A text value corresponding to the data in the cell: "b"　　A blank, empty cell "l"　　Label, text "v"　　Value or anything else
"format"	A text value corresponding to the format in the cell:

Formulas and Functions

Text Value Returned	Format
"G"	General
"F0"	0 or #,##0
"F2"	0.00 or #,##0.00
"C0"	$#,##0 ($#,##0)
"P0"	0%
"P2"	0.00%
"S2"	0.00E+00
"D4"	m/d/yy or m/d/yy h:mm
"D1"	d-mmm-yy
"D2"	d-mmm
"D3"	mmm-yy
"D7"	h:mm AM/PM
"D6"	h:mm:ss AM/PM
"D9"	h:mm
"D8"	h:mm:ss

Note: If you need to use cell information in a macro, use the GET.CELL macro command.

Example:
=CELL("row",D15:G15)
=CELL("format",D15)

Returns:
15
"P2" if cell D15 has been formatted to display percentages as 0.00%

COLUMN(reference)
Number of columns in *reference*

COLUMN returns the number of columns in the area specified. If *reference* is a range, COLUMN returns the column numbers as a horizontal array. *Reference* cannot refer to multiple areas, such as those contained in POPULATION in the example given for AREA.

Example:
=COLUMN(D5)
=COLUMN(D5:G20)

Returns:
1
[1,2,3,4]

COLUMNS(array)
Number of columns in *array*
COLUMNS returns the number of columns in the array specified. *Array* must be entered in the proper form.

Example:	Returns:
=COLUMNS(D5:G20)	4
=COLUMNS[1,2,3;4,5,6]	3

INDIRECT(text,type)
Contents of the cell from its reference
INDIRECT is one way of getting the contents of a cell. You do this by specifying the name of the cell or its address in either A1 style or R1C1 style. If you use the name of a cell, enclose it in double quotation marks.

Examples:
Assume that cell D5 contains the text "F22" and cell F22 contains the value $542.35. The function

=INDIRECT("D5")   Returns 542.35

Assume that cell A1 contains the text "R2C2." Then the function

=INT(INDIRECT(R1C1,FALSE))   Returns 1

ISBLANK(value)
Returns TRUE if *value* is blank
ISBLANK tests a cell to see whether it is blank. If it finds an empty cell, it returns TRUE; otherwise it returns FALSE.

Example:	Returns:
If C5 contains 0, =ISBLANK(C5)	FALSE
If C5 contains "TRUE", =ISBLANK(C5)	FALSE
If C5 is blank, =ISBLANK(C5)	TRUE

ISERR(value)
Returns TRUE if *value* is any error value except #N/A

ISERROR(value)
Returns TRUE if *value* is any error value

These two functions test for the presence of error messages. ISERR tests for any error value except #N/A; ISERROR tests for any of the *Excel* error values: #N/A, #VALUE!, #REF!, #DIV/0!, #NUM!, #NAME?, or #NULL!. If anything other than the specified contents is found, it returns FALSE.

Example:

ISERR and ISERROR are particularly useful in formulas and macros where you want to find errors or unusable values in a calculation. For instance, suppose you wanted to average the numbers in cells C50:C55, but you wanted to be sure there were numbers in each of those cells before you started, since if all of them were blank, you'd get the error message #DIV/0! If you used the formula

=IF(ISERROR(AVERAGE(C50:C55)),"Blanks",
   AVERAGE(C50:C55))

you'd get the message "Blanks" in the current cell if *Excel* found all of the cells in C50:C55 to be blank, but the program would compute the average if they all contained numbers.

ISLOGICAL(value)
Returns TRUE if *value* is a logical value

ISLOGICAL tests for the presence of TRUE or FALSE or a value that can be interpreted as TRUE or FALSE.

Example:	Returns:
=ISLOGICAL(A14)	TRUE if A14 contains the value TRUE
=ISLOGICAL(A14)	FALSE if A14 contains $243.75

ISNA(value)
Returns TRUE if *value* is the error value #N/A

ISNA looks specifically for the error value #N/A. This is useful in checking for errors as a result of earlier calculations.

Example:	Returns
=ISNA(D42)	FALSE if D42 contains the error value #NUM! or the values $750 or TRUE

Chapter 6

ISNONTEXT(value)
    Returns TRUE if *value* is not text
        ISNONTEXT checks for the presence of anything other than text and returns TRUE if it is not text or FALSE if it finds text.

Example:	Returns:
=ISNONTEXT(E18)	TRUE if E18 contains a number or a logical value
=ISNONTEXT(E18)	FALSE if E18 contains "Name"

ISNUMBER(value)
    Returns TRUE if *value* is a number
        ISNUMBER checks for the presence of a number and returns TRUE if it finds one or FALSE if it finds anything else.

Example:	Returns:
=ISNUMBER(B35)	TRUE if B35 contains a number
=ISNUMBER(B35)	FALSE if B35 contains TRUE

ISREF(value)
    Returns TRUE if *value* is a reference
        ISREF checks *value* for a reference and returns TRUE if finds one or FALSE if it finds anything else.

Example:	Returns:
=ISREF(Salary)	TRUE if *Salary* is a range name

ISTEXT(value)
    Returns TRUE if *value* is text
        ISTEXT checks *value* for the presence of text and returns TRUE if it finds text or FALSE if it finds anything else.

Example:	Returns:
=ISTEXT(F12)	TRUE if F12 contains "Mary Smith"

N(value)
    Translates *value* into a number
        The function N evaluates whatever you specify and translates what it finds into a number.
        If you enter or refer to a number as the argument, N re-

turns that number. If the argument is or refers to TRUE, N returns the value 1. If the argument is or refers to anything else, N returns 0.

Generally, *Excel* translates values as indicated above, regardless of the presence of the N function. It's provided here to make *Excel* compatible with other spreadsheet programs.

Example:	Returns:
=N("4/15/88")	0, because "4/15/88" is text
=N(5)	5
=N(C5)	1 if C5 contains TRUE

NA( )

Error value #N/A

The NA function is usually used to mark empty cells so that in a calculation that might otherwise include cells which should have values, the error message #N/A! will flag the situation. This situation commonly occurs when you don't have all the data you need to complete a spreadsheet.

The NA function inserts the value #N/A where it's entered. You can also type the value #N/A directly into the cell.

If you use the NA function, you must include the parentheses, or *Excel* reports a syntax error.

Example:

Suppose you have values as shown below.

	L	M	N	O
33	15	25	35	45
34	247		134	105
35	101	#N/A	125	117

AVERAGE(L33:O33)	Returns 30
AVERAGE(L34:O34)	Returns 162
AVERAGE(L35:O35)	Returns #N/A!

ROW(reference)

Returns number of rows in *reference*

ROW returns the number of rows in the area specified. If *reference* is a range, ROW returns the row numbers as a horizontal array. *Reference* cannot refer to multiple areas, such as

Chapter 6

those contained in POPULATION in the example given for AREA.

Example:	Returns:
=ROW(D5)	5
=ROW(D1:G4)	[1,2,3,4]

ROWS(array)

Returns number of rows in *array*

ROWS returns the number of rows in the array specified. *Array* must be entered in the proper form.

Example:	Returns:
=ROWS(D1:G4)	4
=ROWS[1,2,3;4,5,6]	2

T(value)

Translates *value* into text

The T function returns *value* as text, if possible. If it encounters text, T returns whatever was specified as *value*. Otherwise, T returns " ", as empty text.

Generally, *Excel* translates values as indicated above, regardless of the presence of the T function. It's provided here to make *Excel* compatible with other spreadsheet programs.

Example:	Returns:
=T(C5)	"4/15/88" if C5 contains the date value 4/15/88
=T(B48)	"TRUE" if B48 contains the logical value TRUE
=T(TRUE)	" "

TYPE(value)

Returns type of *value*

TYPE returns a number indicating the data type of *value*. Numbers returned are as follows:

Value	TYPE returns
number	1
text	2
logical value	4
error value	16
array	64

Example: Returns:
=TYPE(A5)   1 if A5 contains 365
=TYPE(D1)   2 if D1 contains "March"

Lookup Functions
CHOOSE(indexnumber,value1,value2,. . .)
Uses *indexnumber* to select a value from *values*

CHOOSE works a bit like the IF function in that it allows you to return results depending on the values you specify. It differs from IF in that you can have a number of items to consider rather than one item for a True condition and one item for a False condition.

It also works somewhat like the LOOKUP functions except that CHOOSE works with any of the values referenced in the argument list rather than just those arranged in table form.

The arguments for CHOOSE can be range references as well as individual values. This allows some interesting possibilities for calculations:

=SUM(CHOOSE(Offset,C5:C9,D5:D9,E5:E9))

The function above lets you sum the results of the three ranges shown, depending on whether the named cell (Offset) contains a 1, 2, or 3.

You can also use CHOOSE in a macro with GOTOs as the value arguments. For instance, you could use the following functions in a macro:

=CHOOSE(Counter,GOTO(First),GOTO(Second),
   GOTO(Third))

Example: Returns:
=CHOOSE(A5,"Pass",   "Pass" if A5 contains 1
"Fail","Conditional")
=SUM(D23:CHOOSE   SUM(D23:D40) if F2 contains 3
(F2,D32,D36,D40))

HLOOKUP(lookupvalue,table,rownumber)
Finds a value in *rownumber* of *table* selected by *lookupvalue*

The functions HLOOKUP and VLOOKUP let *Excel* find values from a table in much the same way you scan a table. HLOOKUP assumes the values are stored in ascending order

Chapter 6

from left to right in two or more rows; VLOOKUP assumes the values are stored in ascending order from top to bottom in two or more columns.

With HLOOKUP, *Excel* scans the top row of *table*, looking for the last value that doesn't exceed *lookupvalue*. Having found that, it drops down the number of rows indicated in *rownumber* and returns the value it finds there.

Example:

HLOOKUP lends itself nicely to dealing with tax tables. For instance, suppose you wanted to determine the amount of straight-line depreciation for property, using a table that shows the percentages for properties with various standard useful lives. Below is such a tax table.

Depreciation rate for recovery period, by years:

	AA	AB	AC	AD	AE	AF	AG
10		3	5	7	10	15	20
11	1	33.33%	20.00%	14.29%	10.00%	5.00%	3.75%
12	2	44.45%	32.00%	24.49%	18.00%	9.50%	7.219%
13	3	14.81%	19.20%	17.49%	14.40%	8.55%	6.677%

where rows 11 through 13 are for years 1, 2, and 3 in each category.

If, in its third year, you wanted to determine the depreciation for an item with a seven-year life, the HLOOKUP function would look like this:

=HLOOKUP(7,AB10:AG13,3)

which returns the value 17.49 percent.

If you wanted to determine the depreciation for the second year of an item with a 15-year life, the function would look like this:

=HLOOKUP(15,AB10:AG13,2)

which returns the value 9.50 percent.

188

INDEX(ref,rownumber,columnnumber,areanumber)
INDEX(array,rownumber,columnnumber)

Reference in *ref* or *value* in *array* selected by index values

The INDEX function has two forms, one that works with cell references and one that works with arrays. The cell-reference form uses a reference to one or more cell ranges, in *ref*. If *ref* contains more than one range, use the optional argument, *areanumber*, to indicate which range is to be considered. Array reference 1 uses a reference to an array constant and returns a value or array of values.

Both forms use numbers to refer to rows and columns within the range(s) specified: 1 is the first row within the range, regardless of its actual row number, 2 is the second row, and so on. The same principle is used to number columns within a range.

Example:

Suppose you have the following table, listing, among other things, various types of lettuce seeds for your nursery. It's keyed to a stock number as follows:

	A	B	C
35	Simpson	1.85	B-59535
36	Bibb	2.10	B-58982
37	Buttercrunch	1.95	B-59543
38	Great Lakes	1.95	B-59550
40	White Cos	1.95	B-59014
41	Ruby	1.95	B-59048
42	Tango	2.10	B-59600

To obtain the stock number of Buttercrunch seeds, you'd use an INDEX function that looked like this:

=INDEX(A35:C42,3,3)

It would return "B-59543".

In array form, an array must be entered instead of a reference to a range or set of ranges. For instance,

=INDEX([2,4,6;20,40,60],2,2)

returns the value 20.

Chapter 6

LOOKUP(lookupvalue,lookupvector,resultvector)
LOOKUP(lookupvalue,array)
Value in a table selected by *lookupvalue*

The LOOKUP function has two forms—one which works with vectors, and one which works with arrays.

A vector is an array that contains only one row or one column. The vector form of LOOKUP inspects *lookupvector* for *lookupvalue* or the largest value that doesn't exceed *lookupvalue*, moves to the corresponding position in *resultvector*, and returns the value it finds there.

The array form of LOOKUP looks in the first row or column of *array* for *lookupvalue*, moves down or across to the last cell, and gives the value of that cell.

The array form of LOOKUP is very similar to HLOOKUP and VLOOKUP in that all three forms search tables. However, while HLOOKUP inspects the first row and VLOOKUP inspects the first column, LOOKUP searches according to the dimensions of the array. If the array has the same number of columns and rows, or if it has more columns than rows, LOOKUP inspects the first row; if the array has more rows than columns, LOOKUP inspects the first column.

Additionally, HLOOKUP and VLOOKUP let you index within the table; LOOKUP always returns the last value in the row or column.

Example:

	A	B	C	D	E	F
1	1	2	3	4	5	6
2	red	orange	yellow	green	blue	violet

In the table above,

LOOKUP(5,A1:F1,A2:F2)	Returns "blue"
LOOKUP(3.5,A1:F1,A2:F2)	Returns "green"
LOOKUP(2.999,A1:F1,A2:F2)	Returns "orange"

MATCH(lookupvalue,lookuparray,matchtype)
Index of a value selected by lookup value.

Match returns the relative position of the element in *lookuparray* that satisfies *lookupvalue*, according to the value of *matchtype*. You can choose three types of matches:

MATCH finds order of *lookuparray*

1, or omitted	Largest value that is less than or equal to *lookupvalue*.	Must be in ascending order: −2, −1, 0, 1, 2, . . . A–Z, FALSE, TRUE.
−1	Smallest value that is greater than or equal to *lookupvalue*	Must be in descending order: TRUE, FALSE; Z–A; . . . 2, 1, 0, −1, −2.
0	First value that exactly matches *lookupvalue*	Can be in any order

MATCH gives the position of the matched value, not the value itself. If *matchtype* is 0 and *lookupvalue* is text, *lookupvalue* can contain the wildcard characters * and ?.
Examples:

	A	B
1	Month	Mean Temp.
2	1	57
3	2	59
4	3	64
5	4	69
6	5	73
7	6	74
8	7	71
9	8	70
10	9	72
11	10	69
12	11	65
13	12	60

Chapter 6

The function:	Returns:
=MATCH(9,A2:A13,0)	9
=MATCH(9,A2:A9,1)	8
=MATCH(9,A2:A13,−1)	#N/A! because the range is incorrectly ordered for type −1

VLOOKUP(lookupvalue,table,columnnumber)
Finds a value in *columnnumber* of *table* selected by *lookupvalue*

VLOOKUP inspects the first column of *table* for a value that is less than or equal to *lookupvalue*. It then indexes over *columnnumber* of columns and returns the value it finds there.

Like HLOOKUP, VLOOKUP lends itself nicely to tax-table work. For instance, suppose you want the program to determine your tax based on your taxable income and status. (You actually could use *Excel* to determine tax amounts by using the current year's tax tables from the appropriate IRS document and a combination of lookup functions and mathematical operations.) A portion of a tax table might look like this:

	AZ	BA	BB	BC	BD
		Single	Mar/joint	Mar/sep.	Head hshld
10	30050	6363	4647	7054	5317
11	30100	6380	4661	7071	5331
12	30150	6398	4675	7089	5345
13	30200	6415	4689	7106	5359
14	30250	6433	4703	7124	5373
15	30300	6450	4717	7141	5387
16	30350	6468	4731	7159	5401
17	30400	6485	4745	7176	5415
18	30450	6503	4759	7194	5429
19	30500	6520	4773	7211	5443A

VLOOKUP function to determine the tax for a single taxpayer with a taxable income of $30,335 looks like this:

=VLOOKUP(30335,AZ10:BD19,1)

and returns the value 6450.

Text Functions

CHAR(number)
ASCII character corresponding to *number*

CHAR returns the ASCII character that is equivalent to the decimal number you specify. *Number* can be in the range 1–255. See the ASCII chart in Appendix B.

Example:	Returns:
=CHAR(72)	H
=CHAR(52)	4
=CHAR(35)	#

CLEAN(text)
Removes control characters from *text*

Some ASCII characters are not printable. If you want *text* to include only printable characters, use CLEAN to remove non-printing characters.

Example:	Returns:
=CLEAN(Buffer)	The string of characters stored in the cell named *Buffer* minus any nonprinting characters.

CODE(text)
ASCII code of the first character in *text*

CODE is the inverse of CHAR except that it returns only the code of the first character in the text string you specify as an argument.

Example:	Returns:
CODE("Animal")	65

DOLLAR(number,decimals)
Rounds *number* and gives it as text in currency format

DOLLAR converts the *number* you specify to the format $#,##0.00 or ($#,##0.00). If the number you give for *decimals* is positive, it specifies the number of digits to the right of the decimal point. If the number you give for decimals is negative, *number* is rounded to the left of the decimal point.

The important difference between using DOLLAR to format a number and using the currency format on it is that DOL-

LAR returns the value as text, while the currency format leaves it as a number.

If you omit *decimals,* *Excel* assumes it to be 2.

Example:	Returns:
=DOLLAR(543.21)	"$543.21"
=DOLLAR(543.21,−2)	"$500"

EXACT(text1,text2)

Tests to see whether *text1* and *text2* are exactly the same

EXACT returns the value TRUE if *text1* and *text2* are exactly the same. If they're not identical, EXACT returns the value FALSE.

The arguments *text1* and *text2* must be text values or references to text values.

Example:	Returns:
=EXACT("this","this")	TRUE
=EXACT("this","that")	FALSE
=EXACT("This","this")	FALSE

FIND(findtext,withintext,startnumber)

Finds *findtext* within *withintext*

FIND allows you to search a specified section of text for a specific character string and returns the character number of the point where *findtext* first occurs within that text. (The first character of *withintext* is character 1.)

The text to be searched is specified as *withintext* and may be the name of a cell containing text. You indicate what you want to find as *findtext*. FIND is case-sensitive, and you may not use wildcard characters in *findtext*.

Startnumber, which is optional, is the character number in *withintext* where you want Excel to start looking for *findtext*.

If *startnumber* is larger than *withintext* or is 0 or a negative value, or if *findtext* is not found in *withintext,* FIND returns the error message #VALUE!.

Example:	Returns:
=FIND("A","Ampersand")	1
=FIND("a","Ampersand")	7
=FIND("and","Ampersand")	7
=FIND("and",CHAR)	7 where the cell named CHAR contains the text "Ampersand"

FIXED(number,decimals)

Rounds *number* and gives it as text

FIXED rounds the *number* you specify to *decimals* number of digits to the right of the decimal point, adds a period and commas as necessary, and returns the result as text.

If *decimals* is negative, the number is rounded to the equivalent number of digits to the left of the decimal point. If you omit *decimals*, it's assumed to be 2.

The important difference between using FIXED to format a number and using the Format Number command on it is that FIXED returns the value as text, while the Format Number command leaves it as a number.

Example:	Returns:
=FIXED(54321)	"543.21"
=DOLLAR(543.21,−2)	"500"
=DOLLAR(9876543.21,3)	"987,654.321"

LEFT(text,charnumber)

Extracts first *charnumber* characters of *text*

LEFT counts the characters in *text* and copies the leftmost *charnumber* of them into the current cell.

If *charnumber* is omitted, it's assumed to be 1.

Example:	Returns:
=LEFT("Paul Gauguin",6)	"Paul G"
=LEFT("80386-inspired architecture",5)	"80386"
=LEFT(A22,7)	"FY 1987" if A22 contained the text string "FY 1987: 3rd Quarter"

LEN(text)
Length of *text* in characters

LEN measures the length of *text* and returns the number of characters it finds. LEN is particularly useful when you're preparing to insert text of uncertain length into some other cell. In some of these cases, it may be useful to widen the cell width to accommodate the full length of the text string.

Example: Returns:
=LEN("Puyallup")   8
=LEN(NAME)   25 if the first cell of the range named
                                 NAME has text that is 25 characters
                                 wide

LOWER(text)
Converts *text* to all lowercase

LOWER is the opposite of UPPER in that LOWER makes all characters in *text* lowercase, whereas UPPER capitalizes all letters in *text*.

Example: Returns:
=LOWER("JANUARY")   "january"
=LOWER("First Friday")   "first friday"
=LOWER(B22)   "prices" if cell B22 contained
                                 "Prices"

MID(text,startnumber,charnumber)
Extracts *charnumber* of characters from *text*, starting at *startnumber*

MID allows you to extract a specified number of characters from *text*, beginning anywhere you want to within the text string.

If *startnumber* is less than 1, or if *charnumber* is negative, MID returns the error message ‰VALUE!. If *startnumber* is greater than the length of text, the result is " ", the empty text value. If *startnumber* plus *charnumber* takes you past the end of text, the result will be all the characters up to the end of text, with no spaces or fill characters added.

MID can be useful in a situation where some other manipulation has removed all spaces from text and you need some of the characters from within that compacted text.

Example: Returns:
=MID("Here'sasampleofcompactedtext",8,6)   "sample"
=MID("4007 Hall Blvd. NE",6,20)   "Hall Blvd. NE"

PROPER(text)
Converts text to initial capitals

PROPER capitalizes all text strings it finds in *text*. It considers anything that follows a space or punctuation to be a text string.

Example: Returns:
=PROPER("JAN FEB MAR APR")   "Jan Feb Mar Apr"
=PROPER("It's a boy!")   "It's A Boy!"

REPLACE(oldtext,startnumber,charnumber,newtext)
Replaces *charnumber* characters in *oldtext* with *newtext*

REPLACE allows you to selectively replace characters in text. You have to specify how many characters from the beginning of text for the operation to start and how many characters are to be replaced.

Example: Returns:
=REPLACE("Proj. Mgr: Linda   "Proj. Mgr: Duc Ng"
Smith",12,11,"Duc Ng")
=REPLACE("Review   "Review 6/1/88"
12/1/87",8,7,"6/1/88")

REPT(text,number)
Repeats *text* as designated by *number*

REPT allows you to repeat a character or set of characters the number of times you specify.

Example: Returns:
REPT("=*= ",4)   "=*= =*= =*= =*= "
REPT("phth",5)   "phthphthphthphthphth"

RIGHT(text,charnumber)
Returns rightmost *charnumber* characters in *text*

RIGHT counts the characters in *text* and copies the rightmost *charnumber* of them into the current cell.

If charnumber is omitted, it's assumed to be 1.

Example: Returns:
=RIGHT("Paul Gauguin",7)   "Gauguin"
=RIGHT("123WistfulVista,Tustin,   "90022" ⟨inch⟩
CA90022",5)

SEARCH(findtext,withintext,startnumber)

Searches *withintext* for *findtext*, starting at *startnumber*

SEARCH lets you pinpoint a specific text string and returns the character number within the specified text where it was found.

The text string you're after is *findtext* and the text you want to search is *withintext*. If *withintext* is extensive, you can help SEARCH speed up the process by specifying the optional *startnumber*; if omitted, it's assumed to be 1.

SEARCH is not case-sensitive, meaning that *findtext* can be entered in any combination of upper- and lowercase letters. You may also use the wildcards * and ? within *findtext*.

If *startnum* is 0 or less or is greater than the number of characters in *withintext*, SEARCH returns the error message #VALUE!.

Example: Returns:
=SEARCH("5","11223344556677889900")   9
=SEARCH("i","April")   4
=SEARCH(" ","false start",2)   6
=SEARCH("?tart","false start")   7

SUBSTITUTE(text,oldtext,newtext,instanceno)

Substitutes *newtext* for *oldtext* in *text* as indicated by *instanceno*

SUBSTITUTE works like REPLACE, except that you specify the text you want to replace, whereas with REPLACE, you have to specify the number of characters from the beginning of text for the operation to start and how many characters are to be replaced.

If you specify *instanceno*, only that instance of *oldtext* is replaced and the others are left alone.

Example: Returns:
=SUBSTITUTE("data query",   "data queries"
"y","ies")
=SUBSTITUTE(Min.Height,   substitutes the text value "6
"5'10"","6 ft.")   ft." in the cell named
                                       Min.Height
=SUBSTITUTE("hi de di",   "hi de ho"
"hi","ho",2)

TEXT(value,textformat)
Converts *value* to text using *textformat*

    TEXT lets you reformat a *value* and store it as text.

    The major difference between formatting a value with any of the Format commands and using TEXT to do so is that TEXT stores the result as text, while the Format command leaves the value as it was.

Example: Returns:
=TEXT("5/25/1988","mmm d, yyyy")   "May 25, 1988"
=TEXT("1234.567","00.00%")   "1234.57%"

TRIM(text)
Removes spaces from *text*

    TRIM compacts a text string, leaving only one space between words.

Example: Returns:
=TRIM("145   4467   9887")   "145 4467 9887"
=TRIM("125   Howard   Ave.")   "125 Howard Ave."

UPPER(text)
Converts *text* to uppercase

    UPPER converts all of the text you enter (or reference as an argument) to uppercase letters. It's the inverse of LOWER.

Example: Returns:
=UPPER("february")   "FEBRUARY"
=UPPER(C5)   "TOTAL AMOUNT DUE" if C5 contains the text "Total Amount Due"

VALUE(text)
Converts *text* to a number

VALUE translates a text representation of a number to its numeric value. It works on any of the number, date, or time formats recognized by *Excel*. (If *text* is not in one of those formats, you'll get the error message #VALUE!.)

Generally you don't have to use VALUE to translate this form of text to a number, since *Excel* automatically does this conversion where appropriate. VALUE was included to make *Excel* compatible with other worksheet programs.

Example:	Returns:
=VALUE("April 15, 1988")	4/15/1988
=VALUE("15:58:00")- VALUE("11:10:00")	0.2, the serial number equivalent to 4 hours, 48 minutes

Database Functions

Each of the database functions uses the same three arguments: *database*, *field*, and *criteria*.

Database is the range of cells that comprises the database. This range must be a contiguous range of cells organized into records (rows) and fields (columns). The argument given for *database* can be either a range name, such as Prices, or range coordinates, such as D55:G61. If you've used the Data Set Database on a selected range, *Excel* has automatically named the range Database.

Field identifies which fields, or columns, are to be used within the function. Each field must have an identifying name (at the top of the column) which may be used as text in the *field* argument (*w/Discount*, *Net*). You may also use a number to indicate which field within the database is being referenced in the *field* argument: 1 for the first field, 2 for the second, and so on.

Criteria is the range of cells that contains the database criteria. This is the table that has been previously constructed to indicate criteria for manipulating the data in the database. The *criteria* argument can be entered as a range or range name. If you've used the Data Set Criteria command on the criteria table, *Excel* has already named the range Criteria, and you can simply specify Criteria as this argument.

Note: If the Data Set Database and Data Set Criteria commands have created these named ranges, do not use *Database* and *Criteria* as text surrounded by quotation marks.

DAVERAGE(database,field,criteria)

Average of numbers in specified *field* of records in *database* matching *criteria*

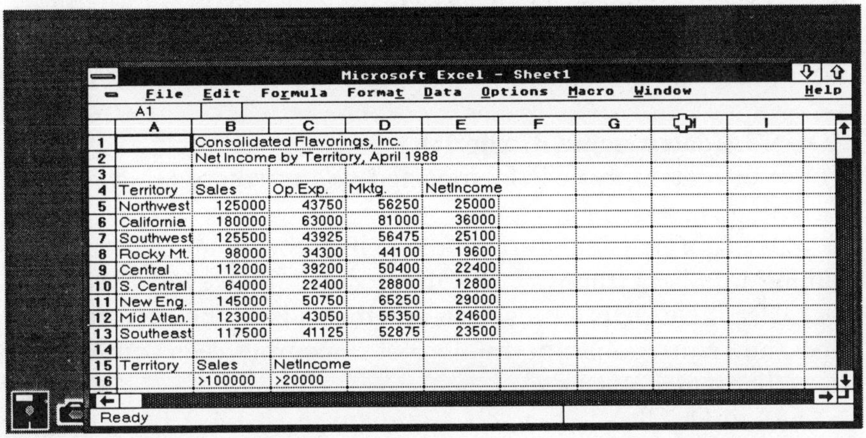
Microsoft Excel - Sheet1

File Edit Formula Format Data Options Macro Window Help

A1

	A	B	C	D	E
1		Consolidated Flavorings, Inc.			
2		Net Income by Territory, April 1988			
3					
4	Territory	Sales	Op.Exp.	Mktg.	NetIncome
5	Northwest	125000	43750	56250	25000
6	California	180000	63000	81000	36000
7	Southwest	125500	43925	56475	25100
8	Rocky Mt.	98000	34300	44100	19600
9	Central	112000	39200	50400	22400
10	S. Central	64000	22400	28800	12800
11	New Eng.	145000	50750	65250	29000
12	Mid Atlan.	123000	43050	55350	24600
13	Southeast	117500	41125	52875	23500
14					
15	Territory	Sales	NetIncome		
16		>100000	>20000		

Ready

Figure 6-11. Sample Database

DAVERAGE looks only at the numbers in the *field* you've specified, and calculates the average of the numbers it finds there. In the sample database above,

=DAVERAGE(Database,"Sales",A16:C16)=132571.4

the average sales for the territories with sales of over $100,000 and net income over $20,000.

=DAVERAGE(Database,"NetIncome",A15:C16)=26514.29

the average Net Income for the territories with sales of over $100,000 and net income over $20,000. As with the other functions, once you have typed the function into a cell, you can change the data in your database and the function is automatically recalculated unless you have turned off the Recalc option.

DCOUNT(database,field,criteria)

Count of numbers in specified *field* of records in *database* matching *criteria*

Like COUNT, DCOUNT inspects the records (cells) in the specified field and returns a count of the ones that contain numbers. However, the number it returns includes another screening: The cells counted also contain numbers that match the criteria specified.

In DCOUNT, the *field* argument is optional. If it's not specified, DCOUNT inspects all records in *database* and returns the count of the ones that contain numbers and also match the selection criteria.

DCOUNTA(database,field,criteria)

Count of nonempty cells in specified *field* of records in *database* matching *criteria*

DCOUNTA counts nonempty cells rather than cells containing numbers (the way DCOUNT does). However, like DCOUNT, DCOUNTA also screens the cells in the field specified and returns only the number of nonempty cells containing data that match *criteria*.

As in DCOUNT, the *field* argument in DCOUNTA is optional. If it's omitted, DCOUNTA inspects all records in the database, returning the number of nonblank cells that match the criteria specified.

DMAX(database,field,criteria)

Maximum of numbers in specified *field* of records in *database* matching *criteria*

DMAX inspects the column specified as *field* and returns the largest number there that matches the criteria specified.

Example:

In the database shown in Figure 6-11,

=DMAX(Database,"Sales",A15:C16)=180000

DMIN(database,field,criteria)

Minimum of numbers in specified *field* of records in *database* matching *criteria*.

DMIN inspects the column specified as *field,* and returns the smallest number there that matches the criteria specified.

Example:

In the database shown in Figure 6-11,

=DMIN(Database,"Sales",A15:C16)=112000

DPRODUCT(database,field,criteria)

Product of numbers in specified *field* of records in *database* matching *criteria*

DPRODUCT multiplies the values in *field* that match the criteria specified and returns the resulting product.

DSTDEV(database,field,criteria)

Estimate of standard deviation of a population, based on a sample, using numbers in specified *field* of records in *database* matching *criteria*

DSTDEV gives the standard deviation of a sample population, cells of which are entirely located in *field* and have been screened to match the specified criteria. DSTDEV is the database equivalent of STDEV.

DSTDEVP(database,field,criteria)

Standard deviation of a population, based upon the entire population, using numbers in specified *field* of records in *database* matching *criteria*

DSTDEVP gives the standard deviation of a complete population, cells of which are entirely located in *field* and have been screened to match the specified criteria. DSTDEVP is the database equivalent of STDEVP.

DSUM(database,field,criteria)

Sum of numbers in specified *field* of records in *database* matching *criteria*

DSUM totals the numbers in *field* which match the *criteria* specified. In the example in Figure 6-11,

=DSUM(Database,"Sales",A15:C16)=928000

DVAR(database,field,criteria)

Estimate of variance of a population, based on a sample, using numbers in specified *field* of records in *database* matching *criteria*

DVAR gives the standard deviation of a sample population, cells of which are entirely located in *field* and have been screened to match the specified criteria. DVAR is the database equivalent of VAR.

DVARP(database,field,criteria)

Variance of a population, based on the entire population, using numbers in specified *field* of records in *database* matching *criteria*

DVARP gives the variance of a complete population, cells of which are entirely located in *field* and have been screened to match the specified criteria. DVARP is the database equivalent of DVARP.

Matrix Functions

MDETERM(array)

Determinant of *array*

The matrix determinant, or MDETERM, is a number derived from the values in the array you specify. It is usually used to solve systems of mathematical equations that involve several variables.

The number you specify as *array* must be a numeric array with an equal number of rows and columns.

For example, in a three-column, three-row array, the determinant is found as follows:

$$A1*(B2*C3-B3*C2)+A2(B3*C2-B1*C3)+A3(B1*C2-B2*C1)$$

The number specified as *array* can be a cell range (A1:C3) or an array constant, such as [1,2,3;4,5,6;7,8,9]. If the array does not contain an equal number of rows and columns, or if any of the cells are empty or contain text, MDETERM returns the error message #VALUE!.

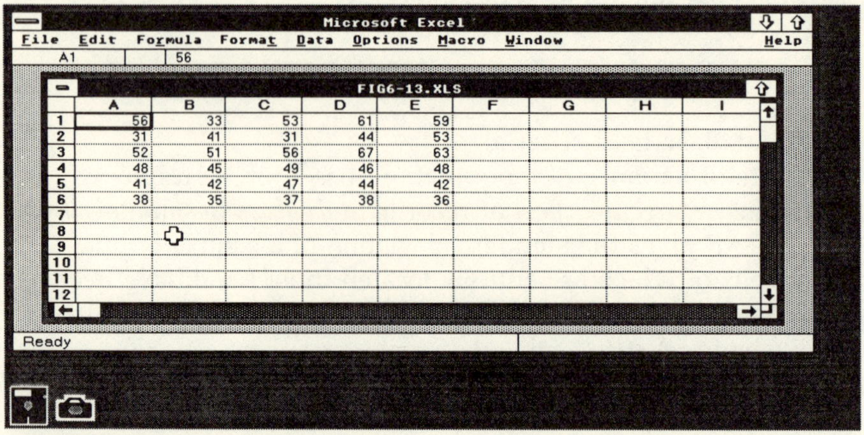

Figure 6-12. Matrix in a Spreadsheet

In the spreadsheet in Figure 6-12,

Example:	Returns:
=MDETERM(C4:E6)	648
=MDETERM(A1:C3)	6745
=MDETERM(A1:E6)	#VALUE! because there are more rows than columns in the array specified

MINVERSE(array)
Inverse of *array*

The inverse matrix is used, like the determinant, in solving equations involving several variables. The product of a matrix and its inverse is the identity matrix, the square *array* in which the diagonal values equal 1 and all the other values equal 0.

Formulas that return arrays must be entered as array formulas. Do this by pressing Ctrl + Shift + Enter and then entering the formula. (If you're using a mouse, press Ctrl + Shift when you click the check box in the Formula bar.)

Using the sample spreadsheet shown in Figure 6-13,

Example:	Returns:
=MINVERSE(A1:E6)	#VALUE! because it's not a square array.

MMULT(array1,array2)
Product of two arrays.

MMULT multiplies two arrays, given as *array1* and *array2*, and returns the product.

In the spreadsheet shown in Figure 6-12,

Example:	Returns:
=MMULT(A1:B2,C1:E2)	3991
=MMULT(A1:C3,D1:E3)	8419
=MMULT(A1:C3,D1:E2)	#VALUE! because the first array has more columns (3) than the second array has rows (2).

TRANSPOSE(array)
Transpose *array*

The TRANSPOSE of an array rearranges array values so that the first row is arranged as the first column, the second row becomes the second column, and so on.

Example:
Suppose the array specified contained values as shown below.

	A	B	C	D	E
1	20	30	40	50	60
2	100	200	300	400	500

Then the function

=TRANSPOSE(A1:E2)=[20,30,40,50,60;100,200,300,400,500]

and the returned values would look like this.

	A	B
1	20	100
2	30	200
3	40	300
4	50	400
5	60	500

Chapter 7
Printing

Using a spreadsheet is a wonderful way to organize and analyze any set of numbers. Manipulating financial figures, engineering data, or even scientific calculations are some of the actions you might be involved with. In each case, the spreadsheet provides a useful working environment in which number juggling can take place.

To show the information in your spreadsheet to others, you could call them over to look at your computer, but what if they aren't in your office? There would also be a problem if they want to look at the figures several times instead of just once.

The easiest way to solve this problem is to print the data—the hardcopy of a spreadsheet or graph you have created from your spreadsheet.

Setting up Your Printer

Using a printer with *Excel* is very important. Because of *Excel*'s design, however, first make sure the appropriate printer driver has been installed.

When you first start using *Excel*, run the Setup program to install your printer to work with the program.

Installing a printer from Setup requires very little work. First, start the Setup program by getting to a DOS prompt. Make sure you insert the appropriate Setup disk in your disk drive and enter the following:

    a:setup

This runs the Setup program from the A: disk drive. Follow the instructions in the program to install a printer driver that allows you to use your printer with *Excel*.

However, if you are now using *Excel*, and would like to add a printer to those you already have, run the Control Panel application rather than rerun Setup. (The main advantage to rerunning Setup is that you can set or reset additional options besides that of the printer.)

Chapter 7

The Control Panel lets you install a printer while you are still within *Excel*. This procedure is somewhat different from the Setup installation procedure. While you're using *Excel*, select the Application Control Menu, and choose the Run command.

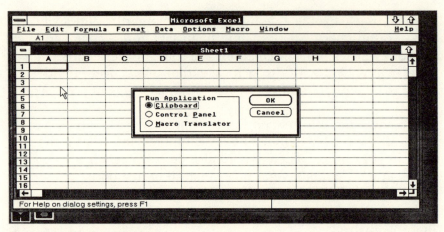

Figure 7-1. The Run Window

This window allows you to select from one of three separate applications you might want to use. In this case, choose the Control Panel by first pressing the P and then the Enter key.

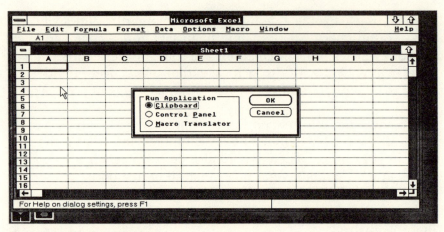

Figure 7-2. The Control Panel

Once you have reached the Control Panel, select the Installation menu to install your new printer by pressing Alt + I. From the menu presented, select the Add New Printer command.

Insert the disk containing the printer control file you want installed in your disk drive. When you're sure the disk is in the designated disk drive, press the Enter key.

Now choose the printer you want to install. Use the arrow keys to move the highlight until your printer is selected; then press the Enter key. *Excel* loads and installs the printer driver.

If you have more than one printer attached to your computer, you can install their drivers at one time and then use the File Printer Setup window to shift back and forth between them as needed. *Excel* lets you use them at the same time, printing different things simultaneously.

To establish this multiple printer capability, first install all of the printers you plan to use. Use the Connections Ports command on the Control Panel to link the different printers to the various communication ports they're attached to. You can then use the Printer Setup window to bring up an active printer, sending individual print jobs to the various machines.

Page Layout

When you print, there are a number of decisions you must make regarding both *what* you want to print, and *how* you want to print. The area of the printout, the format in which it is printed, and what, where, and how it is printed all need to be addressed.

What you want to print can be narrowed down to a simple set of decisions. First, what are you working on? Spreadsheets and graphs are handled in different manners.

If you're going to print a section of your spreadsheet, define, or select, the print block you'll be using. Then, open the File Printer Setup window, so you can define some of the general page layout details.

Using the File Printer Setup Command

Specifically, you need to tell *Excel* the orientation, paper size, resolution, and paper source your printer is using. Defining the orientation of the page means choosing between Portrait (vertical orientation) or Landscape (horizontal orientation) modes.

The paper size you choose is somewhat different. There are various sizes available such as legal, European fanfold, and U.S. letter. Select the appropriate button for the paper type you're using. (Your choices will vary somewhat according to the printer you have installed.)

Chapter 7

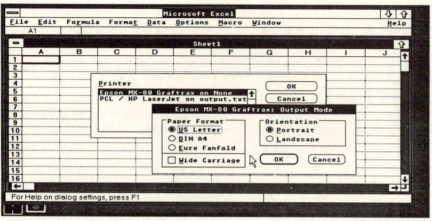

Figure 7-3. The MX-80 File Printer Setup Window

Your printer also determines your paper source. Some printers, such as the Epson MX-80, can have only a single source of paper. In this case, you can choose between automatic sheet-feeding (the printer automatically feeds in the paper) and manual loading (you load each sheet of paper individually before printing).

Printers such as the HP LaserJet, however, have a multiple-feed capability. Here, you not only have the option of manually loading the printer or having it automatically loaded, but you can also choose which bin you want to have your paper come from.

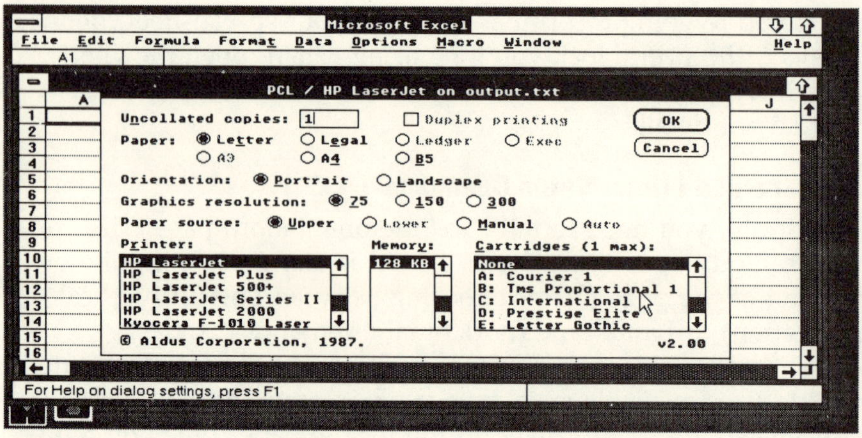

Figure 7-4. The HP LaserJet Printer Setup Page

Finally, choose the graphics resolution you want your printer to use during printing. Printer resolutions are usually defined in terms of a certain number of dots per inch (dpi). (Note that your printer determines whether you have a resolution choice.)

With many laser printers (such as the HP LaserJet series), the resolution ranges from 75 dpi to over 300 dpi. In some cases, however, the resolution does not list a dpi size—instead, the choices of *high* and *low* resolution are presented. Remember that while a high resolution print is of better quality, it usually takes longer to print. As a result, if you're going to print a page that is all text, or that does not need to be a crisp image, you may want to use low resolution for your draft copies.

Using the Printer Setup Command

After you've finished with the Printer Setup window, open the Page Setup window. Here you define several different items, each of which is important to the actual page layout used by your printout.

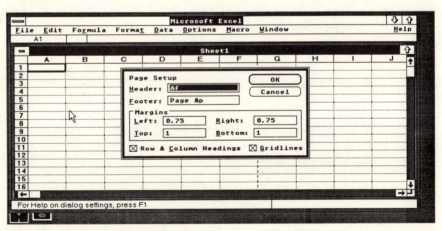

Figure 7-5. The Page Setup Window

Headers and footers. First, what header and footer do you want to appear on your printout? A header is one or more lines of text that appears at the head of a page, staying consistent from one page to the next. A footer is a similar group of text that appears at the bottom of a page.

Your header and footer might be anything—the page number, the date, or a special identification for your company. The default header for *Excel* is the date, while the default footer is *Page &* (which prints out the page number). To alter the header or the footer, select either Alt + H or Alt + F and then, in the dialog box, enter the header or footer as you want it to appear.

The table below indicates the special codes you can use with your headers and footers:

Code	Definition
&&	Print an ampersand.
&B	Bold the left, right, or center part of the header or footer.
&C	Center the following characters.
&D	Print the date.
&F	Print the document's name.
&I	Italicize the left, right, or center part of the header or footer.
&L	Left-align the following characters.
&P + *number*	Add the *number* amount to the current page number and print it as the document's page number.
&P − *number*	Subtract the *number* from the current page number and print is as the document's page number.
&P	Print the current page number.
&R	Right-align the following characters.
&T	Print the time.

For example, the following directions in the header box:

&CAnnual Report&R1989

prints *Annual Report* at the center top of each page and *1989* at the right top.

Margins. Next, you may need to redefine the margins used by your printer. For each of the margins you wish to change, first select the appropriate margin box and then enter the size (in inches) of the new margin that you want the printout to have.

Row & Column Headlines and Gridlines. Next, tell *Excel* if you are using Row & Column Headings and Gridlines by selecting the highlighted character for that option. If an option is already checked, that option has been selected. If you wish to turn off an option, simply select the option again and the check disappears.

Printing a graph. The majority of the options to print a graph are the same for printing a spreadsheet or a macro sheet. Each of the printing windows is changed somewhat, however.

The Page Setup window is altered only slightly. Instead of the Row & Column Headings and Gridlines options, you are given a different selection: the size of the graph. There are three different selections you are allowed to make when deciding the size of the graph:

- Screen Size
- Fit to the Page
- Full Page

Selecting Screen Size makes the printout the same size as the image of the graph you see on the monitor. Selecting Fit to Page or Full Page options generate somewhat larger printouts.

Page breaks. When you create the page layout for your computer, the segment of the spreadsheet you designate to be printed is automatically broken up into page-sized pieces. If you want, you can control where the vertical and horizontal page breaks are placed, using the Manual Page Breaks capability of *Excel*.

When a manual page break is placed in the spreadsheet, the remaining page breaks are recalculated from its location. As a result, the rest of the spreadsheet is reformatted, based on that one page break.

To position a manual page break:

- Move the cell cursor to the cell you want to use to define your page breaks. To define horizontal (page length) page breaks, place the cell cursor in the extreme left column on your spreadsheet in the cell below where you want the page break to occur.
- To define the vertical (page width) page breaks, place the cell cursor in the top row of your spreadsheet, in the cell immediately to the right of where you want the page break to occur.
- If you want to define both the horizontal and vertical page breaks, place the cell cursor in the cell below where you want the horizontal page break, and to the right of where you want the vertical page break.

Chapter 7

- Once you have correctly positioned the cell cursor, open the Options menu and select the Set Page Break command. The page break is set on the spreadsheet so you can see where it occurs.

If you decide you don't want that page break after all, move the cell cursor to the cell where you defined the page break, and open the Options menu. Instead of the Set Page Break command, you'll see the Remove Page Break command. Select this command, and the page break is deleted.

If you've defined a vertical and horizontal page break, and decide you want to eliminate only one of these components, move the cell cursor so it is positioned on the page break you want to remove (but isn't positioned for the page break you want to remain). When you select the Remove Page Break command, only one of the page breaks is eliminated.

Row and Column Labels

Suppose you are printing a large spreadsheet, and you decide it would be useful to include row or column labels with your data to help you keep track of your data. The offhand solution might be to determine where the page breaks are, and then insert sets of labels intermittently throughout your data. But there is actually a way to have *Excel* do the work for you.

First, create the set of row or column labels you want used in your printout. Simply enter them in a set of adjacent rows or columns. You can use more than one row or column, but remember, the more space you use for row or column labels, the less room is available per page for your data.

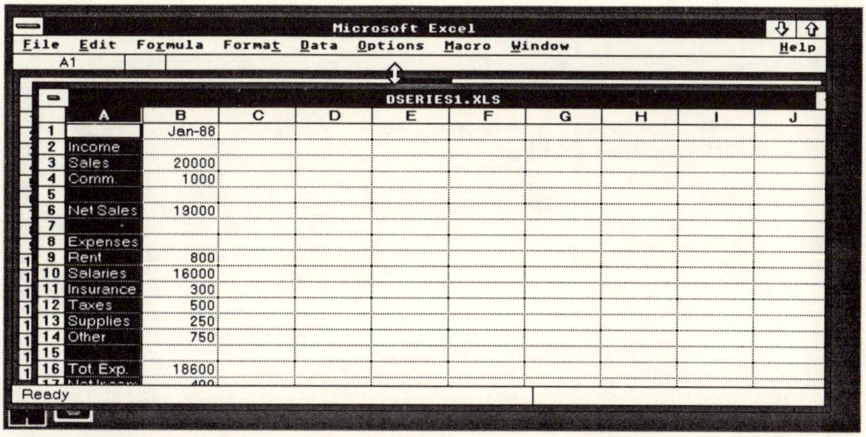

Figure 7-6. Row Labels

Once you have created the labels, there are two more steps to take. Select the rows or columns you want to use for labels. If you're going to use both row and column labels, you'll need to make a multiple selection.

Next, choose the Options Set Print Titles command. The selected rows and columns will be used to generate your row or column titles, as appropriate to their positions.

Previewing

When you've finished laying out the spreadsheet, you should take a look at your finished pages. If you were using any normal spreadsheet program, you'd have to print a draft copy of the spreadsheet to do this.

Since you're using *Excel*, however, Preview lets you view the pages in rough form before they're printed.

To use the Preview capability:

- Choose File Print Preview command.
- Check the Preview box.
- Press the Enter key.

Chapter 7

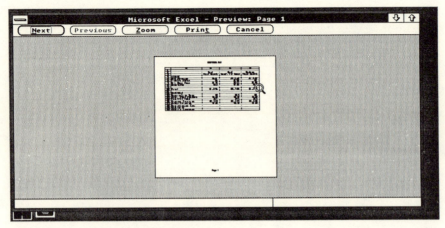

Figure 7-7. A Previewed Spreadsheet Page

This presents a preview display of the first page of your printout. To move through the printout and view the other pages, select the Next command. If you wish to go back and view one of the previous pages, select the Previous command until the page you want appears on the screen. If you want to take a closer look at one of the pages, use the Zoom command to expand that particular page.

If you don't like the way any part of the printout appears, cancel the printout by pressing the Esc key. You can then return to your spreadsheet and correct those parts of the printout that you think need work.

Printing a Complete Document

You may find that you need a printout of the whole spreadsheet versus a printout of a selected range. This is especially the case with cell-by-cell printouts, or when you are printing a spreadsheet with some sort of analysis where you need to see not only the analysis, but the assumptions behind it. (Before you print, make sure there are no selected cell ranges in your spreadsheet.)

When you're ready to print your spreadsheet:

- Select the File Print command. This displays the Print window appropriate to your printer.

Printing

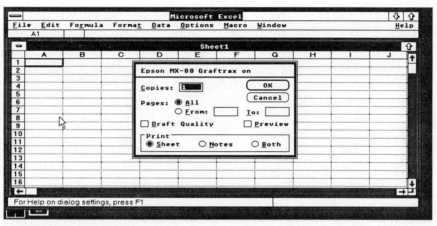

Figure 7-8. The Print Window

- Enter the number of copies you want printed.
- Make sure the All Pages button has been selected on your printout. If it isn't selected, press Alt + A.
- Choose your print quality.
- Do you want to print just the spreadsheet, just the notes, or both? In either case, make sure the appropriate button is highlighted before going any further.
- Finally, do you want to preview your spreadsheet? Remember, Preview lets you catch almost all of the more obvious mistakes in the layout of your spreadsheet—before you use the time and resources of your printer. To select the Preview option, make sure the Preview box has been checked.
- Start your print. If you're using the Preview option, you should be looking at the first of the Preview pages when you press the Enter key. When you're finished using Preview, and are satisfied with your printout's appearance, select the Print button from the buttons at the top of the screen. If you want to make changes to your document, select the Cancel button and your printout is canceled.

If you aren't using Preview, when you press the Enter key, which chooses OK, you immediately start your print run. (To cancel the print procedure, simply press Esc.)

Printing Part of a Spreadsheet

But what if you want only selected ranges within your spreadsheet printed?

Chapter 7

One of the best elements of *Excel*'s range printing capability is being able to select and print portions of the spreadsheet that aren't necessarily adjacent or of similar size.

There are several steps to take before using this unique printing capability. First, select the range(s) of the spreadsheet to be printed. To select the first range,

- Move the cell cursor to one corner of the range.
- Press the F8 key to choose the Extend mode. Use the cursor keys to select the range.
    To select more than one range, hold the Shift key down and again press the F8 key. This invokes Add mode, and you should move the cell cursor into the new range so you can select it.
- When finished selecting the ranges to be printed, open the Options menu and select the Set Print Area command. (Taking any other action deselects your cell ranges.)

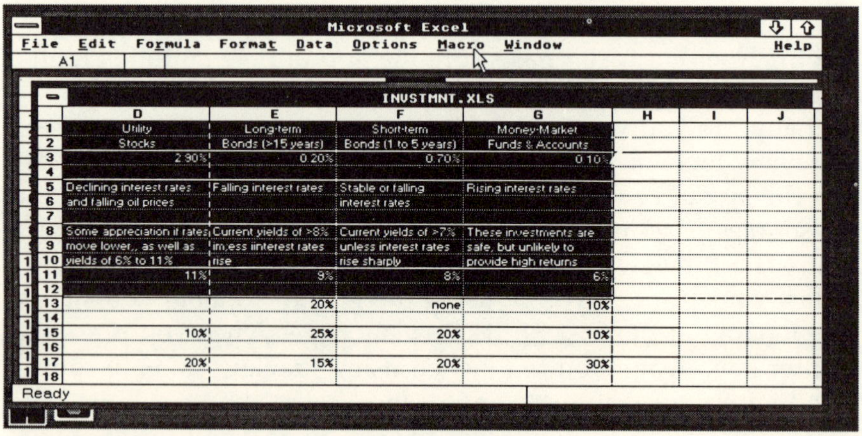

Figure 7-9. Selected Sections of a Spreadsheet

Establishing the print area creates a named range called Print_Area. Invoking the File Print command automatically prints the Print_Area range as long as this named range exists.

The Print_Area range can be deleted. (This does not eliminate the contents of the cells, but it does eliminate the range that those cells are a part of.)

To eliminate the Print_Area range:

- Choose the Formula menu and select the Define Name command. This opens the Define Name dialog box, where whatever is included in your ranges can be edited.
- Select the Names in Sheet region, and highlight the Print_Area name.
- Choose the Delete command and the range is eliminated from your spreadsheet. (Note that Undo does not work with the Delete Name command.)

Printing to a File

You may want to print all or part of a spreadsheet to a separate file, and then print that file at some other time by *copying* the file to your printer. The procedure for this is a bit complex, so it is recommended only for more advanced users.

First, set up a file as a printer, so *Excel* creates the print image in that file instead of your printer.

Simply put, alter the WIN.INI file to include the filename where you want to send an illustration. To alter the file, use a word processor or text editor capable of generating what is variously known as a *text only* or *ASCII format* file. Some word processors capable of doing this are MicroPro's *WordStar* and *WordStar2000*, and Microsoft's *Word* and *Windows Write* word processors.

The WIN.INI file stores the defaults for a number of different settings, some of which aren't useful in *Excel*. Certain parts of the WIN.INI file, however, are important to *Excel*. In this case, the element that needs to be altered is contained in the [ports] section.

To establish your output file:

- Start the word processor and access the WIN.INI file.
- Move down to the [ports] section, and insert a blank line.
- Enter the name and file location where the printouts will be saved, followed by an equal sign (=). Don't enter anything else unless you are planning to change some other default.

As an example, if you wanted a file saved under the filename *output* in your *c:\windows* directory, you would need to add the following line to your [ports] section:

C:\WINDOWS\OUTPUT.PRN=

Chapter 7

After editing the WIN.INI file, exit the word processor, *Excel*, and *Windows*. Next, restart *Excel* and *Windows* (if *Windows* is being used). Once *Excel* is running again, use the File Control menu to access the Control Panel.

Follow the steps below to connect your file to a "printer" to create the actual output. When the file is generated, it will contain not only the actual data, but a number of formatting characters that are configured to mean something to the printer. The file should be connected to same type of printer that will eventually print the file.

First, open the Installation menu and make sure the correct printer driver is loaded. (The printer driver must be installed as part of *Excel*, even if it isn't yet connected to anything.) If the printer driver hasn't been installed, use the Add New Printer command to install it. If the printer driver has been installed, nothing else needs to be changed on the Installation menu.

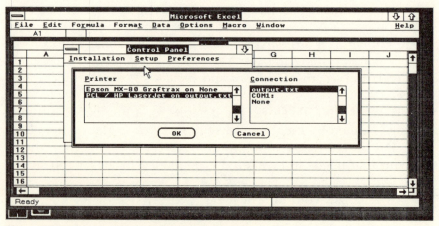

Figure 7-10. Connecting an Output File to a Printer

Open the Setup menu and select the Connections command. Move the Printer highlight until the appropriate printer driver has been highlighted. Then select the Connection menu and highlight the output file instead of one of the access ports on your computer. This allows you to output through that printer driver to the output file, instead of to a real printer.

Now that the output file has been electronically connected to *Excel*, use the File Printer Setup command to select that printer and make it active. Whenever a file is printed, its output goes to that output file, with the file being treated as if the printer really were attached to it.

The Spooler

Print spoolers, which let users send more than one job to the printer at a time, have been in the computer industry since the first of the big multiuser computer systems became available. The print jobs are placed in sequential order as they are sent from the user and each eventually prints, while the user continues with other work.

Print spoolers are relatively new to the personal computer market, first appearing in approximately 1985. As a result of the tendency toward faster computers and interoffice networks, and the resultant traffic jams as everyone tried to use the same printer, print spoolers were borrowed from larger computers and made available on various microcomputers.

Because of this increasing need for a print spooler, *Excel* comes with the Spooler utility program as part of the package, letting you send several printouts to a printer at virtually the same time. They are then printed in sequence.

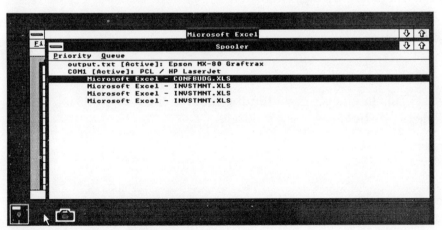

Figure 7-11. A Series of Print Requests in Line

A print spooler (in general) and the Spooler (in particular) first take control of the actual printer, then ask the printer to form its print requests into a line, also known as a *queue* (in much the same way that a ticket taker at a movie theater makes a crowd form a line, admitting people one at a time). Once the current print requests are formed into a single queue, the first print request is sent to the printer, while new print requests are placed at the end of the queue to wait their turn.

The biggest advantage of the Spooler utility in *Excel* is that it works behind the scenes of *Excel*, using processor time only when *Excel* is idle. This lets the computer be used for other tasks while a file is printing.

If you disable the Spooler utility, print information is generated directly by the *Excel* program. Since the program is busy printing, other computer tasks cannot be accomplished.

The only advantage in not using the Spooler is a gain in computer memory. Since the Spooler program takes up some of your computer's memory, fitting a large file, *Excel*, and Spooler into the computer's memory at the same time may be impossible. There may be no choice as to whether you can use Spooler or not.

To disable the Spooler, change your WIN.INI file using the same procedure described in the previous section to create an output file. First, find the line in WIN.INI that reads

spooler = yes

and change it to

spooler = no

This line appears within the first ten lines of the WIN.INI file, so it should be easy to locate.

```
         C:WIN.INI   FC=563 FL=29 COL 11              INSERT ON
                < < <      M A I N   M E N U      > > >
    --Cursor Movement--    | -Delete- | -Miscellaneous-  | -Other  Menus-
^S char left  ^D char right|^G  char  | ^I Tab   ^B Reform| (from Main only)
^A word left  ^F word right|DEL chr lf| ^V INSERT ON/OFF  |^J Help   ^K Block
^E line  up   ^X line down |^T word rt|^L Find/Replce again|^Q Quick  ^P Print
     --Scrolling--         |^Y  line  |RETURN End paragraph|^O Onscreen
^Z line down  ^W line up   |          | ^N Insert a RETURN |
^C screen up  ^R screen down|         | ^U Stop a command  |
beep=yes                                                                  <
CursorBlinkRate=700                                                       <
DoubleClickSpeed=500                                                      <
device=PCL / HP LaserJet,HPPCL,COM1:                                      <
MinimizeMSDos=yes                                                         <
spooler=no_                                                               <

[devices]                                                                 <
Epson MX-80 Graftrax=EPSONMX,output.txt                                   <
PCL / HP LaserJet=HPPCL,COM1:                                             <
                                                                          <
[HPPCL,None]                                                              <
FontSummary=C:\WINDOWS\FSNone.PCL                                         <
                                                                          <
[ports]                                                                   <
1HELP  2INDENT 3SET LM 4SET RM 5UNDLIN 6BLDFCE 7BEGBLK 8ENDBLK 9BEGFIL 10ENDFIL
```

Figure 7-12. Disabling Spooler Within the WIN.INI File

Disabling the Spooler causes print requests to be sent directly to the printer from *Excel*.

A print job's priority can be altered from within the print queue. To view the print queue, select the Spooler icon.

When you open the Spooler window, a display of the currently active printing queue, as well as a short menu bar which lets you use the Priority and Queue menus appears.

To open the Spooler window:

- First make sure the print job is started.
- Press Alt + Esc until the Spooler icon appears and is selected.
- Then press Alt + space bar to select the Control menu.
- Select the Restore command. The Spooler window appears.

Once the Spooler starts, it prints items one after another.

To raise the priority of an item and have it printed as soon as possible, select it, open the priority menu, and choose the High priority option. The item is automatically bumped to the front of the print line.

Conversely, an item can be changed from high to low priority by using the Priority menu. Simply highlight the item in question, open the Priority menu, and select Low.

To stop the printout queue temporarily for some reason, choose the Queue menu and select the Pause command. This temporarily freezes all of your printout queues. Then you can complete the appropriate task (such as reloading a printer with paper) and restart the queue when finished. To restart the queue, choose the Queue Resume command.

To stop printing an item, use the Queue Terminate command. Select the item on the printing queue, open the Queue menu, and select the Terminate command. That item stops printing immediately.

To stop the entire printing queue or if the files in the Print queue have been printed, select the Priority Exit command to return to your spreadsheet. (Closing the Spooler while files remain in the print queue causes any files waiting to be printed to be terminated.) A confirmation box appears. Choose the appropriate button.

While you can define as many printers as you have communications ports, you are limited to a total of 20 print jobs per port. In order to make more than 20 copies of a single page, a series of separate print jobs must be started, each containing no more than 20 copies.

Networking Printers

If your computer, instead of being a stand-alone system, is part of a network that you or your company uses, you can use the facilities in *Excel* to print files, not only on a local printer, but on any printer attached to the network. As a result, several different computers can use a single printer, or one computer can make use of more than one printer at the same time.

If you are using a networked series of printers, but you have your system configured as if it were a stand-alone system, you will want to exit *Excel*, restart the Setup program, and reconfigure your software so it is aware of the presence of the network. If your system is configured to think it is a stand-alone program, you will have an extreme problem when it comes to using anything that isn't directly connected to your computer.

Once you have your system configured to make use of the network, you can begin to create files for use elsewhere on the network. If your network is using printers that already have drivers available under *Excel*, you can establish those printers as part of your initial defaults, selecting from among them when you want to print something. If you are using printers that aren't already defined by *Excel*, you will need to get the printer driver file from the manufacturer before you can use your printer with *Excel*.

Printers Supported by *Excel*

HP LaserJet and LaserJet compatible printers

Apple LaserWriter and LaserWriter compatible printers

IBM Personal Pageprinter

IBM Proprinter

IBM Graphics printer and Graphics printer compatibles

Epson FX-80 and FX-80 compatible printers

Hewlett-Packard plotters, such as the 7470A, as well as H-P compatible plotters

PostScript-driven printing devices

Any printer or plotter compatible with Microsoft Windows v2.0 or higher.

Once you have installed the appropriate printers, use the Printer Setup menu from within *Excel* to select from among them for your print jobs.

One of the benefits of *Excel*'s multiple printer capability is the ability to simultaneously start print runs on as many printers as are connected to your machine and *Excel*. Since *Excel* comes with a print spooler as part of the software package, you can use that print spooler to stack print jobs at various "locations" within the system. To make use of the multiple-print capability inherent in *Excel*, you will need to follow a relatively simple procedure.

First, start a regular print run. Select the printer you want to use, and start the printout of a file you currently have loaded.

Figure 7-13. Printing a Single File, Viewed from the Spooler Window

Chapter 7

Second, access and print another file. This can be done by windowing back to an already loaded file, or by opening the file afresh. Now, use the Printer Setup menu to select the printer you want to use with this particular file. This could be the same printer you're already using, in which case the printout would be stacked up in the print queue for that printer. It could, however, be a different printer. In this case, the file would start printing immediately. Now you have a multiple print run. See how simple that was?

If you want to print more files, just repeat the procedure for each file you want to start printing. If you want to check the status of your different print runs, just open the Spooler window to take a look at how things are going.

Printing Charts

To print a chart,

- Make sure the chart window is active.
- Choose File Print.
- Choose the OK button.

Printing a chart is similar to printing a spreadsheet or macro sheet. In fact, the basics of printing are essentially identical, from selecting what is to be printed, to defining the page layout and printer to be used, to previewing the final printout, to actually finishing the printout.

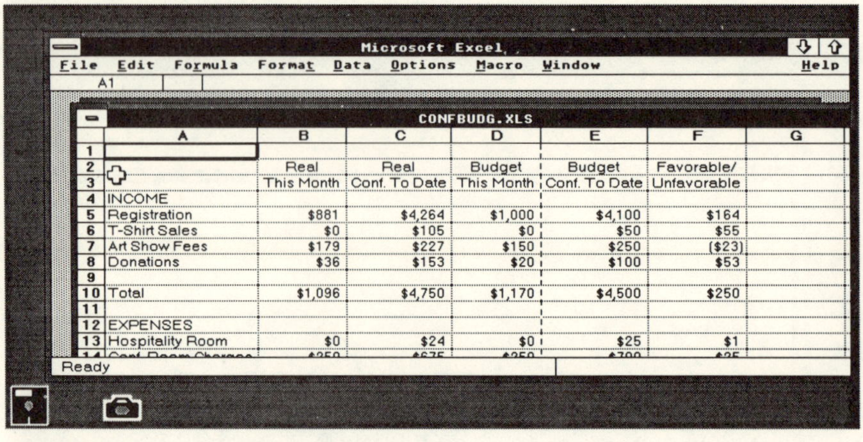

Figure 7-14. Information in a Spreadsheet

But there are some differences that stem not from the type of file *Excel* creates, but instead from the way a chart and a spreadsheet present data.

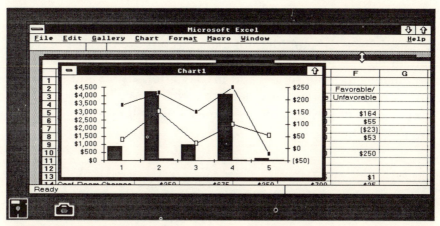

Figure 7-15. Information in a Chart

The major difference between a spreadsheet and a chart is that, while a spreadsheet conveys information by presenting a set amount of data, a chart is intended to present its information by impression. As a result of this difference, while a spreadsheet will look better in a better typeface, or with a somewhat different page layout, there are a different set of factors governing the layout of a chart.

The first of these is contrast. With a spreadsheet you can isolate data by placing it in different columns or lines. When you're using a chart, individual elements need to be visually broken up. You can use different textual or colored fill patterns to separate the different data groups. As a result, using bright blue, black, and deep red as fill colors (if you are using a color-capable printer) is a good method of separating your data.

The second important element in designing your chart is format. As a general rule, you should match the type of chart you use with the general format of its data.

(There is a very good discussion of the various chart types as well as the various formats of information they best represent contained in the Chart section of the *Excel Reference Guide*.)

Another element to keep in mind when you design a chart is its audience. Is your reader more interested in a quick, general comprehension of the numbers involved in your graph? If so, you might want to create a bar, column, or pie chart.

If your reader is more interested in individual figures, as well as how they relate, instead of a basic overview, you might be better advised to use an area, line, or scatter graph.

Finally, be careful of what you put into your graph. Just as all spreadsheets are not just numbers, graphs are not just derived from numbers. Additional elements, such as titles, gridlines, legends, names for data series, and markers (for scatter and line charts) are all important additions to a chart. Weigh carefully the effect of each of these elements you add upon the total picture of your graph.

Chapter 8
The Database

Databases can be extremely useful tools. Just like a card file, they allow you to store and sort large amounts of information in an easy-to-use format.

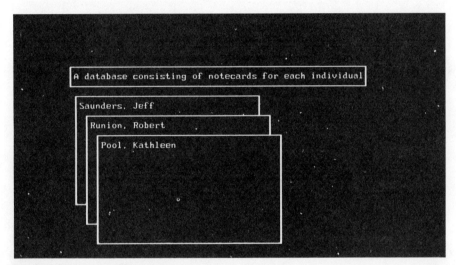

Figure 8-1. A Card File Database

But unlike a card file, a database lets you do more with your information than merely store it. You can execute automated searches for particular information, merge and sort different databases, and create reports about your database—all with just a few keystrokes.

The database in *Excel* is a restructuring of the regular spreadsheet. This is a common method of creating a database, because it has two inherent advantages: Spreadsheets and databases can be created essentially one from another because the standard display format for a database is basically the same as that used for a spreadsheet; and, all of the data in the database can readily be exchanged with the spreadsheet format you presumably use.

Admittedly, there are some problems with using a spreadsheet for a database. One big problem that persisted until the advent of spreadsheets with a file-linking capability was that it

Chapter 8

was virtually impossible to link data between two different database files. This meant you had to create completely separate databases for something as closely linked as an invoice register and the individual invoices.

Another problem in using a spreadsheet as a database is that since the program is originally created as a spreadsheet, it will never be able to perform database functions as well as a purpose-designed database program.

Fortunately, *Excel* has at least in part dealt with both of these problems. As a result, *Excel* performs much better as a database now than many of the commercially available databases did as little as five years ago.

Setting Up a Database

Before you begin designing a database, you need to understand some of the basic terms that are used.

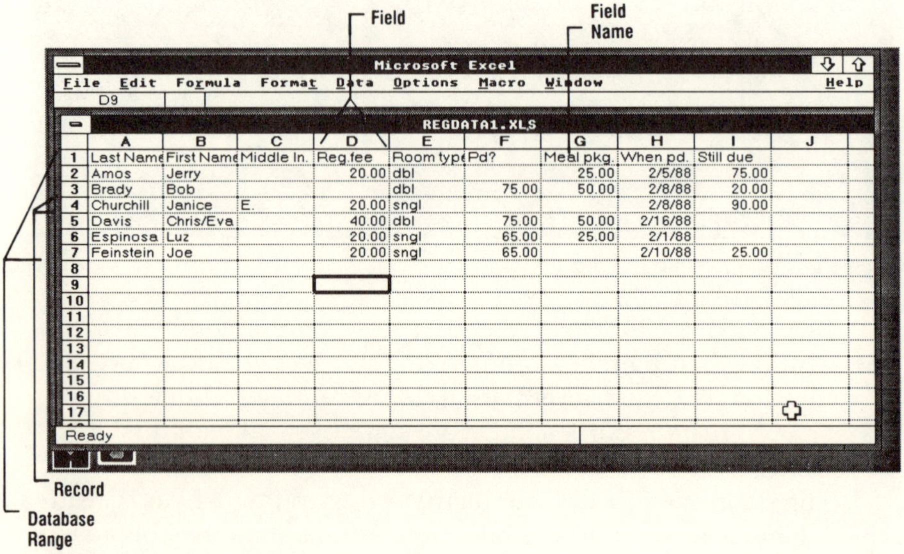

Figure 8-2. A Sample Database

A *database* is the entire file in which you store information.

The *database range* is the area of your worksheet used to store database information. You will use the Database Set Range command to define where on the worksheet you want the database range to be.

230

A *record* is a single entry. It is a specific segment of the worksheet containing all the data that pertains to a single item in the database. In the case of *Excel*, a single record in the database occupies one line of your database.

A *field* is a specific category of information stored in your database. A given field occurs in each individual record across the entire database. When you look at a database in *Excel*, a field appears as a column of information.

A *computed field* is just like a regular field, with one notable exception: Instead of entering it when you enter the rest of the record, it is computed by *Excel* from information you enter elsewhere.

A *field name* is the name used to identify data stored in a particular field. In most cases—and always in *Excel*—the top row of the database will contain the field names.

The first database action is to define exactly what you want to store. Are you storing client contract information, stock inventories, or sales order records? For each different type of data to be stored you need to create a different type of database.

Once you decide exactly *what* to store, determine *how* to store it. Specifically, you need to decide how many and what type of fields you are going to have in your database.

As you create the database, keep in mind several important factors. Each of these is part of the limitations imposed by *Excel*, and you should keep track of them as you design and work with your database.

First, when you begin using your database, include several blank records at the end of it. The reason for this is simple: Whenever you put a new record into the database, you insert it somewhere above the bottom blank line. As long as you insert new records *above* the blank line, you are in good shape; if you try to insert a record *below* the blank line, you will need to redefine the database.

Second, there is a limit to your database. You can have no more than 256 fields and 16,383 records. While this may seem like a lot of records and fields, some complex databases would go through that kind of capacity very quickly. As a result, you need to be cautious with what you ask the database to do.

Third, there is a peculiar limit to the number of databases you can have on a single worksheet. Since *Excel* recognizes as a database only the range named *Database*, theoretically you can

Chapter 8

have only a single database on a given worksheet. However, since it is quite easy to rename a range, one workable solution is to have names for more than one range on a worksheet, but have only one range at at time named *Database*. As a result, you can store several different sets of data on a single worksheet, even though you can only work with one of them at a time.

	A	B	C	D	E	F	G	H	I
2	Amos	Jerry		20.00	dbl		25.00	2/5/88	75.00
3	Brady	Bob			dbl	75.00	50.00	2/8/88	20.00
4	Churchill	Janice	E.	20.00	sngl			2/8/88	90.00
5	Davis	Chris/Eva		40.00	dbl	75.00	50.00	2/16/88	
6	Espinosa	Luz		20.00	sngl	65.00	25.00	2/1/88	
7	Feinstein	Joe		20.00	sngl	65.00		2/10/88	25.00
8									
9									
10	Event	Room	Day	Timeslot	Guests	Equipment			
11	Costuming 101	Carmel	Friday	afternoon	Butterfield, Trir	1 mic			
12	Meet the Gues	Thunderbird	Friday	evening	Feist, Kidd, Mc	2 Mics			
13	Blood Drive	Thunderbird	Saturday	afternoon	Stanford Blood	lights			
14	Masquerade	Thunderbird	Saturday	evening	Montana, Cabr	2 mics, 2 spots, sound			
15	Practical Hanc	outside	Sunday	morning	S.C.A.	none			
16	Plagiarism for	Fir	Sunday	afternoon	Maitz, Gropat,	Imic			
17	Regency Danc	Monterey	Sunday	evening	B.A.E.R.S.	1 mic, tape deck			
18	Bulwer-Lytton	Fir	Monday	morning	Murphy, Rice,	2 mics			

Figure 8-3. Several Different Databases on a Single Worksheet

Fourth, the only kind of value *Excel* allows as a field name for a database is a *text constant*. As a result, you can't use

- numbers
- logical values
- error values
- empty cells
- formulas

as field names. This doesn't mean you can't enter one of these as a text constant and display it that way.

Fifth, a field name can be no longer than 255 characters.

Finally, two basic points: Every record of your database is required to have the same fields, even if some records do not have data in each field. Also, *Excel* ignores capitalization when it is working with the database, which means *Smith* and *smith* are seen as identical.

Creating Your Database

The first thing you should do is define the area of the worksheet to be used for a database—if the worksheet will be used *only* as a database, you are fine; if you put a database into a worksheet containing other data, however, be sure the data and database remain separate.

Next, enter field names into the first row of the area you are eventually going to use for a database. Remember to enter only one field name per cell.

Now enter your starting records into the rows below the field names. You don't have to enter every record at this time, but it may be useful to enter some now so you'll have something with which to test your database.

Select the entire database range. This should include all the field names, the records you just entered, and the block of blank records you should leave at the end of your database.

Open the Data menu and select the Set Database command to define the range you selected as the database. *Excel* names the range you defined *Database*.

A Simple Database

Suppose you want to create a simple database to keep track of a phone list containing contact information for your business associates. You want the phone list to have basic information for each entry, such as company, name, phone number, and address. You also want to be able to add new people as your business grows, yet keep the phone list sorted.

Here's how to do this.

- Choose the range you want to use as your database. For this particular type of database, open a new file since there isn't much else you will want to put in the same file.
- In the A column of your spreadsheet, type the first field of your database, LASTNAME. This entry should be a single word with no spaces.
- Press the right-arrow key to move the active cell one cell to the right. Now enter the next field name in your database, FIRSTNAME.
- Repeat the previous step, entering the other field names you want in your phone list—PHONENUM, ADDRESS1, ADDRESS2, CITY, STATE, ZIP, and COMPANY.

Chapter 8

- Now select the area of the worksheet you want to be your database. This must include all fields that make up the database and as many rows as necessary for the database to work. As a good starting region, use A1–I15.
- Now open the Data menu and choose the Set Database command. This takes the area you have selected and tells Excel that it is now a range named *Database*.

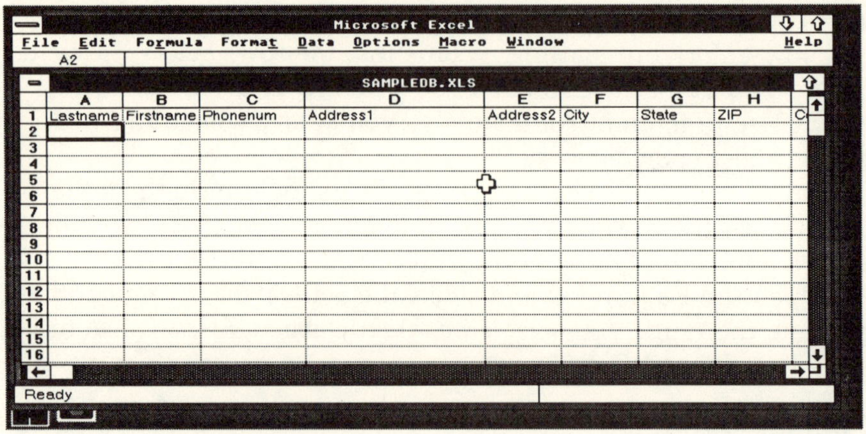

Figure 8-4. A Blank Database

- Now you are ready to enter the information for your database. You might want to try the several sample records listed in the following table. For example, enter *Blaker* in cell A2, directly under the fieldname LASTNAME. Enter *John* in the cell B2, directly under the fieldname FIRSTNAME, and so on.

> John Blaker, Ford Aerospace, 3000 Fabian Way, Palo Alto CA, 94305, (415) 555-1212
> Angela Jones, Artistic Solutions, Red Lion Plaza, San Jose, CA, 95123, (408) 767-1111
> Mike Siladi, Baycon, 1234 N. First St., San Jose, CA, 94891, (408) 321-5678
> Kathleen Pool, NorWesCon, University of Washington, GW-10, Seattle, WA, 98122, (206) 547-2769

Now you have a sample database entered into your spreadsheet.

Editing Your Database

There are a number of editing rules you will want to keep in mind when using the newly created database.

At some point, you'll almost certainly need to edit the database. When you do, use the same techniques as for editing a worksheet.

If you want to add a new record, use the Edit Insert command to place the new record in your database. Make sure you insert the new record above the last record of your database. If you accidentally insert it somewhere after the last record, you will have to redefine the database range. Also, if you did not include a blank row at the end of the database, you will need to redefine its range each time you add records to the end of the database.

If you delete or add records in the middle of the database, *Excel* will automatically adjust the range accordingly; as a result, you won't have to redefine the range.

Avoid deleting the last record in the database range since this affects the defined range. The easiest way to get around this problem is to keep the last record in the database permanently blank.

Finally, you can sort or reorder your database records as much as you want—this won't change a thing. Whenever you sort the records or fields of your database, *Excel* automatically compensates without distorting the defined range.

Defining a Data Form

There are not that many database tasks that can't be made somewhat easier by using a *database form* in place of the main database. Using *Excel* as a database program, you can view, add, edit, delete, or search for specific records within the database any time you choose. The only thing you can do with a regular database that you can't do with a form is extract records.

Whenever you define a database, you have also essentially defined a database form. In reality, *Excel* redefines the form whenever you choose the Data Form command, using the current configuration of your database as the guide from which to create the form.

To use a Data Form:

- Define your database.
- Choose the Form command from the Data menu. Your Data Form appears.

Chapter 8

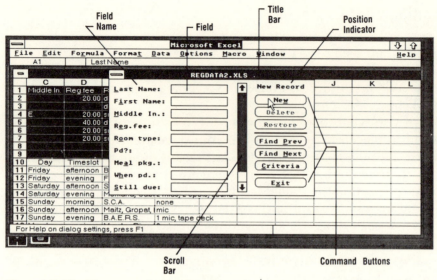

Figure 8-5. The Elements of a Database Form

There are a number of different ingredients in a database form. The first column in your data form is the various field names. Next to that column appears the field information for the particular record you are viewing.

You may notice there are two different kinds of data fields displayed. One type of field has a box around the data while the other does not. There is a simple enough reason for this: A field with a box around it (a text box) can be edited; conversely, a field without a box around it cannot be edited. There are several possible reasons for this. The field might be a computed field, resulting from either a formula or a database function; alternately, the field might be part of a locked section of your worksheet.

In the upper right-hand corner, you may notice a small line that says something like this:

2 of 33

This is the *position indicator*. It tells you the position of the record you are currently viewing, relative to the rest of the database. In the preceding example, the record is the second one in a total of 33.

An important factor to note is that the position indicator only counts those records that have data in them; blank records are ignored.

An extra useful feature is that whenever you scroll to the first blank record after the last nonblank record, the position indicator will change to read

New Record

instead of the position count given elsewhere in your database.

Moving About Within the Data Form

The navigational commands for moving about in your Data Forms are similar to those used for moving about any other window in *Excel*.

Movement	Action
To select a field	Press Alt + the key for the underlined letter in the field name.
To choose a command button	Press Alt + key for the underlined letter in the button.
To move to the same field in the next record	Press the down-arrow key.
To move to the same field in the previous record	Press the up-arrow key.
To move to the next field in the same record	Press the Tab key.
To move to the previous field in the same record	Press the Shift + Tab key.
To move to the first field in the next record	Press the Enter key.
To move to the first field in the previous record	Press the Shift + Enter key.
To move to the same field ten records forward	Press the PgDn key.
To move to the same field ten records back	Press the PgUp key.
To move to the last record	Press the Ctrl + PgDn key.
To move to the first record	Press the Ctrl + PgUp key.
To move and edit within a field	Use the Home, End, left-arrow, right-arrow, and Backspace keys.

Chapter 8

Adding and Deleting Data

Once you create a database, there are a number of things you can do with it. You can change an existing record, insert a new record, or delete an existing record—all with the touch of a few keys. These actions change depending on whether you are editing the database or a data form.

When you want to change a record in the database, the first thing you should do is find the appropriate record. Move the cell cursor so that the field within the record you want to change is highlighted, and edit the cell contents accordingly. The same editing guidelines that apply for editing worksheet cells apply to editing the database.

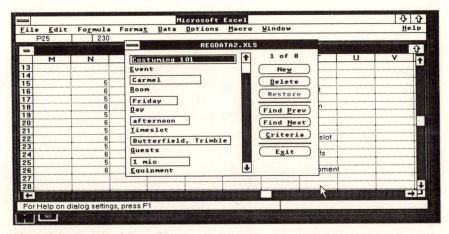

Figure 8-6. An Edited Data Form

If you are going to edit your record while using the data form, the procedure is somewhat different. You should use the cursor movement keys described above to move about from field to field within the data form and to move about within a given field.

Adding new records also differs somewhat between data forms and the database. The reason for this is that *Excel* is first and foremost a spreadsheet. While the data form automates the procedure somewhat, there are several limitations when you are adding a new record directly to the database.

To add a new record from within the data form, first make sure you are looking at the data form for your database. If you

238

are using the keyboard, select the New button; this will cause *Excel* to scroll to the first blank record after the last nonblank record. At this point, the position indicator changes to

New Record

instead of showing which record this is. (If you are using a mouse, either select the New button or drag the scroll box to the end of the scroll bar. In either case, the results will be the same as for using the keyboard.)

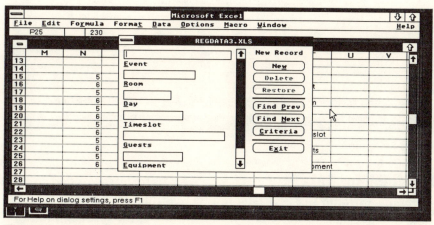

Figure 8-7. A New Record

Now that you have a blank record displayed, all you need to do is enter the information into the individual fields for your new record.

Something you should take note of is that when you are using the data form method of entering a new record, *Excel* automatically extends the database range if necessary. This occurs when two conditions are met: There are no blank records at the end of the database; and, there is room below the database to extend its range.

Deleting data in your database involves essentially the same procedure as inserting data. If you are working directly with the database, you can simply delete the row containing the record you want removed; if that isn't practical, erase the record individually.

Chapter 8

If you are working with the data form, activate the worksheet and data form mode and find the record you want to remove. Display the record and select the Delete button. As a precautionary measure, you will be asked to confirm your decision to delete the record.

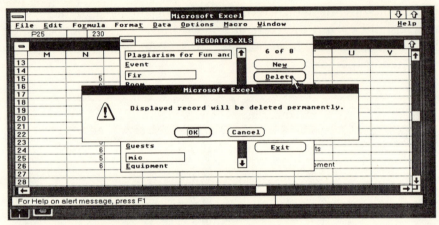

Figure 8-8. Confirming a Deletion

Searching for Data

Searching for data in *Excel* falls under two distinct headings. First, there are *specific data searches*. These can be conducted from either the regular database or from a data form. The second type of search in *Excel* is *criteria matching*. This is a more generalized search format that cannot be performed from within the data form, although it can be performed from the database.

Specific data searches can basically be described as any data search that uses only comparison criteria. As a result, since they don't use computed criteria, they can be run from within the database structure as well as from a data form.

Searching for Specific Data with the Data Form

To create a specific data search:

- First, isolate the fields in which you want to set up your search criteria.
- Access the data form by opening the worksheet that contains your database and selecting the Data Form command.
- Choose the Criter͏ͅ   ͏ͅtton to inform *Excel* that you want to de-

fine a search criteria. You'll notice that the data form window alters to some extent, with several of the buttons changing their operations.
- Enter the information you want to search for into the appropriate fields of the data form. (For example, if you have a field called *Last Name* and you wanted to search for all clients with the last name *Smith*, enter *Smith* into the Last Name field.)

Once your search criteria are defined, choose either the Find Next or Find Prev button to find the nearest occurrence of the criteria you specified. Each time you select this button, *Excel* pages either forward or backward through the database, finding the appropriate occurrences that match your search criteria.

When you finish searching through the database from the form, select the Exit button to leave the data form environment.

Searching for Specific Data with the Database

Searching in the database is handled differently. Instead of using the predefined data form, you create a separate range that contains the search parameters you want to use. The range—called a *criteria range*—is completely separate from the database range, although it must be on the same worksheet as the database range you are going to search.

When you create a criteria range, there are a number of restrictions you must obey. The first and most important is that the minirange you create must list both fields and values for which you want to search.

Because of the format you are forced to use, your criteria range will always be at least two rows high by one column wide. When you create your crteria range, place each field you want searched in a separate column with the values you want searched for in the rows below.

When the criteria range is completed, you must indicate to *Excel* that it is a criteria range:

- First, select the criteria range you have created.
- Next, open the data menu and choose the Set Criteria command. The named range you have just created is called *Criteria*.

A criteria range created on the worksheet can be used with more than just comparison criteria. Unlike searching in the data

Chapter 8

form, you can also use computed criteria to help define what you are searching for.

Defining Search Criteria

Search criteria, in general, fall into one of two catagories: *comparison criteria* and *computed criteria*. Between the two of these, you can define practically any search profile you can think up.

These criteria are roughly what they sound like: Comparison criteria compare field values within the database with a value or values you predetermine; computed criteria compare a field value with a value calculated either from several values within the database or from values both within the database and outside of it.

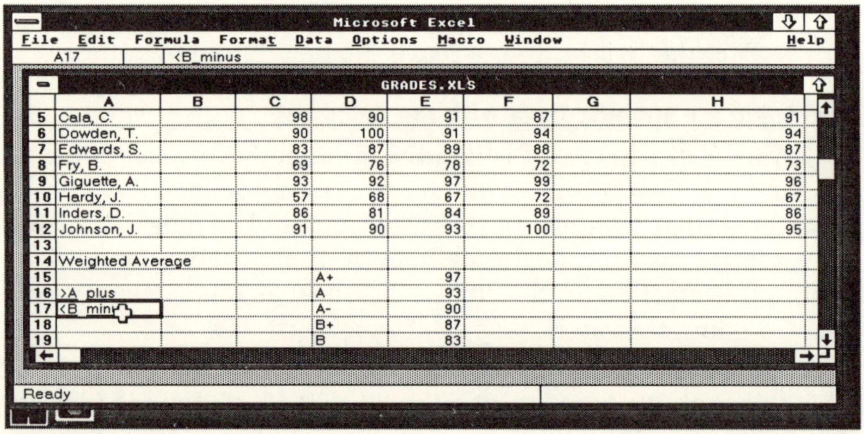

Figure 8-9. A Comparison Criteria Field

When you create a comparison criterion, you actually have greater latitude than you may think. While at first glance it might appear that you have to create an exact match for your search (looking for either a precise value or a single set of text); the definition capability of *Excel* allows you to be less specific on exactly what you want to search for.

Text searches in the database can use the actual text you are searching for as well as a variety of operators that let you define wildcard searches. In addition, the rules for text searches allow for both exact and inexact definitions of text to be found.

The ? character is a single-character wildcard. You can use it in place of a single character you want to broadly define in the text search. A search entry such as:

Sm?th?

could actually result in several different acceptable results:

smythe   smith
smithe   smotho

or anything else that fulfills the appropriate conditions.

The * character, on the other hand, is a variable-length wildcard that can contain any number of characters. There is a particular danger in using this wildcard—if you place regular text after the asterisk, it will actually be ignored during the search.

As a result, a search for something like

sm*th

could produce the following results, all of which are acceptable:

smith   smooth
smythe   smile
smack   smitten

As you can see, not all of the entries have "th" at the end. This particular command searches for text prior to the asterisk. Once that text has been duplicated, the entry is considered a match.

When you search for a particular text set such as *Smith*, what you are actually searching for is any entry that starts with *Smith*. As a result, you can wind up with more than just the *Smith* entries—you can also wind up with entries such as *Smithson* or *Smithfield*.

There is a way to avoid this and search for only precise matches. Instead of entering just the text you want, you can also search for an exact match by entering an example such as the following:

= " = smith"

This matches only the entries reading *smith*. *Smith, smithereens*, and other near matches won't be found.

Also, value matches don't have to be between precise figures. Using the various numeric operators, you can search for a wide variety of numbers with a single entry. Following is a short listing of the different numeric operators and what they do.

Operator	Definition
=	Equal to
>	Greater than
<	Less than
>=	Greater than or equal to
<=	Less than or equal to
<>	Not equal to

It is important to remember that any comparison criterion must begin with one of the comparison operators.

If you want to find values falling within a range, you can use more than one row of comparison criteria to show that range.

Computed Criteria

Computed criteria are a different breed from comparison criteria. A comparison criterion simply looks at the values it already has and compares them with the value stored in the appropriate field of a given record. A computed criterion takes not just the one pair of values into account, but also values from elsewhere in the database, on the worksheet, and even from other files.

There are a few restrictions when using computed criteria. A computed criterion will only return TRUE or FALSE. The formula you use to define the computed criterion can refer to as many fields as you want, provided the field is mentioned either by name or by reference in the first record of your database. Finally, the formula can refer to a constant value either within the database or outside of it. If the value is located outside the database, you will need to use *absolute* references rather than *relative* ones.

When you use your comparison criterion during a search, you should be aware that the formula is evaluated exactly once for each record being searched; so long as the record returns either a TRUE value or a nonzero number, the record is selected. If

The Database

the record returns a FALSE value, a zero, text, or an error value, it is ignored and the search continues to the end of the database.

	A	B	C	D	E	F	G	H
5	Cala, C.		98	90	91	87		91
6	Dowden, T.		90	100	91	94		94
7	Edwards, S.		83	87	89	88		87
8	Fry, B.		69	76	78	72		73
9	Giguette, A.		93	92	97	99		96
10	Hardy, J.		57	68	67	72		67
11	Inders, D.		86	81	84	89		86
12	Johnson, J.		91	90	93	100		95
13								
14	Weighted Average							
15				A+	97			
16	<97			A	93			
17	>83			A-	90			
18				B+	87			
19				B	83			

Figure 8-10. A Comparison Criterion

One thing you can do to make your searches work more easily is give each field a proper *Excel* name using the Formula Define Name command. This actually saves you some trouble later on if you wind up creating a computed criterion to search your database.

You don't necessarily need to search for a single criterion at a time. You can also create search criteria that search for sets of criteria.

When you are ready to combine your criteria, there are three different possibilities: You can search for one set of criteria *and* another set; you can search for one set of criteria *or* another set; or, you can search for some combination of criteria *and/or* other criteria.

When you create your search criteria set, you'll notice that you can have more than a single row of criteria established. This is where the combination capability of *Excel* is generated.

Basically, each separate line of the search request contains a separate set of criteria, all of which are run within the single search request.

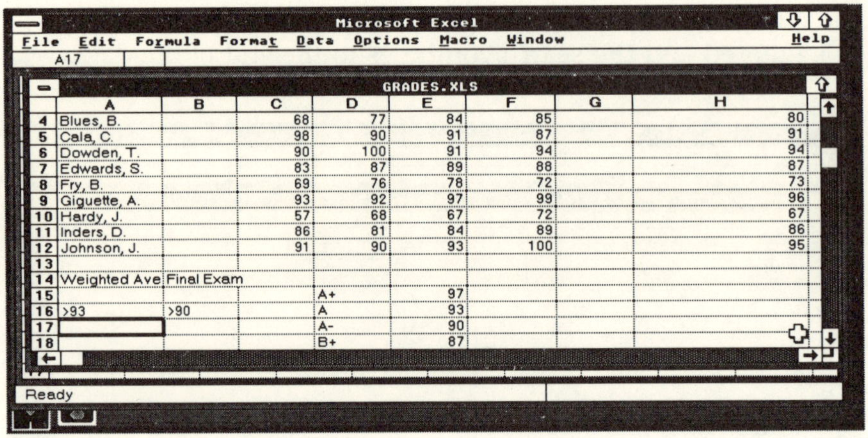

Chapter 8

Figure 8-11. An *And* Search Criterion

If you place more than a single criterion on a line, therefore, you are creating a this *and* that search.

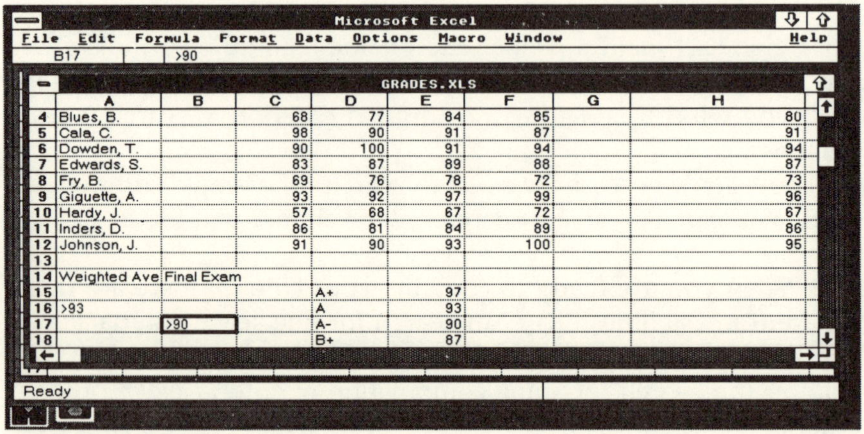

Figure 8-12. An *Or* Search Criteria Set

If you place the entries on seperate lines, you are creating a this *or* that search.

246

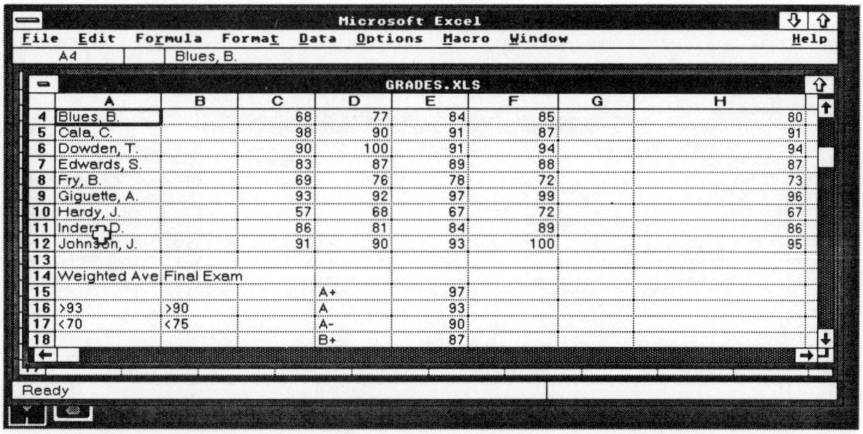

Figure 8-13. A Combined Search

You can also mix the two search formats to produce a mixed *and/or* search. Using this capability, you can accomplish a very complex multifield search of your database with relatively little effort.

Sorting

Sorting the information in your database is a highly useful capability, allowing you to list your database sorted by everything from zip code, to amount due, to a particular date.

You can specify up to three different fields, called *sorting keys,* to control the sort. Although you are limited to only three sorting keys for any one sort, the sort can be repeated if you want the database sorted even further.
To sort your database:

- First select the range from your database you want to have sorted.
- Next, open the Data menu and select the Sort command.

Chapter 8

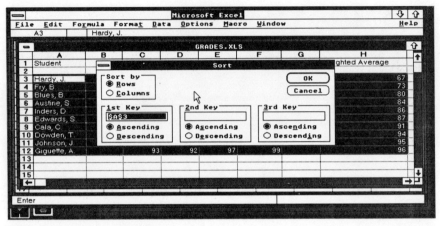

Figure 8-14. The Sort Window

You will want to sort your database by rows because sorting by columns simply sorts the different fields by whichever record you happen to choose as the sorting key. Therefore, make sure the Rows button has been selected. If the Columns button is selected, change the selection back to Rows.

- Choose your sorting keys. Find the field you want to use to primarily control the sort. This will be the first key. Enter a cell reference from within that field to designate the field as a key.

  If you want the database sorted by more than one key, select the second key and third key options, and put cell references from the appropriate fields in the boxes.
- Choose whether you want each key sorted in ascending or descending order. *Excel* sorts in the following order for ascending sorts:

    Numbers
    Text
    Logical Values
    Error Values
    Blanks

Within each category, the sort is also subdivided. Numbers are sorted from the lowest negative number to the highest positive number.

Text character numbers are those appearing as text, not as

numeric values. Also, you should be aware that *Excel* completely ignores the case of a given letter when it sorts. As a result, uppercase and lowercase letters are considered equal.

For logical values, FALSE is sorted before the value TRUE.

When you sort in descending order, the sort order is completely reversed, with one exception: Blank cells in *Excel* are always sorted last.

- Choose the OK button. The database is sorted.

To reverse the effects of your sort, choose the Edit Undo command immediately after executing the sort.

Extracting Data

Instead of using the search option, which merely highlights the records matching your search criteria, it is possible to copy the records you want into a separate area of the worksheet, called an *extract range*.

There are a few prerequisites to making use of an extract range. First, locate an area on your worksheet to which you want to copy your extract. This area must be outside the database, but is otherwise just like any other range on your worksheet. It doesn't need to have a special range name assigned to it. This range should contain enough rows to fit all the records you're going to be extracting. If there aren't enough rows, then only enough records to fit the range are extracted.

Next, prepare the extraction range by deciding which fields you want copied into the range and then enter those field names into the first row of your extract range. All field names you want copied into your extract range must be in the first line. If the field names don't appear there, the field information won't appear in the extract.

The next step is to define a separate criteria range to use to control the extract. Enter into it the information that defines how the records are to be selected, as illustrated in the previous section. Once you know the criteria are correct, be certain the range is correctly defined as a named range.

Now, select the extraction range. There are several ways to do this. If you only want to extract a limited number of records, select that number of rows below the description line you just created. If, on the other hand, you want to extract every record

Chapter 8

that meets your criteria, select the description line. This extracts every record that fits your extraction criteria.

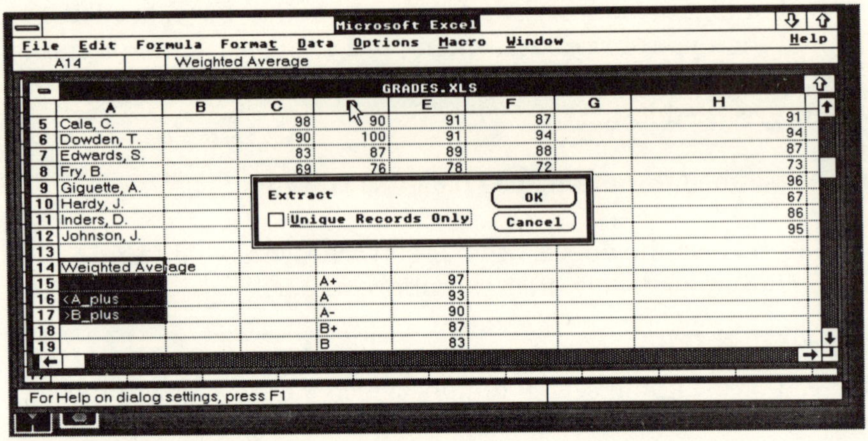

Figure 8-15. The Data Extract Dialog Box

Now you are ready to perform your extraction. Open the Data menu and select the Extract command. If you want to extract only one copy of records that are repeated or partially repeated, turn on the Unique Records Only check box. Now, select the OK button to start the extraction.

Using Database Functions

There are a number of worksheet functions specifically designed to function within the database. In each case, they replicate the regular worksheet function. For a complete listing, consult Chapter 4.

Chapter 9
Graphs and Charts

When it's necessary to show someone what you're doing with a spreadsheet, the person is often more interested in a *summary* of what the data says, rather than the raw data. One of the easiest ways to create such a summary is to graph the data in a chart.

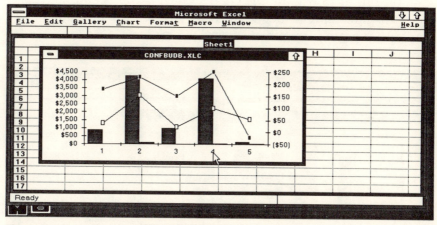

Figure 9-1. Data Summarized in a Chart

Reasons for using a chart are relatively simple. Charts provide a simple, straightforward, easily comprehended overview of spreadsheet data, illustrating trends and correlations in a manner that can be readily grasped.

Some charts are better suited to displaying particular types of data. Pie charts, for example, are better at showing a breakdown of a given sum while scatter charts are better at showing correlations between different values. Bar charts are preferable for showing how a given set of numbers might change over time. You should select the type of chart best suited to the data you'll be using to create the chart.

Creating a Chart

Creating a basic chart in *Excel* is very simple. (Each of the steps below are discussed in more detail later in this section.)

Chapter 9

- Select the cells you want to use as data for your chart.
- Choose the File New command.
- Choose Chart.
- Choose OK.

Because a basic chart isn't always enough, *Excel* allows for some creativity when generating charts.

When creating a chart, remember you can use more than one range, which means you can create charts that make use of more than one range when computing a given series. This also means you don't need to use the pie chart, which is the beginning choice for most spreadsheets; instead, you can use any other chart appropriate for your purposes.

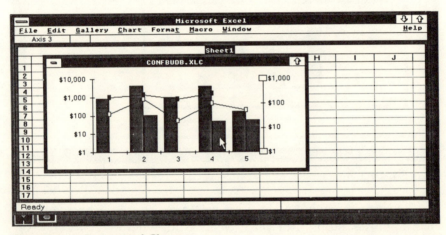

Figure 9-2. A Customized Chart

To create a chart, first select the cells you'll be using in it. Each set of numbers becomes a completely separate series within the chart, with virtually no limit to the number of series that can be simultaneously displayed.

Selecting cells in *Excel* for use with a chart is extremely simple. At least one cell in your spreadsheet is always selected—the one the cell cursor is in. To select more cells, you need to select a data series. First,

- Place the cell cursor so that it is at the beginning of the cell range you want selected.
- Press the F8 (Extend) key once, and use the cursor keys to ex-

tend the highlighted area on the spreadsheet so that it covers the area you wish to select. Remember that a single series must be a rectangle of some sort.

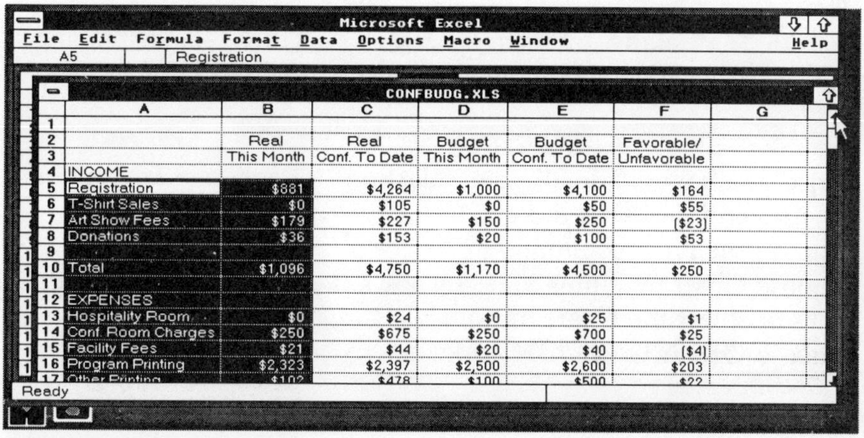

Figure 9-3. A Selected Series

To select more series at the same time, press the Shift + F8 key to add another series to the one already selected. Move the cell cursor to where your new series is going to begin and press the F8 (Extend) key again. Now highlight the new series you want appended to your previous selection.

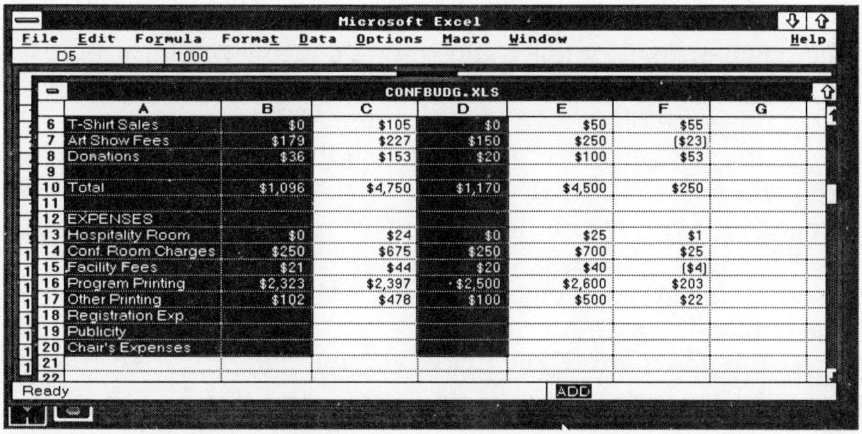

Figure 9-4. Two Series Selected

Chapter 9

Using this procedure, you can select as many series as needed. It turns out that just as there is no limit to the number of ranges you can add to a chart, there is also no practical limit to the number or orientation of the series you can simultaneously select.

Note that taking any action besides selecting cells or making use of the selections results in the entire spreadsheet being deselected.

- Once you have made all your selections, choose the File menu by pressing the Alt + F key.
- Choose the New command.
- Choose Chart by either pressing the C key or using the cursor keys to select the Chart button.
- Choose OK. A basic chart appears.

A Simple Example

In this example, we'll use the sample worksheet you already created. If you haven't created one, go back to Chapter 3 and follow the directions for creating a worksheet. Once you have the worksheet prepared, you are ready to begin creating a chart.

- Select the information you want displayed on the graph. In this case, we want to display the actual expense information but not the totals. Therefore, begin by moving the cell cursor to cell A5.
- Press the F8 key to begin selecting information, and then press the down-arrow key twice and the right-arrow key once, selecting cells A5, A6, A7, B5, B6, and B7.
- Now press the Shift + F8 key, to enter ADD mode.
- Move the cell cursor to cell A11, using the down-arrow key. You will note that the selection block did not extend downward while you were moving the cell cursor. This is because you are in Add mode, and not Extend mode.
- Press the F8 key to reenter Extend mode. Now you can select the remainder of your cells.
- Press the down-arrow key twice, and the right-arrow key once, selecting the remaining cells for your chart. Cells A5, A6, A7, B5, B6, B7, A11, A12, A13, B11, B12, and B13 should be selected.
- Open the File menu by pressing the Alt + F key combination.

- Now you can create your chart. Select the New option and when the dialog box appears, choose Chart.
- Now that the chart has been created, it needs to be reformatted so that it makes a bit more sense. While it would be nice to use a Pie chart, *Excel* regards the two separately selected areas as belonging to two different data series. Therefore, we'll use a logarithmic line chart to display the data. Open the Gallery window, and select Line. . .
- When the Line chart gallery is displayed, it is easy to pick out the logarithmic chart from the others. Select the option 6 and then choose OK.

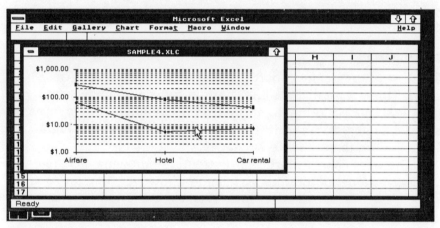

Figure 9-5. Completed Chart

As you may notice, there are two separate data series displayed on the chart. The upper line is the data series for the hotel, airfare, and car, while the lower line displays the amounts for the different meals.

Predesigned Charts

There are seven different basic chart types to choose from in *Excel*, as well as a predefined *Preferred* type you can set yourself.

Chapter 9

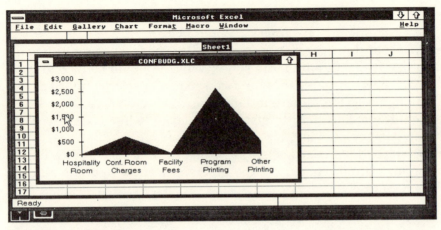

Figure 9-6. An Area Chart

Area Charts

The first of the defined chart types in the Gallery is the Area chart. This is essentially a line chart with the area underneath each line shaded to highlight the cumulative effect of one or more series changes. As a result, the amount of the change is highlighted more than the rate of change.

The Area chart is particularly useful for showing a change in value over a period of time. Remember, however, that an Area chart is always, in whatever form it takes, going to be a stacked chart of some sort. The result is that the chart is always scaled to the largest sum in the chart, not the largest single value. This may result in the overall scale of the chart being much smaller than you would otherwise expect it to be.

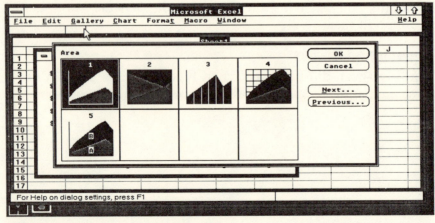

Figure 9-7. The Gallery of Area Chart Types

As you can see, there are a number of different types of area charts. Four of these formats are the same basic chart with variations in what is included. The fifth chart, selection 2, is constructed as a 100-percent area chart. As a result, data input to that particular chart format displays quite differently from the other four formats.

The first format generates a basic area chart. It comes without any embellishments and consists of only the data series you selected, now plotted into an area graph format. This format is useful for getting a good grasp of the essentials.

The second format is the 100-percent area chart discussed earlier. This format is more useful when you are trying to compare the performance of several sets of values. As a result, while the relative performance of the different series is emphasized, the actual performance of each series may be less easy to determine.

The third and fourth area charts are otherwise standard with plotting lines—either vertical, or vertical and horizontal—plotted as part of the chart. Use chart formats if you need to determine precisely where the values on the chart lie. Use the vertical-only format if you only need to track the increments by which the series are marked. The vertical and horizontal format is more useful if you need to determine the actual values of the various data points.

The last of the predetermined area chart formats is one that includes the various series labels as part of each region. This makes differentiating between the various series much easier. This format is especially useful when your chart is too large to fit a proper legend on the page.

Bar Charts

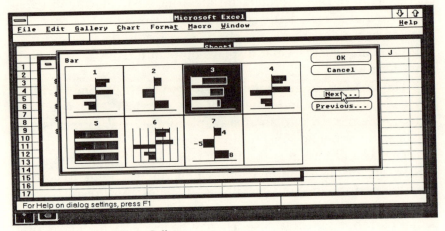

Figure 9-8. The Bar Chart Gallery

Bar charts contain a basic design philosophy: simplicity. Their format is easy to understand—a bar is proportionally sized to the value of the data point. As a result, bar charts are both easy to comprehend and widely used.

Because of the bar chart's orientation, *Excel* differentiates between bar and column charts: Bar charts are oriented along vertical axes; column charts are oriented along horizontal axes (a horizontal axis gives a better representation of time passing).

The first of the Bar charts in the gallery is the standard bar chart. Each new series is plotted along the length of the axis, with new series set side by side, touching each other. In this chart format, positive values are plotted to the left of the axis and negative values are plotted to the right. The result is that you see what you get—a normal bar chart.

The second format is a single-value bar chart. This chart takes each data point in the series and creates a separate bar for it. The result is that every data point is treated as a separate series with a single value in that series.

The third format is a stacked-bar chart. In this case, instead of placing the different series next to each other, they are stacked one on top of the other. As a result, not only does the format allow you to take a look at relative values of the different data points, it also gives you a good opportunity to see the cumulative effect of all the series. A good example of using this format is to compare the sales performance of several stores. In addition to showing how the different stores perform, you can also see the cumulative sales performance of all the stores.

The next format is a straightforward bar chart with one alteration for aesthetic purposes: Instead of having the series placed side by side, they are slightly overlapped, allowing each value position to take up less space than it might in a regular bar chart. This format might be preferable when you have series with large numbers of data points.

The fifth bar chart format is a 100-percent stacked-bar chart. This format is similar to the regular stacked bar, with one major exception: Instead of plotting the cumulative series against an absolute scale, they are plotted against a relative scale. Each data point is only as large as its value contrasted with the sum of the total for that particular value point. To illustrate this, if one series contained a constant value while the other series contained increasing values, the region for the first series would actually decrease across the graph.

The sixth format is a regular bar chart with one alteration: Gridlines are included, making it is easier to find the different values that make up the chart. These gridlines are simply an aesthetic touch you may or may not like. If you want them as part of your graph, choose this format for the easiest path.

The last preset bar chart design is again, a straightforward bar chart but with the addition of value labels. This is another way of providing the same utility available with the gridlined chart. You may decide this is a preferable way to establish the values in your chart.

Chapter 9

Column Charts

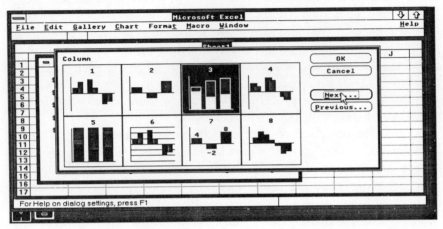

Figure 9-9. The Column Chart Gallery

Column charts are basically the same as bar charts, with the exception of their being reoriented into horizontal format. Column charts, in general, are better at providing a sense of time passing than bar charts, and are probably more useful for time-oriented data series.

The preset column charts are essentially identical to the Bar chart presets, with one significant exception—the last of the Column chart presets is a block column chart format. Instead of each data point in the series forming a single long rectangle with the length proportional to the data point value, in this case, the data point value is used to create a block of the appropriate size with the separate blocks stacked next to each other. Because of this display format, you should use only a single series with this chart, as any more would tend to cover the previous series' data.

Note that all of the comments for the bar chart presets are equally applicable to the appropriate Column chart format.

Line Charts

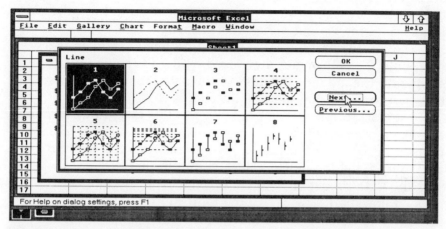

Figure 9-10. The Line Chart Gallery

Line charts are very useful when you are trying to emphasize a rate of change in a series. Instead of emphasizing the values as would a bar or column chart, a line chart visually emphasizes the rate of change of a series through the viewers' judgements of the line format of the chart.

The first of the predetermined chart formats in the Line Chart Gallery is a basic line chart with markers. Each individual data point is plotted and assigned a marker, with each series having a different marker. The different values within a given series are then connected by a line to illustrate any changes in values. This format of line chart is useful in almost any situation in which you need to have a visual display of rates of change between and inside various series.

The second line chart format is also a standard line chart; however, there are no markers included in it—they were in the previous chart format. As a result, while the values are plotted on the chart and the data points are connected via series lines, there are no individual data point markers. This particular chart format is more useful for situations in which you have no real need to show the individual values in the series, only the trends those series take.

The third line chart format is a markers-only chart. This is again similar to the first of the formats; the exception is that the connecting lines have been removed instead of the data point markers. This chart format is useful for situations in which you are interested in the trends your data series take and the individual values, but when you don't necessarily need to track the performance of the various series in any detail.

The fourth chart format is a basic gridlined chart. In this case, only the data values are placed with grids so you can more easily find the individual values of the data points. Otherwise, the chart format is the same as the first one.

The next format is also gridlined. In this case, however, both axes have been gridded. Use this format when you have a large number of data points within a given series and you want to be able to track the individual values within the series.

The sixth predetermined chart format is a logarithmically gridded line chart. This is like the fourth format, but with one difference: Where the data values in the previous chart format were evenly distributed, in this case, they are compressed as the values increase. As a result, it becomes much easier to determine the values of the lower-value data points. In addition, in the low-value regions of a line chart, this format makes it somewhat easier to determine the performance of the various series in your chart.

The next chart format is a vertically linked line chart. In previous chart formats, the individual data points within a series are linked by a line, indicating they are part of a common set of values. In this chart format, however, instead of linking values within a series, values with a common marker value are linked by the line. This chart format is particularly useful for drawing attention to values (such as dates) that share a common marker value.

The last of the line chart formats is a vertically linked line chart with a twist. Because of the structure of the chart, it becomes a maximum-minimum-median chart. In this format, all the data points are plotted, but without markers, and a line is drawn between those data points that share a common marker value. Next, a new data series is created and plotted using markers only, showing the median value at each set of marker values. This chart format can be particularly useful for analyzing the performance across a period of time of selected groups of values, such as stocks, bonds, or commodities.

Pie Charts

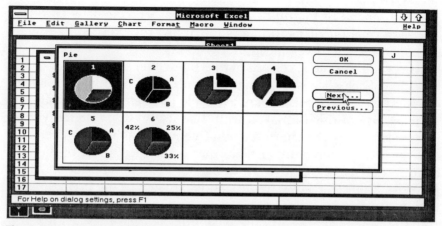

Figure 9-11. The Pie Chart Gallery

The Pie chart format has several limitations that need to be understood before you use it with your data. First and foremost, a pie chart can be used with only one value series. This means defining a large number of values for a single graph will create a single pie chart with a large number of very thin slices that may not have as much in common as you would like. The second restriction is that all pie charts are created in the form of a 100-percent chart of some kind, much like a 100-percent bar or column chart.

    Pie charts are a result of an interesting form of charting. The entire chart is proportionally scaled with individual chart slices proportionally scaled to both the slices they represent and the whole chart. In other words, the entire area of the chart is set so that it is equal to the sum of the data series being used to create the chart. Each slice of the pie chart is then sized so that it is proportionally sized to the individual data point it represents.

    The first of the predesignated pie chart formats is a bare bones pie chart format. Nothing is included on the chart page aside from the actual pie chart. The only assistance provided in the chart is that each pie slice is marked with a different texture, allowing you to visually diversify the different slices. All other extra elements available with pie charts are included in the other predesignated formats. This chart format is most useful when you

Chapter 9

want quick breakdown of the data, rather than a presentation-quality chart.

The second of the predesignated pie chart formats is an otherwise normal pie. This format is much like the preceeding one in that only a single diversification method is used. In this case, however, all the pie slices are marked with the same format of texturing. Each slice is then marked with an individually assigned label, much as series labels are available in other chart formats. To make use of this format, it would be useful to predefine your marker labels for the chart, allowing you to establish the chart quickly and conveniently. This format is the most basic of the chart formats you would want to use for actual presentation. It provides a quick, readily understandable view of the breakdown within a given data series.

The next format is an otherwise unlabled pie chart with a single slice *exploded*. (In this usage, *exploded* means "separated from the rest of the chart" rather than "destroyed.") Using this format, you can more readily establish charts when you want to quickly draw attention to a particularly important data point. This format is very useful for situations in which you need to point out one special value for some reason.

The fourth pie chart format is like the previous one in almost every respect; however, instead of exploding a single chart slice to highlight it, all slices are exploded so they can be more easily viewed. As a result, each slice can be checked individually without consideration of the others.

The next preset chart format is a labeled pie chart. However, this format is somewhat different from the previous labeled chart format in that it includes elements of both that chart and of the textured format. This makes it much easier to see which section a given label is referring to. This format is a much better choice when you are going to be using chart labels, since the differentiated pie segments allow your viewers to visually separate the different segments.

The last of the preset pie chart formats is, again, a standard pie chart with a single modification: Instead of having text labels, each segment has a label consisting of the percentage of the total chart the associated slice represents. This lets you quickly determine what proportion of the whole each slice contains. This graph format is useful when you need to be able to quickly determine the relative size of a given segment of a graph.

Scatter Charts

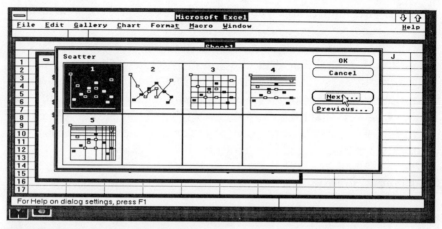

Figure 9-12. The Scatter Chart Gallery

Scatter charts are used almost exclusively for determining correlations between different sets of values and, as such, become very useful in statistical studies. When you use scatter charts, you should always be sure to provide both series you are attempting to correlate when you define your chart.

The first of the predefined scatter charts in the gallery is the basic two-dimensional scatter chart and is mainly useful for determining if there is a correlation between two different series of numbers. When you define the graph, remember that each graph series needs to have *two* (not one) separate sets of numbers defined for it.

The second predefined scatter chart is otherwise normal with the various data points linked in the order they are presented in the data series. This format can be useful in when you need to demonstrate a very positive or linear correlation in your chart.

The next format is a standard scatter chart with both horizontal and vertical grids. As a result, all the data points in the chart are plotted in a manner that allows you more ease in correlating specific values. The greatest single use for this particular chart format is when you need to determine the values of the different points on the chart.

Fourth on the scatter chart gallery is a logarithmically scaled scatter chart. This is only lined in one dimension, however, so while the one axis is compressed, the other is proportionally distributed along its length. This sort of scatter chart is most useful when you need to be able to determine a correlation for the lower values in your chart, and you are less interested in correlating the higher values.

The last of the predetermined scatter chart formats is a two-dimensional, gridded scatter chart, constructed with a logarithmic scale on both axes. This format determines that large values in both dimensions are compressed while the smaller values are not. This can be very useful in some cases when your series covers a broad region, yet you need to demonstrate a correlation at low values that is just as valid as at much higher values.

Combination Charts

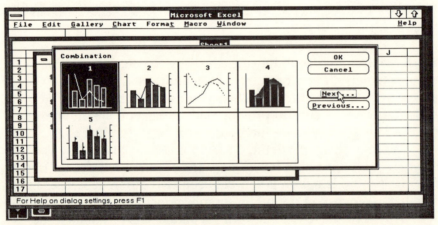

Figure 9-13. The Combination Chart Gallery

Combination charts are useful when you want to show the relationship between one type of data and another. Since *Excel* provides the capability to merge certain types of charts into a single chart, you can demonstrate these relationships. A number of the more commonly combined chart formats are already created in *Excel*.

The first of the combined charts is a merged line and column chart. When you define it you should take care to define both of the chart series you intend to use. This format is mostly useful when you need to combine a column and line chart. It is important to note that you do not want to put too many series in the column chart—you might very quickly confuse your viewer regarding which is the column graph and which is the line graph.

The next format is a combined line and column chart with two separate value axes. This format is useful when you want to display both sets of data in the same graph, but one set is very much out of scale with the other. In this case, you can rescale the second value axis so that it is more appropriately sized for the entire graph.

The third combined graph format is actually two line charts combined into a single chart. This may seem silly to do since you can accomplish the same thing by putting two separate series in a single line chart, but this format has a very important difference: The two lines in this chart use completely different value axes. Since the two series are on a very different scale, one series would be an almost flat series along the bottom of the chart, and the other would appear virtually normal. This chart format, therefore, is very useful when you want both line charts displayed, but the values on the two charts are grossly out of scale with each other.

The next combination format is a combined area/column chart with a single-value axis. This format is appropriate when you need to emphasize the line portion of a combined line and column chart.

The last of the predefined combined chart formats is a merged column and high/low/median value chart, displayed with separate value axes. A good example for using this is a chart on which you are simultaneously showing both the performance of something and its value—such as a company's profitability versus its stock performance.

The last of the gallery selections is the Preferred chart format. In this case, the chart selected is the one you have already designated as the format you prefer to use. Keep this format on hand for a particular chart format you frequently use.

Using the Gallery

The gallery allows you a great deal of flexibility in defining your charts. For all the different chart types, you can bring up a predefined chart format as well as store a particularly favored format or formats.

In addition, you can use the gallery to switch between various chart formats when you can't decide which one you want for your final output.

The Gallery windows are similar to each other, the only real difference being what type of chart format is stored in each window. Once you have learned the applicable commands for one window, you have learned them for all windows.

When you open a Gallery window, you're given a great deal of control over your chart. Using just the Enter, N, P, Esc, and cursor keys, you can easily reformat a chart.

When you look at the Gallery window, notice one of the chart selections has a darkened background while the others all have light backgrounds. The format with the darkened background is the one currently selected within that Gallery window.

There are two ways to change the selection. The first is to use the cursor keys to move the selection highlight through the different formats. The down- and right-cursor keys move you forward through the selections, while the up-and left-cursor keys move you backward through the selections. When you are using this method, remember the selections are looped, so moving forward through the last selection brings you back to the beginning.

The second method of changing the selection is to use the number keys (across the top of your keyboard) to directly choose the format you want highlighted. Simply press the number of the new format and the highlight jumps to that selection.

Choose the Next or Previous buttons to scroll back and forth through the various Gallery windows, just as if you were selecting them from the Gallery menu. Use them to rapidly scroll through the chart formats to select a format appropriate for your purposes.

To exit the Gallery window without selecting anything, either press the Esc key to activate the Cancel command, or use the tab key to select the Cancel button and press the Enter key.

Choose the OK button to designate the currently highlighted graph as active. *Excel* reformats your selected data into that format and displays it onscreen.

Customizing Your Chart

When you customize a chart, you'll discover three basic alterations you can make to chart elements:

- Reformat already existing chart elements.
- Add and format new chart elements.
- Redefine the data series.

Excel places each item appearing as part of a chart into one of several classes of objects:

Chart
Plot area
Legend
Axes
Chart text
Chart arrows
Gridlines
Each seperate data series
Drop lines
Hi-lo lines

Selecting a chart object. Throughout the remainder of this chapter, you'll need to select the different parts of your chart in order to change them. From the keyboard, use the up- and down-cursor keys to move and select between classes of objects; use the left- and right-cursor keys to move and select between objects within each class. Using the mouse, point to the chart object you want to select, and click.

Of the classes just listed some are present automatically when you define your chart and some need to be explicitly created before they can be manipulated. The elements present when you begin working on your chart are limited. Things like legends, chart text, and chart arrows are almost certainly not going to exist. Similarly, if you want gridlines, you'll have to create them as a new element in the chart unless you selected one of the particular chart formats that explicitly contains gridlines. You can, however, expect certain things to be already exist: the chart and plot area, the data series, and the axes. If any of these objects are missing, something is very wrong, indeed.

Reformatting what you already have in your chart is the first step. (Usually, you should plan on working with what you already have on the chart before you think about adding new elements. Adding new elements before you have handled the original chart elements very rapidly leads to a cluttered, unreadable, and unusable chart.)

When altering things in your chart, manipulate them one object at a time. This lets you see the results of your changes (to make sure you haven't completely wrecked your chart) before proceeding on to the next modification.

Classes of chart objects are dealt with in this manner because you can either move the selection within a class of objects, or you can change the selection from one class to another when you are selecting something in your chart. As a result, being able to distinguish one class of chart objects from another allows you to work that much more quickly.

When you first select objects, notice that either white or black boxes spring up around the object in question. The color of the box determines whether you can alter a given chart object directly from the keyboard. If an object is bound by black boxes, you can move or size it directly from the keyboard and format it directly with commands. If it is bound by white boxes, you cannot move or size it directly and only some such items—like the axis labels or legend—can be reformatted with commands.

Your selection may cause something to appear in the formula bar. If you select a text entry, it appears in the formula bar where it can be edited. If you select a series marker, the formula *Excel* uses to define a series appears in the formula bar, allowing you to edit that, too.

Changing the Background

The most obvious object you might change is the background of your chart. This is called the *chart area* and can be reconstructed from the Chart menu into one of a variety of formats. In addition to changing the background pattern, you can also change the borders and colors used in the display.

The first step in this process is to select the entire chart. If you wish to use the Chart menu to select your chart, open the Chart menu and choose the Select Chart command. Alternately, you may select the chart using the keyboard or a mouse.

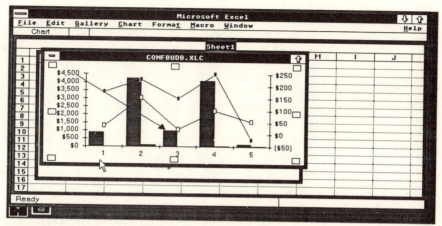

Figure 9-14. Selecting the Chart

Next, open the Format menu and select the Patterns command. This displays the various formatting options for your chart's background.

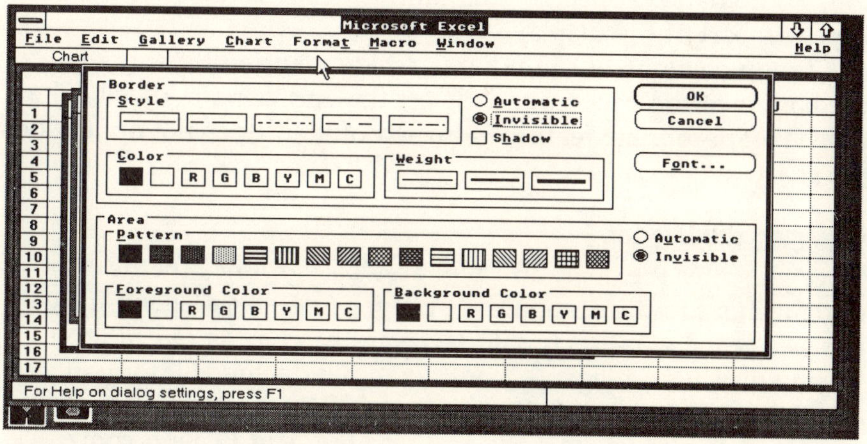

Figure 9-15. The Chart Format Window

This command lets you alter the texture of the chart's border as well as its background format. You are also able to change the colors used in displaying or printing your chart (if your monitor is color capable). The colors *Excel* supports in a charting environment are black, white, red, green, blue, yellow, magenta, and cyan.

Finally, press the Enter key to select the OK button. This activates your selections.

Chapter 9

Changing the Plot Area

The next object you would probably think to alter is the plot area. This is the region including both axes where *Excel* plots your data.

Select the plot area either by using the keyboard or by using the Select Plot Area command from the Chart menu.

Open the Format menu and choose the Patterns command. Using the window this command displays, you can adjust both the background and border of the plot area.

To add a border to the plot area, first select the Automatic command from the Border section of the window. Without this button selected, you cannot display the plot area border. Next, choose the weight and then the style and color of the plot area border you want displayed.

The procedure for altering the plot area background is quite similar: Select the Automatic button and then define the pattern and colors you want to use for the display.

Activate these new element changes by selecting the OK button. Your chart reappears—this time with the features you selected as part of the display.

If you change your mind and decide you don't want either the border or the background, select the appropriate Invisible button. The appropriate feature is turned off and does not appear on the chart.

Changing the Legend

Once you alter the chart and plot area background, the next important thing to think about is the legend. A chart legend makes it easier to tell what each data series in the chart is referring to. When you create a legend, it automatically includes information on all the different series in the chart.

Open the Chart menu and choose the Add Legend command. This creates a legend on the right side of the chart with each data series labeled using the data series name from the series formula.

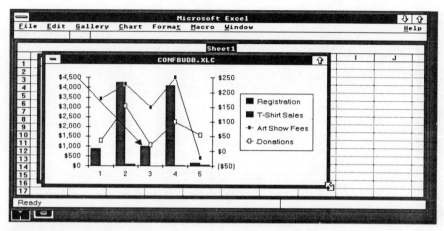

Figure 9-16. A Chart Legend

To change the text of the labels, you must edit the text of the series formula. For more information on this, see the section on editing chart series formulas.

If you want, you can reformat the legend into something different from its original appearance. To do this or to move the legend, first select the legend and choose the Legend command from the Format menu. A dialog box appears, containing a number of options for positioning the legend as well as exactly how you want it formatted. Choose the position, fonts, and border and background patterns for the legend; then choose OK.

If you decide you don't want to have a legend after all, open the Chart menu and select the Delete Legend command.

Changing the Chart Axes

Alterations to your chart axes include removing them, formatting them, and using them to add gridlines to your chart.

Chapter 9

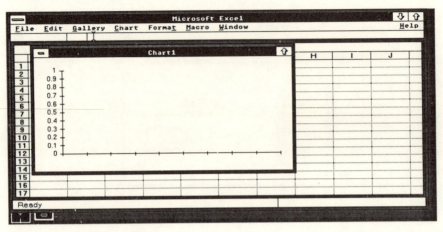

Figure 9-17. The Chart Axes

Normally, when you create a chart (unless it is a pie chart) it comes with a set of axes included. If you really don't want one or both of those axes present on your chart, use the Axes... command from the Chart menu. When you activate this command, a dialog box is displayed, allowing you to turn off the chart axes. If your chart has an overlay, you can also alter the axes on the chart from this window.

Each of the boxes containing an X corresponds to a chart axis that will be displayed. If you wish to turn an axis off, hold down the Alt key and press the appropriate key. Once you have selected all the axes you want to adjust, choose OK to return to your chart and activate your selections.

To return the chart axes you removed, open the Axes dialog again, turn on the appropriate selections, and choose OK. This method lets you change your mind about chart axes as often as you want.

You don't necessarily need to turn your chart axes on or off. If you don't like the way they look, you can reformat them to fit better within your chart's overall appearance.

Reformatting your chart axes covers a relatively broad range of possibilities. You can alter things specifically on the Category axis or the Value axis, or on both axes at once.

When you reformat your chart, the areas you will be working on fall into three broad categories, all controlled from the Format menu. If you wish to change where the axes of your chart intersect or make numeric adjustments to your chart, use the Scale command. If you want to reformat the text attached to the chart axes, choose the Font command. If you otherwise want to reformat the physical appearance of the chart axes, choose the Patterns command.

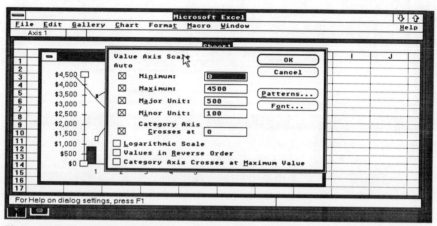

Figure 9-18. The Scale Window

Changing the scaling of your chart axes demands a number of different decisions. You must decide whether you want the computer to generate the chart axes, what the scaling of the chart axes is, and where you want the axes to cross. If you don't want the computer to automatically generate any of these values, then you also need to decide what you want these values to be. In addition, you need to establish whether or not you want to use a logarithmic scale or a reverse scale and whether you want the axes to cross at the maximum possible value.

To change the scale, choose the Scale command from the Format menu; then, in each case, select the check box appropriate to what you want. If you want the feature turned on, make sure there is an *X* in the box. If not, you should be certain the box is empty. In addition, if you are turning off any of the automatic features, you will need to input a hard value to replace the value the computer would otherwise generate.

Chapter 9

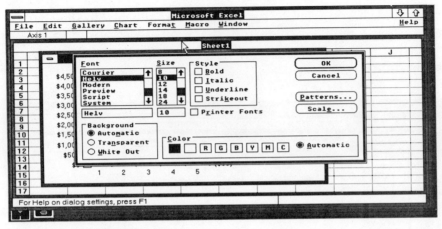

Figure 9-19. The Fonts Window

To change the text that comes with your chart axes, use the Fonts window. Depending on your desires and the equipment installed in your computer, you can have your choice of a wide variety of fonts, type sizes, and typefaces.

In addition, you can choose the color used for the display, what you want the background to look like, and whether you want to use different fonts on your printer.

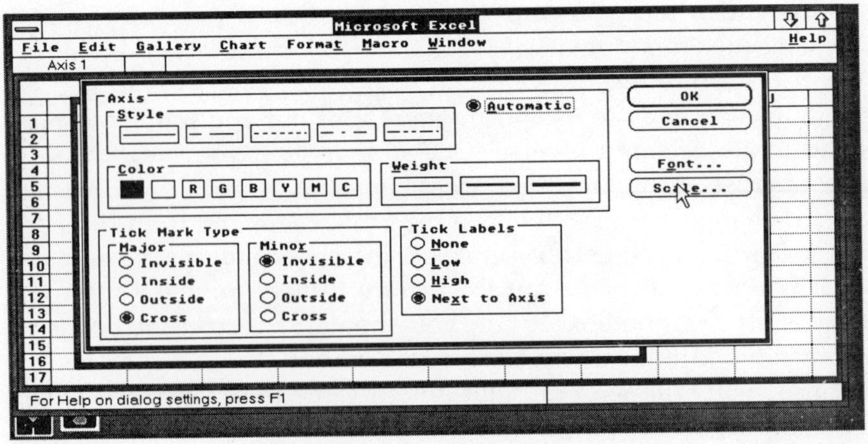

Figure 9-20. The Patterns Window

Depending on what else you want to do with your chart, you can change the appearance of each of your chart axes using the Patterns window. This window is very similar to the Patterns windows used to reformat the Chart Area and Plot Area. In this case, however, there is no fill used.

This window also controls the appearance and location of the tick marks and tick labels appearing on your chart axes. From here, you can reformat and reposition your major tick marks, add or alter minor tick marks, and remove or reformat the appearance of your tick mark labels. With both major and minor tick marks, you are given the choice of not having them, or having them inside, outside, or crossing the chart axes.

Depending on which window you open, you can jump from one window to another using the Font, Scale, or Patterns buttons that appear in the windows. Using this facility, you can change several features at the same time without reopening the Format menu.

Remember, no matter what you are going to change, first select the axis you will be working with, select the option you want to work with, and then edit it as appropriate.

Changing Chart Text

A number of different items can be edited under the heading *chart text*. These include chart title and subtitle, axes titles, data point labels, and other unattached text.

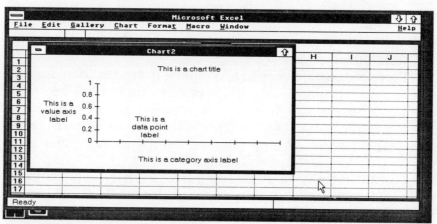

Figure 9-21. Text Locations in a Chart

Most of the text types you use in your chart fall under the heading *attached text*. These are all controlled through the Attach Text command on the Chart menu.

Chapter 9

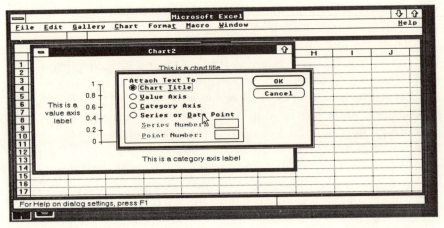

Figure 9-22. The Attach Text Window

When you select this command, you should know beforehand both where you want to locate the text and what it should say.

From the Attach Text dialog, choose the text location by selecting one of the buttons and then choosing OK. If you want to enter a text attached to a particular series or data point, you will also need to provide the series number and point number before you select the OK button.

After you select the location for your text, *Excel* presents you with a default entry for that text block. At the same time, the default text is displayed in the edit bar. Here, you can edit it just as you would the contents of a spreadsheet cell.

There is one difference in text editing for charts. If you were editing text in a spreadsheet and wanted to insert a line break, you would simply skip down a row and continue entering text. In a chart, however, all text in a particular location is treated as a single cell's contents. As a result, you insert line breaks by pressing the Ctrl + Enter key combination.

You are also able to include as a label a reference to another spreadsheet. This is in addition to the automatically created and updated formulas controlling the appearance of the chart.

To create an external reference formula for chart text, you need to understand the format used for the reference label as well as the restrictions placed on the formula you are using. There are three rules you must follow when creating your formula:

278

- The worksheet to which the formula is referring must be open when the formula is created.
- The external reference can only refer to a single cell. You can use a named range to accomplish this, but the named range can only apply to a single cell and not to a cell range.
- The external reference can be an absolute reference or any type of constant such as text, a number, data, time, logical value, or an error value.

So long as these rules are obeyed, almost anything can be imported as a cell reference for your chart.

Next, you need to construct the formula that will actually import the text to your chart. This formula is fairly similar to those used to define the different series in that it contains the same basic elements.

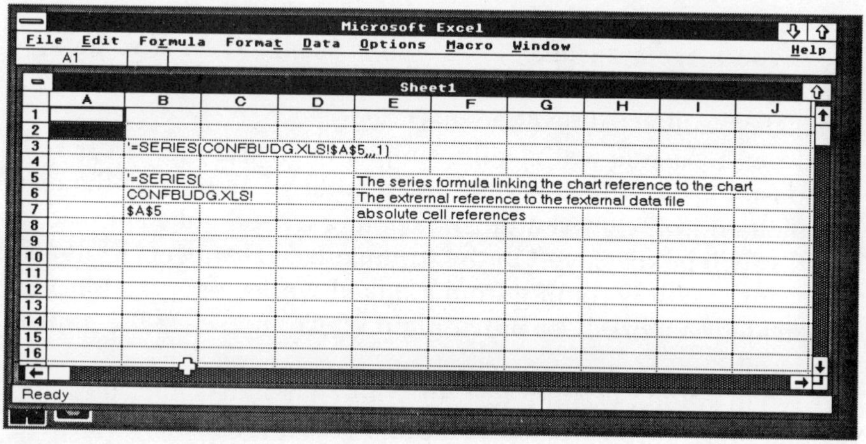

Figure 9-23. The Syntax of a Reference Formula

Once you have created this formula, all chart text linked to the spreadsheet is automatically updated regarding changes in the spreadsheet, just as the series values in the chart are updated according to changes in the values of the spreadsheet.

The other kind of chart text you can include in your worksheet is called *unattached text*. This kind of text is used for subtitles, comments on chart objects or data, emphasizing elements of the chart, and other similar things.

To add unattached text, first make sure none of the other text already in the chart is selected. Enter the text you want to appear on your chart. As you type, the text appears in the formula bar where you can edit it as you deem necessary. Such text follows all the rules that apply to regular attached text, including insertion of line breaks using the Ctrl + Enter key combination. After typing your text block, press the Enter key and the block of text will appear on the chart.

The text is surrounded with black selection boxes so you can edit things such as size and location of the text block.

If you want, you can also link unattached text to a cell in your spreadsheet. The procedure for using a link with unattached text is quite similar to that used for attached text. First, make sure none of the text on your chart is selected. Next, type an equal sign. Open the spreadsheet window for the data you want linked and select the cell you want referenced. Alternately, you can simply type the appropriate cell reference formula in the formula bar. Once you have the correct formula displayed in the formula bar, press Enter.

If you make a mistake, as everyone seems to do at some point, it's easier to either edit or reformat the text rather than eliminate the affected text and start over.

To edit existing text is quite simple. First, use the cursor keys or mouse to select the text that needs editing. As long as the text is contained in the chart and isn't coming from a linked spreadsheet, it will be displayed in the formula bar. However, if the text you want to edit is coming from a linked worksheet, you'll need to activate the worksheet providing the text and select the appropriate cell.

When editing existing text for your chart, the same rules apply that were in force when you originally entered the text. Inserting a line break, for instance, can still be accomplished using the Ctrl + Enter key combination. Once you finish editing the text, either select the enter box or press the Enter key; the revised text will appear in your chart.

Changing chart text's formats. You can also change format appearance of chart text by altering the typestyles, changing the orientation and alignment of attached text, and adding borders and backgrounds to the text.

Graphs and Charts

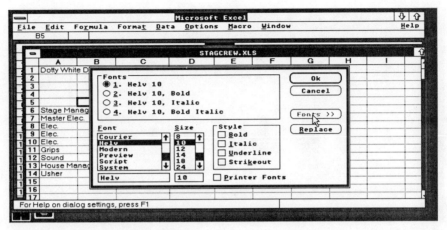

Figure 9-24. Some Available Fonts

In all three cases, reformatting involves only a few simple steps:

- First, select the text.
- Next, select one of three diferent commands on the Format menu. If you want to change the color, font, style, or font size, choose the Font command. If you want to change the orientation or alignment of the text, choose the Text command. If you decide to reformat the background and borders used for your text, select the Patterns command.
- The text selected in your chart is altered.

The best possible way to determine what you can do with fonts and display options available on your computer is to experiment with the different combinations; see which ones work for your particular system.

Moving unattached text. When it is first created, unattached text just sits. It occupies space in the middle of your chart, which is probably not where you want it to be. You can move and resize the text to work better with your chart.

Chapter 9

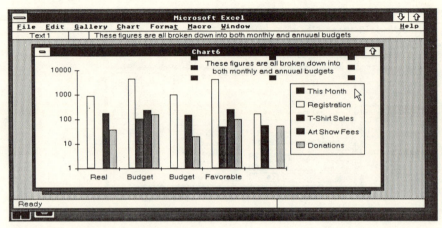

Figure 9-25. Selected Unattached Text

- First select the text you want to move.
- If you use a mouse, drag the text block to its new location, and you're finished.
- If you use the keyboard, open the Format menu and select the Move command.
- Use the directional cursor keys to move the positioning box to the location where you want the text. If you need to make fine adjustments of the box location, hold the Ctrl key down while you use the directional cursor keys.
- When finished with your adjustments, press the Enter key to confirm the positioning.

Resizing unattached text.

- Select the text you want resized.
- With a mouse, point to one of the black selection squares and drag it to enlarge or shrink the positioning box.
- With the keyboard, first open the Format menu and then choose the Size command. Use the directional cursor keys to enlarge or shrink the positioning box until it is the size you want. To make finer adjustments in size, use the Ctrl + Cursor key combination as just described.
- When finished with your adjustments, press the Enter key to confirm the positioning.

Deleting chart text.

- Select the text in question. If you gave the text block borders or backgrounds, use the Format Patterns command to change them back to Invisible.
- Press the Backspace key and then the Enter key. The text is deleted.

Chart Arrows

Chart arrows are useful items as highlights for key points on your chart, or as pointers from text to certain chart elements.

You can add as many arrows as you like to your chart. All you need to do for each arrow is open the Chart window and select the Add Arrow command.

Once you have created an arrow, you can position and size it so that the arrow is pointing at what you want emphasized.

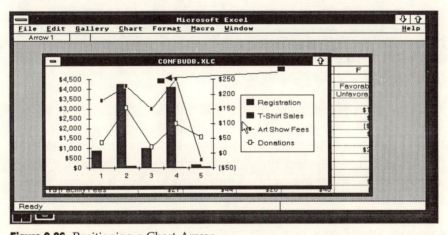

Figure 9-26. Positioning a Chart Arrow

To move a chart arrow:

- Select the arrow.
- Open the Format menu and choose the Move command.
- Use the direction keys to shift the arrow about. For fine movements of the chart arrow, hold down the Ctrl key while you use the direction keys. If you are using a mouse to move a chart arrow, simply drag the arrow into position.

Chapter 9

Resizing an arrow involves only a little more work than moving the arrow. Select the arrow in question and select the Format Size command. Use the direction keys to size the arrow until it is correct. For finer control, use the Ctrl + Cursor key combination as you would for moving an arrow. If you are going to resize a chart arrow using a mouse, drag the black selection squares until the mouse is the size and orientation you want.

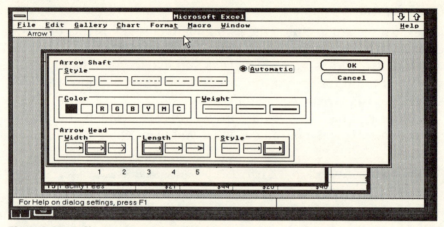

Figure 9-27. Different Arrow Possibilities

You don't necessarily need to use the basic chart arrow format—you can alter the appearence of the arrow using the Format Patterns window. Select the arrow you want to change, open the Format menu, and select the Patterns command. Once the window appears, select the options you want to use and when you select the OK button, your chart arrow will reformat accordingly.

To delete a chart arrow, select it and choose the Delete Arrow command from the Chart menu.

Using Chart Gridlines

Charts can be very useful tools. They allow you to see at a glance a particular trend in your data. When it comes to examining the specific values of your chart, however, as often as not it can get rather sticky. You have to gauge the values from a scale that isn't very exact and isn't all that conveniently located for most of the chart.

There is a way to make this particular task a little easier (and make your chart a little snazzier at the same time). Use chart gridlines to provide a readily accessible scale against which to judge your chart values.

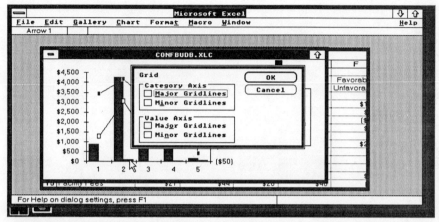

Figure 9-28. The Gridlines Window

Where do you want to place the gridlines on your chart? The most obvious location is along the Value Axis, making it much easier to tell individual values on your chart. However, there are some cases in which you will want to place gridlines along your Catagory Axis as well—especially when you use scatter graphs.

When you select the Chart Gridlines command, a window is opened that allows you to turn on only those gridlines you want to appear in the chart.

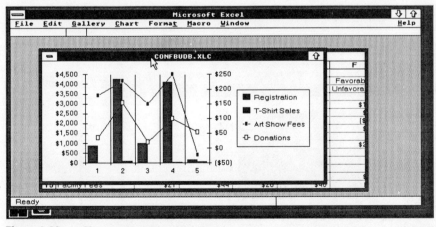

Figure 9-29. A Chart with Major Gridlines

Chapter 9

A *major gridline* is one that appears only at the labeled values on the selected axis. This kind of gridline is useful for subdividing the chart and making it easier to determine individual values. It is also used for aesthetic purposes, making the chart look nicer.

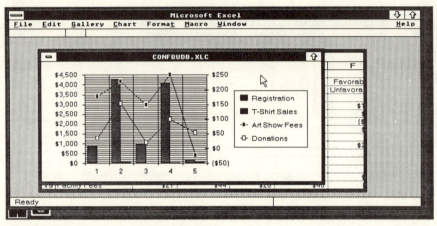

Figure 9-30. A Chart with Minor Gridlines

Minor gridlines, such as used by *Excel*, are subsidiary gridlines that break up the divisions made by the major ones. Their biggest use is in making it easier to determine a specific value in a chart.

After choosing the Gridlines command from the Chart menu, use the appropriate keys to turn on only the gridlines you want to appear in your chart. Also, make sure the gridlines are viable for use with the shading already present. With some of the chart options, you could lose your chart elements in the background.

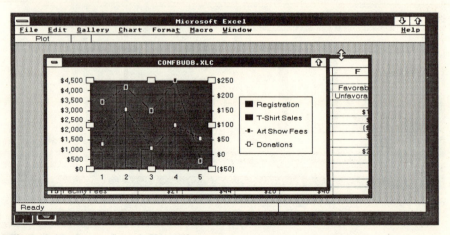

Figure 9-31. Camouflaged Chart Elements

Editing Data Series Definitions

Sometimes the only way to change a chart element is to directly edit the data series definition. To do this, you first need to understand how a data series is put together.

This is what a complete Series Formula looks like:

=SERIES(SERIES7.XLS!$A$16,SERIES7.XLS!$B$15:$J$15, SERIES7.XLS!$B$16:$J$16,1)

What each element means can be quite important to the chart as a whole. So here is an element-by-element breakdown of what the formula does.

Element	Definition
=SERIES	This is the Series function call that tells *Excel* it is looking at a data series for a chart. This must be preceeded by an equal sign and followed by a left parenthesis to mark the beginning of the arguments.
SERIES7.XLS!$A$16	This is the series name argument. It can be an external reference to a single cell or to a string of characters, or it can be the actual series name enclosed in quotation marks. The argument must be followed by a comma.
SERIES7.XLS!$B$15:$J$15	This is the categories argument that allows *Excel* to break up the chart into individual data points. If it exists, it must be an external reference to the block of cells containing your catagories. You can use a cell range argument, a named range, or an array constant for this value, but you must get the file reference correct. This argument also needs to be followed by a comma.
SERIES7.XLS!$B$16:$J$16	This is the Values argument. This argument assigns the block from which each of the individual data points are drawn. It must be an external reference to the file and worksheet cells that contain your values. You can use a cell range argument, a named range, or an array constant to define the cells, but they must be defined. This argument also needs to be followed by a comma.
1	This is the Plot order argument. It must be an integer and must be followed by a right parenthesis to mark the end of the series formula. This argument defines the order in which the data series is actually plotted on the chart.

Now that you know how the series formula is constructed, you can use that knowledge to edit your chart into the format you want it to have.

Chapter 9

To edit the formula, select a marker from the appropriate data series, and press the F2 key. This will bring the data series into the edit box where you can alter it to suit your taste.

One interesting thing is that you don't have to include the series name and category arguments. If you don't want them to appear, simply don't put them into the series formula. What you will wind up with is a formula that looks like this:

=SERIES(,,SERIES7.XLS!$B$16:$J$16,1)

As a result, while the series doesn't include a series name or categories, it still includes the actual data series and the plot order arguments, both of which are essential to the formula.

Using the Format Command

There are several options on the Format Main Chart and Format Overlay windows that let you quickly customize your chart in a way you can't using the Gallery. Simply put, you can create all the different options that are available in the Gallery from these two Format windows.

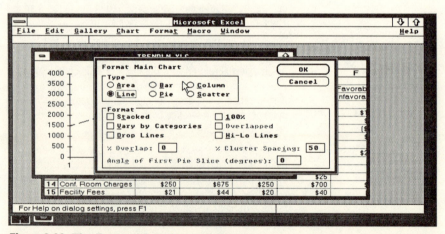

Figure 9-32. The Format Main Chart Window

The reason for this is simple. The Gallery is intended as a readily accessible and easy to use selection of chart formats you can use right away. The two Format windows, on the other hand, are where these formats are created. While the easily accessible window formats are already defined, there are a large number of formats that have yet to be defined that can be created through the Format window.

The top of the window is dominated by the basic selection area. This set of buttons lets you choose the basic chart type you are going to use, and it controls the different options that will be available to you in the different charts.

An Area chart is a line chart, with each subsequent series stacked on top of the previous with the area between shaded.

A Bar chart is a chart consisting of sets of bars, each one proportionally sized to the value it represents. A Bar chart is oriented horizontally.

A Column chart is similar to a Bar chart, but it is oriented vertically.

A Line chart consists of a set of lines, each one representing a single data series. The lines connect the individually plotted data points in the series.

A Pie chart consists of a single data series. The size of the different pie segments corresponds to the proportional size of the different data points.

A Scatter chart consists of a plot of both x and y values for each data point. As a result, it is useful for determining correlations between different sets of values in a given series.

The lower portion of the window includes the different formatting options you can use with your charts. In each case, select which options you want to use by turning on and off the check marks in the various boxes.

The Stacked option allows you to stack the various values on top of each other so you can see not only the individual values, but their cumulative effect. This option is usable with the Area, Bar, Column, and Line graphs.

The 100-percent option lets you redefine the chart so that the highest possible value on the chart is also the highest value plotted. This makes all the values plotted against the scale forced by the single largest value in the chart. This chart format is most useful for providing proportional comparisons of different values. It is usable with the Area, Bar, Column, and Line charts.

The Vary by Categories selection is only useful when you have a single series in your chart. If you activate this option, each individual data point is assigned a different marker (color, pattern, or symbol). This option is usable with the Bar, Column, Line, Pie, and Scatter chart formats.

The Overlapped option allows you to partially or fully overlap the different markers within a given cluster overlap. The amount of overlap is determined from the percentage you enter into the *% Overlap* box. This option is usable with the Bar and Column chart formats.

The Drop Lines option creates a line extending from the highest value in each category to the category axis. This can be useful with certain chart formats in helping determine what values are in which category. This chart option works with the Area and Line chart formats.

The Hi-Lo Lines selection lets you create a line extending from the highest to the lowest value within each category. This format can be very useful in helping determine what the extent of a given range of values is in a chart. The Hi-Lo Lines option is only usable with Line charts.

The % Cluster Spacing selection lets you determine how far apart the different clusters of bars or columns are. The number you enter here is the percentage of the width of a single bar or column. This option is only useful with the Bar and Column chart formats.

The Angle of First Pie Slice option lets you select the angle at which you want the leading edge of the first pie slice to appear. This is measured in a clockwise direction from a vertical axis. This chart option is, obviously, only usable with Pie charts.

Saving a Chart

Once you have created your chart, or when you want to take a break from working on it, you'll need to save it. *Excel* treats each individual chart as a separate file, even though it is interdependent with a given spreadsheet. Use the File menu to save your chart.

When you finish working with your chart the first time, you may want to save it under a singular name so you can remember exactly where it is.

Choose the Save As command from the File menu. A dialog box appears in which you enter the filename you want the chart saved under. Do not enter a filename extension—*Excel* appends an extension automatically.

After entering the filename, you can use the file options. To display them, press Alt + O; the box expands to show you the different file options available.

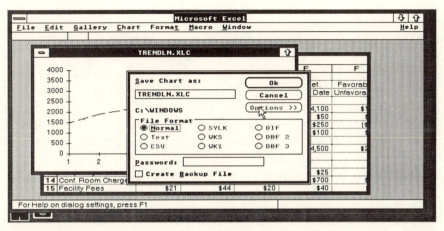

Figure 9-33. The Save As Dialog Box with Options

As you may have noticed, not all the options are usable with charts. You only have a single file format available instead of the range of file formats available for use with a spreadsheet or macro sheet.

You can still automatically back up your charts and assign a password to protect access to your chart. To create a password, press the P key and enter your password. You will then need to enter that password whenever you open the chart.

Otherwise, saving a chart is essentially the same as saving any other file in *Excel*. Use the Save, Save Workspace, or Close commands to save your file. The Save command saves the file and lets you continue. The Save Workspace command saves all the files you have opened at this point and allows you to continue with what you were doing. The Close command, just like elsewhere in the program, saves the file and puts it away until it is opened again.

There is one thing about charts that should be mentioned: Since charts are completely dependent on other files for their data, every time you open a chart, *Excel* asks if you want it updated from the other files. Similarly, if you have updated your chart and decide to quit, *Excel* regards the new changes as reason enough to find out if you want the new information saved.

If you know your data hasn't changed and you are interested in saving time, you'll quickly discover that it is quite easy to say no to rechecking the data. You may decide it is easiest to only update the chart when you have actually changed something in the reference spreadsheet.

Summary

One of the most important things you can do with the charting capability in *Excel* is experiment. While it is possible to list the different chart formats that can be used, in the long run, you must be the deciding factor regarding what works for your data and what doesn't.

Once you have a basic understanding of how charts work in *Excel*, the best thing you can do is play with the program. Find out what you can and can't do and don't be afraid to make a mess. Getting used to charting in this way is actually as beneficial, in the long run, as reading the documentation.

Chapter 10
Using Macros

Excel provides a very large set of macro commands, allowing you to create and execute miniprograms of instructions. These miniprograms can be used anywhere you need them—whether you're constructing or using a worksheet, a chart, or related set of documents.

Just as a computer program lets you take some shortcuts in getting work done—for example, word processing programs and spreadsheets let you create text and financial documents faster and more accurately than with a typewriter and calculator—macros let you get certain kinds of work done faster within a spreadsheet.

Paying attention to outlining before you write a report saves time as does thinking through your work and deciding what functions are repetitive. These functions can then be handled by a macro that can be called whenever the function needs to be performed.

Excel macro instructions let you not only create function-oriented command sequences, but also create menus and dialog boxes. We'll show you how later in this chapter.

What's a Macro?

A macro is a series of commands that tell *Excel* to perform a specific set of actions, such as formatting data, performing complex calculations, printing certain blocks of cells, or prompting the user for certain kinds of input.

Macros can be very simple, very complex, or anywhere in between. Generally, they're referred to by a name you give them, and stored as a type of file.

You can create two kinds of macros with *Excel*:

- *Command macros* carry out some sequence of actions, such as specifying commands, entering data, selecting cells, formatting, or selecting parts of a chart.
- *Function macros* operate like worksheet functions, in that they use values for input, make calculations, and return the resulting values.

Chapter 10

Macros are created and stored on *macro sheets*. A macro sheet looks a lot like a worksheet but differs in a few basic ways. A macro sheet normally displays formulas, whereas a worksheet normally displays values. A macro sheet also begins with wider column widths to better accommodate formulas. When used with a macro, the Formula Define Name dialog box has an extra set of options, since there are different types of macros. Finally, when you use one of the built-in functions, you'll see that while there are many macro functions equivalent to worksheet functions, there are also many more functions that work just with macros.

Think of a macro as something like the programming equivalent of a frozen dinner. There's nothing wrong with preparing a dinner yourself, from scratch, with ingredients you prepare and mix and serve. However, most supermarkets carry packaged frozen dinners, which a lot of people find easier to use than spending the time creating the equivalent meal from scratch. Individual tastes vary, and some people may not like the ingredients in any given dinner; however, if the dinner looks reasonably satisfactory, and can be ready to serve in a minimum amount of time, you may well choose a frozen dinner over one you fix from fresh ingredients.

The parallel isn't exact, but similar thinking goes into using macros. You can create the same procedure every time you need it in a new worksheet, perhaps changing one or two items to adapt it to the current worksheet. Or you can create a macro that performs the procedure in a general way, and call it to save time when you're creating a new worksheet. If you're sharing files in a network environment with one or more other people in your office, you may have the equivalent of a stock of standard macros which can be used in your worksheets simply by calling them.

Macros save you time and effort. They can perform simple tasks, such as making the text in a cell boldface, or more complex tasks, such as calculating the amount of a given mortgage payment that goes to interest and principle. They can also be helpful in simplifying a large worksheet so others can follow your logic, or so you can reduce calculation time. Macros can also be used to create menus and dialog boxes on customized application worksheets to help people who don't normally create worksheets enter data and get calculated results. Plus, you can even use them to run other applications under Microsoft *Windows* version 2.0 or higher.

How Does A Macro Work?

On the disks that came with the *Excel* files, Microsoft provided a number of sample worksheets in the two libraries EXCELCBT and LIBRARY. With the manuals also came a booklet entitled Microsoft *Excel Sampler*. This booklet contains an example of an application to create and print mailing labels from information in an *Excel* database. The files involved are CUSTOMER.XLS and LABEL.XLM, and the example starts on page 66 of the Sampler.

To get an idea of how macros work, open both the files CUSTOMER.XLS and LABELS.XLM, and compare what you see on your screen with the examples shown in the booklet. The macro file LABELS.XLM contains three command macros, each of which performs a different set of actions.

(Incidentally, though the booklet says the macros are on the worksheet CUSTOMER.XLS, they're not; the three macros shown are in the separate, unlinked file LABELS.XLM.)

The original database contains an unsorted list of customer names and addresses. To create a mailing label, all data for each line of the label must be in the same field, so the macro LABEL.SETUP rearranges the data that way. The Setup macro starts on line 1 and continues through line 15.

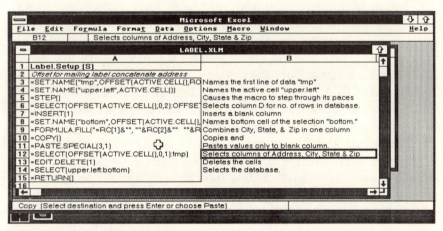

Figure 10-1. Label.Setup Macro

Notice that the name of the macro, Label.Setup (S), is on the first line, and an explanatory line is on line 2. The letter in parentheses indicates that the macro has been designed so you can use

Chapter 10

it with a shortcut key: If you press Ctrl and the letter indicated, the macro runs. Being able to run a macro with a shortcut key is one of the distinguishing marks of a command macro.

The actual macro instructions start with the third line, where the commands begin with an equal sign. These commands are run in logical sequence, ending with the =RETURN( ) command on line 15. Notice that the writer of this macro did something quite commendable: Each instruction is paired with a set of comments in the adjacent column. Comments are highly useful in explaining how a macro works, so another user can decide whether the macro is applicable in a new worksheet.

The Label.Setup macro is run when the CUSTOMER.XLS worksheet is the active document, and the LABEL.XLM macro file is open. Choose the Macro Run command, choose the LABEL.SETUP macro, and press the Enter key to run the macro. Or you can use the shortcut key: Press Ctrl + S. Look at the example in the Sampler to see how your database should appear after this step.

(This macro has been designed to show you the Step ability with *Excel* macros, which allows you to perform the macro's actions one step at a time. Choose Continue and the macro continues to run.)

The next step is to run another macro to rearrange the above data. This macro, LABEL.CREATE, is listed on the same macro sheet. To see it, press the PgDn key or scroll down with your mouse. You won't see the entire macro; if you need to, use the down- and up-arrow cursor keys or scroll further with the mouse. The LABEL.CREATE macro starts on line 17 and ends on line 36.

This macro, like the Setup macro, can be run by using the shortcut key shown. In this case, press Ctrl + C.

When run, the Create macro creates the text necessary for a mailing label, converting the name and address data for each company into three lines of data that fit vertically on ordinary mailing labels. There's also a blank line between the lines of data.

A third macro, LABEL.PRINT, lets the printer know how big the labels are, removes gridlines, and prints the labels. This macro starts on line 38 and ends on line 43. The shortcut key, Ctrl + P, runs the Print macro.

You can construct command macros like these by typing the commands, or you can use Record mode, which turns your keystrokes into macro commands for you. We'll look at the Recorder in more detail in a bit.

The other form of macro is a Function macro. These work much the same way as worksheet functions: You can use the Formula Paste Function to paste the general form of the function in place, and then fill in the arguments with your own data. You can also type the function yourself, starting with an equal sign, and enclose any arguments in parentheses.

Function macros have a particular structure, and because of their complexity, may take some study before you feel comfortable writing them. With a function macro, first specify the type of data you expect as a result of the function macro (the return value). Second, specify an argument function statement for each argument that must be provided when the macro is called. Third, specify the formulas or actions that the macro is to perform. Fourth, specify that the macro is to return to the instruction that called it.

Writing macros is like writing programs and, as such, deserves time and attention to both what you want the macro to do, and to logically constructing the commands. Macros can contain branches to other macros, If-Then statements, prompts for user action, application-specific error messages, and a host of other details that emphasize the similarity between macro construction and programming.

Once constructed, however, it's important to do two things to a macro: test and debug it, and document it.

Testing lets you put the macro through its paces, using different values or cell references and trying different methods of running it so the logic of the macro gets tested. Most people who write macros recognize that this phase is a bit humbling; you run the macro deliberately looking for errors, and when you find them, you have to debug the macro and fix the logic so it does what you want.

A lot of people also overlook the documentation phase, thinking that nobody else will need to figure out how the macro works, and that they'll always remember their own logic. Unfortunately, that just isn't true.

Adding comments to a macro helps both the writer and others understand how the macro works since comments usually detail what is needed in the way of arguments or calling sequences. Comments in *Excel* macros don't interfere with the logic, and take up very little extra memory.

This chapter looks briefly at the macro commands and functions available within *Excel*. A companion book, PC *Excel Business*

Solutions, presents a much more detailed explanation of how to construct and use macros in *Excel*.

The Recorder

Microsoft made it easy for you to create a command macro. Simply choose the Macro Record command, pick a name for your macro, and step through (recreate) the action(s) you want to take. The Recorder opens a macro sheet, gives it the name you've specified, and translates your actions to macro commands (sometimes changing the cell reference style). When you've finished, choose Macro Stop Recorder, and *Excel* closes the macro.

Once the actions have been recorded, they're yours to edit, format, document, or change in any way you need. Cell references are absolute unless you specifically ask that they be relative. (You can change from absolute to relative or vice versa any time during the recording process.)

You may decide to modify the macro in other ways:

- You can create your own dialog boxes and menus that appear with a macro.
- You can prompt the user with ALERT and MESSAGE functions, and ask the user to type in a value with the INPUT function.
- You can suspend macro action with the WAIT function, or have it start automatically when a certain time occurs with the ON.TIME function, or when data arrives from another program with the ON.DATA function.
- You can create loops within your macro, so certain actions get performed several times with IF-NEXT or WHILE-NEXT functions.
- You can use information about the active worksheet, open windows, references, names within the active worksheet or any other to which you have access, and send information to other worksheets or other programs with some of the value-returning macro functions.

The Recorder gives you a simple way to translate your actions to a macro that can be repeatedly used and modified so it performs far more sophisticated actions.

A Simple Exercise

Here's how to construct a simple macro sheet. Let's assume you want a macro that will automatically put a date and time on consecutive lines on your worksheet. The simplest way to do this is to turn on the Macro Recorder as you step through the process. When you've finished, choose the Stop Recorder command.

- Position the active cell on a worksheet where you'd like the date and time to be located.
- Choose the Macro Recorder command. *Excel* presents a dialog box, asking what you want to call the macro. Type a name, perhaps *Datetime*. Excel also suggests the shortcut key to use when you want to invoke the macro: Ctrl + A. If you want to change that, use the Tab key or your mouse to move to the Key box, and type the letter you'd like to use. When the filename and shortcut key are as you want them, choose the OK bar. Notice that the Status bar contains the word Recording to indicate that the Recorder is active.
- *Excel* stores the current date and time maintained by your computer as a serial number. In order to convert it to a date or a time, you'll need to format it. Choose the Format Number command, and in the dialog box, choose the m/d/yy format.
- Type the formula =NOW( ) and press the Enter key. The NOW function retrieves the current date/time serial number, and displays only the date portion, formatted as you specified.
- Press the down-arrow key to move the active cell down one cell.
- This time, you want to format the date/time serial number to reflect the current time. Choose the Format Number command, and in the dialog box, choose the h:mm AM/PM format.
- Type the formula =NOW( ) and press the Enter key. This time the NOW function retrieves the current date/time serial number, and displays only the time portion, formatted as you specified.
- Close the macro by choosing the Macro Stop Recorder command. Nothing changes on your worksheet, except the word Recording disappears from the Status line. Here's how your worksheet looks:

Chapter 10

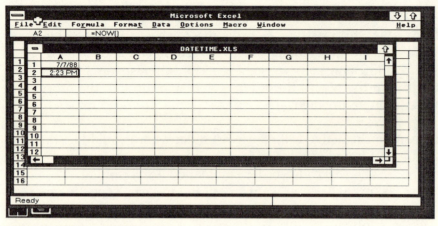

Figure 10-2. Sample Worksheet

- To see the macro, choose the Window menu. In the menu box, you'll see both the current worksheet and *Macro1* listed. Macro1 is the name *Excel* is using for your macro, since you haven't yet saved it. Choose Macro1, and it will appear on your screen.
- The columns aren't wide enough to see all the contents of each line, so use the Format Column Width command to change the column width to 16. Figure 10-3 shows the macro *Excel* has created by recording your steps.

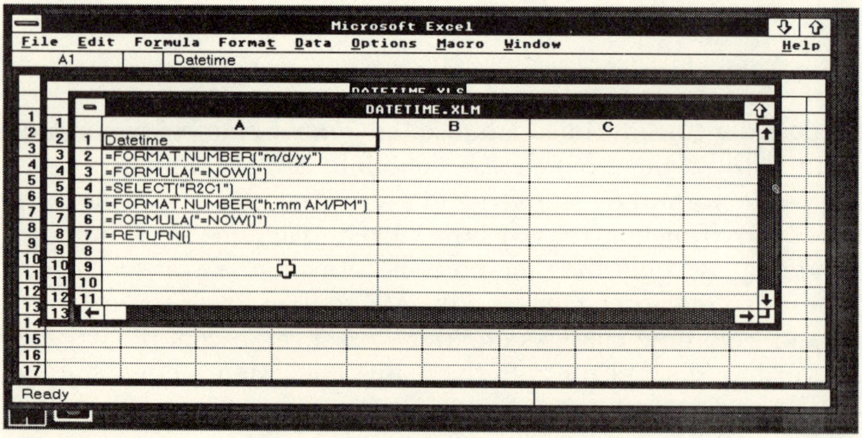

Figure 10-3. Macro Example

Notice that line 4 refers to R2C1, which is a reference to cell A2. If you want your macro to work anywhere, rather than just in cells A1 and A2, edit this line so the reference is to RC.
- Save the macro under a filename, like *DATETIME.XLM*.

Macro Functions

Excel provides you with the following kinds of functions to use in your macros: command equivalent functions, dialog box functions, action equivalent functions, customizing functions, control functions, and value-returning functions.

Command Equivalent Functions

When you execute a command equivalent function in a macro, you perform the same action as if you were choosing the command from a worksheet menu. Arguments specified with a command equivalent function specify options associated with the command.

Following is the macro function equivalent to a worksheet command with its comparable worksheet command.

Macro Function:	Worksheet Command Equivalent:
ACTIVATE	Window (document)
ADD.ARROW	Chart Add Arrow
ADD.OVERLAY	Chart Add Overlay
ALIGNMENT	Format Alignment
APP.MAXIMIZE	Control Maximize (application)
APP.MINIMIZE	Control Minimize
APP.MOVE	Control Move (application)
APP.RESTORE	Control Restore (application)
APP.SIZE	Control Size (application)
APPLY.NAMES	Formula Apply Names
ARRANGE.ALL	Window Arrange All
ATTACH.TEXT	Chart Attach Text
AXES	Chart Axes
BORDER	Format Border
CALCULATE.DOCUMENT	Chart Calculate Document; Options Calculate Document
CALCULATE.NOW	Chart Calculate Now; Options Calculate Now
CALCULATION	Options Calculation

Chapter 10

Macro Function:	Worksheet Command Equivalent:
CELL.PROTECTION	Format Cell Protection
CHANGE.LINKS	File Links
CLEAR	Edit Clear
CLOSE	Control Close (document)
CLOSE.ALL	File Close All
COLUMN.WIDTH	Format Column Width
COMBINATION	Gallery Combination
COPY	Edit Copy
COPY.PICTURE	Edit Copy Picture
CREATE.NAMES	Formula Create Names
CUT	Edit Cut
DATA.DELETE	Data Delete
DATA.FIND	Data Find; Data Exit Find
DATA.FORM	Data Form
DATA.SERIES	Data Series
DEFINE.NAME	Formula Define Name
DELETE.ARROW	Chart Delete Arrow
DELETE.NAME	Formula Define Name
DELETE.OVERLAY	Chart Delete Overlay
DISPLAY	Info Cell; Info Dependents; Info Format; Info Formula; Info Names; Info Note; Info Precedents; Info Protection; Info Value
EDIT.DELETE	Edit Delete
EXTRACT	Data Extract
FILE.CLOSE	File Close
FILE.DELETE	File Delete
FILL.DOWN	Edit Fill Down
FILL.LEFT	Edit Fill Left
FILL.RIGHT	Edit Fill Right
FILL.UP	Edit Fill Up
FORMAT.FONT	Format Font
FORMAT.LEGEND	Format Legend
FORMAT.MOVE	Format Move
FORMAT.NUMBER	Format Number
FORMAT.SIZE	Format Size

Macro Function:	Worksheet Command Equivalent:
FORMAT.TEXT	Format Text
FORMULA.FIND	Formula Find
FORMULA.GOTO	Formula Goto
FORMULA.REPLACE	Formula Replace
FULL	Control Maximize (document); Control Restore (document)
FREEZE.PANES	Options Freeze Panes
GALLERY.AREA	Gallery Area
GALLERY.BAR	Gallery Bar
GALLERY.COLUMN	Gallery Column
GALLERY.LINE	Gallery Line
GALLERY.PIE	Gallery Pie
GALLERY.SCATTER	Gallery Scatter
GRIDLINES	Chart Gridlines
HIDE	Window Hide
INSERT	Edit Insert
JUSTIFY	Format Justify
LEGEND	Chart Add Legend
LIST.NAMES	Formula Paste Name
MAIN.CHART	Format Main Chart
MOVE	Control Move (document)
NEW	File New
NEW.WINDOW	Window New Window
NOTE	Formula Note
OPEN	File Open
OPEN.LINKS	File Links
OVERLAY	Format Overlay
PAGE.SETUP	File Page Setup
PARSE	Data Parse
PATTERNS	Format Patterns
PASTE	Edit Paste
PASTE.LINK	Edit Paste Link
PASTE.SPECIAL	Edit Paste Special
PRECISION	Options Calculation
PREFERRED	Gallery Preferred
PRINT	File Print

Macro Function:	Worksheet Command Equivalent:
PRINTER.SETUP	File Printer Setup
PROTECT.DOCUMENT	Chart Protect Document; Chart Unprotect Document; Options Protect Document;
QUIT	File Exit; Control Close (application)
REMOVE.PAGE.BREAK	Options Remove Page Break
REPLACE.FONT	Format Font
ROW.HEIGHT	Format Row Height
RUN	Macro run
SAVE	File Save
SAVE.AS	File Save As
SAVE.WORKSPACE	File Save Workspace
SCALE	Format Scale
SELECT	Chart Select Chart; Chart Select Plot Area
SELECT.SPECIAL	Formula Select Special
SET.CRITERIA	Data Set Criteria
SET.DATABASE	Data Set Database
SET.PAGE.BREAK	Options Set Page Break
SET.PREFERRED	Gallery Set Preferred
SET.PRINT.AREA	Options Set Print Area
SET.PRINT.TITLES	Options Set Print Titles
SHORT.MENUS	Options Full Menus; Options Short Menus; Chart Full Menus; Chart Short Menus;
SHOW.INFO	Window Show Document; Window Show Info;
SIZE	Control Size (document)
SORT	Data Sort
SPLIT	Control Split
TABLE	Data Table
UNDO	Edit Undo
UNHIDE	File Unhide Window; Window Unhide;
WORKSPACE	Options Workspace

Dialog Box Functions

Dialog box functions are available for every command that brings up a dialog box. Each dialog box function has the same name as the command equivalent function. The only difference is that the function is stated with a question mark.

For instance, the dialog box function for File Save As is *SAVE.AS?* The dialog box function for Edit Insert is *INSERT?*

Some dialog box functions don't display dialog boxes. We'll look at these individually in the sections below.

Action Equivalent Functions

The action equivalent functions listed below neither have command equivalents nor are dialog box functions. Arguments are shown in parentheses. Remember that, if parentheses are shown, they must be included in the function as used, even if they include no arguments.

A1.R1C1(r1c1)
Displays A1 or R1C1 references.
Works the same as choosing the Options Workspace command and turning on the R1C1 check box if the *r1c1* argument is true, or turning off the R1C1 check box if the *r1c1* argument is false.

ACTIVATE(windowtext,panenumber)
Selects a window.
Works the same as activating a pane in a window. *Windowtext* is the name of a window and must be enclosed in double quote marks; *panenumber* is the number of the pane to activate.

ACTIVATE.NEXT()
Selects the next window.
Equivalent to pressing Ctrl + F6.

ACTIVATE.PREV()
Selects the previous window.
Equivalent to pressing Ctrl + Shift + F6.

CANCEL.COPY()
Cancels the selected cell for a copy operation.
Equivalent to canceling the marquee around a selected cell, by pressing the Esc key after you copy or cut a selection.

COPY.CHART(number)
Copies a picture of a chart.
The picture shown depends on the number indicated:

Chapter 10

    1   as shown on the screen
    2   as shown when printed

The COPY.CHART?(number) is also acceptable; it is included for compatibility with Microsoft *Excel* for the Apple Macintosh. In Microsoft *Excel* for Windows, it is the same as the COPY.PICTURE macro function without the (appearance) argument.

DATA.FIND.NEXT()

Finds the next matching record in a database.

DATA.FIND.PREV()

Finds the previous matching record in a database.
Finds the next or the previous matching record in a database. Works the same as pressing the up- or down-arrow keys after choosing the Data Find command. If no matching record can be found, the function returns the value False.

DELETE.FORMAT(formattext)

Deletes a Format Number command format.
Works the same as using the Format Number command to delete the format specified, where *formattext* is the format string and enclosed in double quotes, like "#,##0".

DIRECTORY(pathtext)

Changes directories and returns a new pathname.
Sets the current drive and directory to the path given in *pathtext*, and returns the name of the new path as text. If a drive or directory name is not included in pathtext, it assumes the current drive or directory.

FORMULA(formulatext,reference)

Enters a formula in a cell, or text on a chart.
This function works differently, depending on whether the active document is a worksheet or a chart.
    If the active document is a worksheet, the function enters the formula specified by *formulatext* into the cell specified by *reference*. If no cell is specified, it uses the active cell.
    The formula must be in the same form as if you entered it in the formula bar, but must be enclosed in double quotes. It can be a formula, a number, text, or a logical value. How-

ever, any cell references in a formula must be in R1C1 form. (If you're using the Recorder, *Excel* converts any A1 style references to R1C1 style.)

If the active document is a chart, *Excel* enters text labels or SERIES functions. If formulatext can be treated as a text label and the current selection is a text label, the selected text label is replaced with formulatext. If the current selection is not a text label, the function creates a new text label. If formulatext can be treated as a SERIES formula and the current selection is a SERIES formula, formulatext replaces the selected SERIES formula. If the current selection is not a SERIES formula, the function creates a new SERIES formula.

Example:

=FORMULA(625)	Enters the value 625 in the active cell.
=FORMULA("=R6C*(1+R8C10)")	Enters the formula =F6*(1+$J$8) into the active cell if the active cell is G6.
=FORMULA("=SERIES(" "Name" ",,[1,2,3],1")	Enters a SERIES formula on the chart. Note that, within the text value, you have to enter two sets of double quote marks in order to represent a single quote mark.

FORMULA.ARRAY(formulatext,reference)

Enters an array formula on a document.
Works the same as entering an array formula while pressing Ctrl + Shift + Enter. The function enters the formula specified in *formulatext* as an array formula in the range specified by *reference*, or in the current selection if reference is not given.

FORMULA.FILL(formulatext,reference)

Fills a range with a formula.
Works the same as entering a formula while pressing Shift. The function enters the formula specified in *formulatext* into

the area specified in *reference*, or in the current selection if reference is not given.

FORMULA.FIND.NEXT()
Finds the next cell, as described in the Formula Find dialog box.

FORMULA.FIND.PREV()
Finds the previous cell, as described in the Formula Find dialog box.
These two functions work the same as pressing F7, and Shift + F7 respectively. The function finds the next or previous matching cells on the worksheet, as defined in the Formula Find dialog box. If no match is found, the function returns the value False.

HLINE(numbercols)
Horizontally scrolls the active window by columns.
This function scrolls the worksheet a number of columns to the right or left, depending on the number given in *numbercols*. If the number is positive, the worksheet scrolls to the right that number of columns; if the number is negative, the worksheet scrolls to the left that number of columns.

HPAGE(numberwindows)
Horizontally scrolls the active window one full window at a time.
This function scrolls the worksheet a number of windows to the right or left, depending on the number given in *numberwindows*. If the number is positive, the worksheet scrolls to the right that number of windows; if the number is negative, the worksheet scrolls to the left that number of windows.

HSCROLL(scroll,value)
Horizontally scrolls a document by percentage or by column number.
HSCROLL lets you scroll to the right or left edge of your document, or anywhere in between. If value is True, HSCROLL scrolls to the position represented by the number you specify as *scroll*. If *value* is False or omitted, HSCROLL scrolls to the position represented by the fraction given in scroll. If scroll is

0, HSCROLL scrolls to the left edge of your document; if scroll is 1, it scrolls to the right edge of your document.

To scroll to a specific column, either use the form HSCROLL(colnumber,TRUE) or HSCROLL(colnumber/256).

Examples:

Assuming you're starting from A1, the following uses of HSCROLL all scroll to column 64, 25% of the way across the worksheet:

HSCROLL(64,TRUE)
HSCROLL(25%)
HSCROLL(.25,FALSE)
HSCROLL(64/256)

SELECT(selection,activecell)

Selects a reference.

This is one of two forms of the SELECT function. This is the one used if the selection is on a worksheet or macro sheet. (The following version is used if the selection refers to a chart.)

This function is used to select a cell or cell range, as specified in *selection*, and to make *activecell* the active cell. Both arguments must be preceded with exclamation marks if the A1 reference style is used.

Selection must be either a reference on the active worksheet (for example, !B23:C24, !Netsales, or an R1C1-style reference to the currently active cell such as "RC5:"). If you omit selection, SELECT does not change the selection.

Activecell must be within selection, and may be either a reference to a single cell on the active worksheet, such as !B23, or an R1C1-style reference to the active cell in the current selection, such as was used in the paragraph above.

If you are recording a macro with the Macro Relative Record command and you select something, *Excel* uses R1C1-style references as text. If you're using Macro Absolute Record, *Excel* uses absolute references.

SELECT(itemtext)

Selects an item on a chart.

This is one of two forms of the SELECT function. This one is used if the selection is a chart. The preceding version is used if the selection refers to a worksheet or macro sheet.

Itemtext must be enclosed in double quotes, and refers to a chart object, as follows:

Selection:	Itemtext:
Entire chart	"Chart"
Plot area	"Plot"
Legend	"Legend"
Main chart value axis	"Axis 1"
Main chart category axis	"Axis 2"
Overlay chart value axis	"Axis 3"
Overlay chart category axis	"Axis 4"
Chart title	"Title"
Label for main chart value axis	"Text Axis 1"
Label for main chart category axis	"Text Axis 2"
nth floating text item	"Text n"
nth arrow	"Arrow n"
Major gridlines of value axis	"Gridline 1"
Minor gridlines of value axis	"Gridline 2"
Major gridlines of category axis	"Gridline 3"
Minor gridlines of category axis	"Gridline 4"
Main chart droplines	"Dropline 1"
Overlay chart droplines	"Dropline 2"
Main chart hi-lo lines	"Hiloline 1"
Overlay chart hi-lo lines	"Hiloline 2"
Data associated with point x in series n	"SnPx"
Text attached to point x of series n	"Text SnPx"
Series title text of series n of an area chart	"Text Sn"

SELECT.END(direction#)
Changes the active cell.
Moves the active cell to the edge of the next block, in the direction specified by *direction#*:

Direction#:	Direction:
1	left (same as Ctrl + left-arrow)
2	right (same as Ctrl + right-arrow)

Direction#:	Direction:
3	up (same as Ctrl + up-arrow)
4	down (same as Ctrl + down-arrow)

SELECT.LAST.CELL()
 Selects the cell at the end of a document.
 Selects the cell at the intersection of the last row and last column in your document that contains a formula, value, format, or are referred to in a formula.

SHOW.ACTIVE.CELL()
 Displays the active cell.
 Works the same as pressing Ctrl + Backspace; scrolls the active window so the active cell becomes visible.

SHOW.CLIPBOARD()
 Displays the Clipboard.
 Works the same as choosing the Run command on the Control menu, and selecting Clipboard. Included for compatibility with macros written with Microsoft *Excel* for the Apple Macintosh.

STYLE(bold,italic)
STYLE?(bold,italic)
 Changes font.
 If *bold* is True, *Excel* finds an available bold font and changes the font of the current selection to the bold font. If *italic* is true, it changes the font of the current selection to an available italic font. If no appropriate font is available, *Excel* uses the most similar font available.
    This function is included for compatibility with macros written with Microsoft *Excel* for the Apple Macintosh.

UNLOCKED.NEXT()
 Moves to the next unlocked cell.

UNLOCKED.PREV()
 Moves to the previous unlocked cell.
 Works the same as pressing Tab or Shift + Tab to move the active cell to the next or previous unlocked cell in a protected worksheet.

Chapter 10

VLINE(numberrows)
Vertically scrolls the active window by rows.
Scrolls the active window vertically the number of rows specified in *numberrows*. If numberrows is positive, *Excel* scrolls down; if numberrows is negative, *Excel* scrolls up.

VPAGE(numberwindows)
Vertically scrolls the active window one window at a time.
Scrolls the active window vertically the number of windows specified in numberwindows. If *numberwindows* is positive, *Excel* scrolls down. If numberwindows is negative, *Excel* scrolls up.

VSCROLL(scroll,value)
Vertically scrolls the document by percentage or by row number.
VSCROLL lets you scroll to the top or bottom of your window, or anywhere in between. If *value* is True, VSCROLL scrolls to the row represented by the number you specify as scroll. If value is False or omitted, VSCROLL scrolls to the position represented by the fraction given in *scroll*. If scroll is 0, VSCROLL scrolls to the top row, row 1; if scroll is 1, it scrolls to the bottom of the window, row 16384.
   To scroll to a specific row, either use the form VSCROLL(rownumber,TRUE) or VSCROLL(rownumber/16384).

Examples:
   Assuming you're starting from A1, the following uses of VSCROLL all scroll to row 4096, 25% of the way down the window:
   HSCROLL(4096,TRUE)
   HSCROLL(25%)
   HSCROLL(.25,FALSE)
   HSCROLL(4096/16384)

Customizing Functions
ADD.BAR()
Adds a custom menu bar.
Creates an empty menu bar, and if successful, returns the bar ID number. If 15 menu bars (the maximum number of

custom menu bars allowed) have already been defined, ADD.BAR returns the error message #VALUE!

ADD.BAR doesn't display the new bar. To see the bar, use the SHOW.BAR function.

ADD.COMMAND(bar#,menuposition,menureference)

Adds a custom command.

Adds one or more custom commands described in the menu construction area *menureference* to the menu, at *menuposition in bar number bar#*. Menureference must be to a macro sheet that describes the new command.

Menuposition can be the number of a menu or the text name of a menu. Bar# can be the number of one of the built-in menu bars or the ID number returned by the previously executed ADD.BAR function. The command position of the first command added is returned by the ADD.COMMAND.

Built-in menu bar numbers are:

Number:	Built-in menu bar:
1	Worksheet and macro menu, full menus
2	Chart menu, full menus
3	Nil menu (menu displayed when no documents are open)
4	Info window menu
5	Worksheet and macro menu, short menus
6	Chart menu, short menus

ADD.MENU(bar#,menureference)

Adds a custom menu.

Adds a menu described in the menu construction area *menureference* to the bar with the bar ID number *bar#*. Menureference must be to a macro sheet that describes the new menu.

Bar# can be the number of one of the built-in menu bars or the ID number returned by the previously executed ADD.BAR function.

If ADD.MENU is successful, the menu is added immediately to the right of the existing menus on bar, and ADD.MENU returns the position number of the new menu.

ALERT(messagetext,type#)
Displays a dialog box.
This is the function you use if you want to display a custom dialog box and have the user choose a button.
The dialog box contains the text you specify as *messagetext*, and the type of box displayed depends on the number you specify as *type#*:

When type# is:	Use it to:
1	Tell the user to make a choice
2	Present info
3	Present an error message where no choice is available

ALERT returns the logical value True if the user chooses the OK bar, and False if the Cancel bar is chosen.

Examples:
ALERT("I'm sorry, but I can't let you do that.",3)
ALERT('Data entered will affect other worksheets.",1)

APP.ACTIVATE(titletext,waitvalue)
Starts another application.
Use this function to activate another application with the title bar *titletext*. If titletext is omitted, the function activates *Excel*.
The argument *waitvalue* is used to tell *Excel* to wait before starting the application. If waitvalue is True or is omitted, *Excel* flashes a message indicating it is waiting. If waitvalue is False, *Excel* activates the application immediately.

BEEP(number)
Sounds a warning beep.
BEEP triggers production of an audible tone. Depending on your hardware, you may be able to use the argument *number* to specify different tones. Number may be from 1 to 4, and is interpreted by your hardware as a beep tone. Some hardware, such as an IBM-PC, interpret all numbers used with BEEP as the same tone.

CALL(calltext, argument1,. . .)
Calls the Microsoft Windows library.
CALL is suggested for use only by programmers expert in using the Microsoft Windows dynamic library. Incorrect use could cause damage to your system's operation.

CALL works with the macro function REGISTER, which sets up the parameters for CALL. In using REGISTER, specify the name of the module and procedure you want to use, as well as a text value describing the number and data types of arguments you want to give, and the data type of the return value. REGISTER returns the value of *calltext* to use with the CALL function.

CANCEL.KEY(enable,macroreference)
Alters the Esc key.
Lets you temporarily disable the Esc key during a currently running macro. If *enable* is False or omitted, pressing Esc while a macro is running will not interrupt it. If enable is True and *macroreference* is omitted, the Esc key is reactivated. If enable is True and you specify macroreference, execution jumps to the specified macro location if you press Esc.

CANCEL.KEY only lasts for the duration of the currently running macro. Once the macro stops, the Esc key is reactivated.

CHECK.COMMAND(bar#,menuposition,commandposition,check)
Marks a command.
Adds or removes a check mark beside the command designated. *Bar#* is either the number of one of the *Excel* built-in menu bars, or the number returned by the previously executed ADD.BAR function. *Menuposition* is either the number of the menu or the text form of the menu name. *Commandposition* is either the number of the command or the text form of the command title.

If check is True, this function checks the command; if check is False, it removes the check mark.

A check mark does not affect the execution of the command. Its primary use is to indicate a command or option is in effect.

DELETE.BAR(bar#)
Deletes a custom menu bar.
Deletes the custom menu bar numbered *bar#*. Bar# must be the number returned by the previously ADD.BAR function, and may not be the currently displayed menu bar.

DELETE.COMMAND(bar#,menuposition,commandposition)
Deletes a command.
Deletes the command in the position specified. *Bar#* is either the number of one of the *Excel* built-in menu bars, or the number returned by the previously executed ADD.BAR function. *Menuposition* is either the number of the menu or the text form of the menu name. *Commandposition* is either the number of the command or the text form of the command title.

If the specified command does not exist, the function returns the error message #VALUE!

When a command is deleted, the number used for commandposition for all commands after that is decreased by 1.

DELETE.MENU(bar#,menuposition)
Deletes a menu.
Deletes the menu at *menuposition* in the bar identified by *bar#*. Menuposition is either the number of the menu or the text form of the menu name. Bar# is either the number of one of the *Excel* built-in menu bars, or the number returned by the previously executed ADD.BAR function.

If the menu specified by menuposition does not exist, the function returns the error message #VALUE!

When a menu has been deleted, the number used for menuposition for all menus to the right of that menu is decreased by 1.

DIALOG.BOX(dialogreference)
Displays a custom dialog box.
Displays the dialog box described in the construction area described in *dialogreference*, which may be on a macro sheet or a worksheet. The area pointed to by dialogreference must be seven columns wide and at least two rows high.

If the OK bar in the dialog box is chosen, the function enters values in the fields as specified in the dialogreference area, and returns the item number of the button pressed. Items are numbered sequentially, starting with the item in the second row in dialogreference. If the Cancel button in the dialog box is chosen, the function returns False.

If dialogreference is invalid, the function returns the error message #Value!, and when the macro is run, displays a message indicating the cell in which the error was found.

DISABLE.INPUT(logicalvalue)
Stops all input to *Excel*.
If *logicalvalue* is True, the function blocks all input from the keyboard and mouse, except input to displayed dialog boxes. If logicalvalue is False, it reenables input.

ECHO(logicalvalue)
Toggles screen update on and off.
If *logicalvalue* is True or omitted, the function turns on screen updating while a macro is running. If logicalvalue is False, it turns off the screen updating. Screen updating resumes automatically when a macro ends.

ECHO is particularly useful when running a large command macro, since turning off screen updating lets the macro run faster.

ENABLE.COMMAND(bar#,menuposition,commandposition,enable)
Toggles the gratifying of a custom command.
Enables or disables the command identified by the arguments. *Bar#* is either the number of one of the *Excel* built-in menu bars, or the number returned by the previously executed ADD.BAR function. *Menuposition* is either the number of the menu or the text form of the menu name. *Commandposition* is either the number of the command to be checked or the text form of the command title. If commandposition is 0, the entire menu is enabled or disabled.

If enable is True, the function enables the command. If enable is False, it disables it. Disabled commands appear as grayed and cannot be executed.

If the specified command is one of *Excel*'s built-in commands, or does not exist, the function returns the error message #VALUE!

Chapter 10

ERROR(enable,macroreference)
Specifies an action to take if an error occurs while a macro is running.
If *enable* is False, all error checking is disabled. When error checking of a macro has been disabled, and an error is encountered, *Excel* ignores it and continues.
If enable is True, and *macroreference* is omitted, normal error checking occurs, which means that a dialog box appears when an error is encountered, permitting you to halt execution, single-step through the macro, or continue normal running. If enable is True and macroreference specifies the reference of a macro, that macro will be run when an error is encountered.
WARNING: Both ERROR(True,macroreference) and ERROR(False) result in no warning messages at all. ERROR(False) further suppresses the warning messages that normally are displayed if you attempt to close an unsaved document.

EXEC(programtext,window#)
Starts another application.
Starts the program named *programtext* as a separate program running under Microsoft *Windows* version 2.0. Programtext uses the same form of arguments as the File Run command in the Windows MS-DOS Executive.
Window# specifies how the window holding the program should appear:

Window#:	Window type:
1	normal window
2	minimized window
3	maximized window

If omitted, window# is assumed to be 2.
If the EXEC function is successful, it returns the task ID number of the program started. The task ID number identifies the program running under Microsoft *Windows* version 2.0 or higher. If the function is unsuccessful, it returns the error message #VALUE!

EXECUTE(channel#,executetext)

Carries out a command in another application.

The EXECUTE function executes whatever commands are described in *executetext* in the application that's connected through *channel#*. The channel so designated must have already been opened by the INITIATE macro function.

This function works only if you are running Microsoft *Windows* version 2.0 or higher.

EXECUTE returns the following error messages if unsuccessful:

Message	Meaning
#VALUE!	Channel# isn't a valid channel number.
#N/A!	The application is doing something else.
#DIV/0!	The application doesn't respond, so you've pressed Esc to cancel the command.
#REF!	The application refuses the EXECUTE request.

FCLOSE(file#)

Closes a text file.

Closes the file that has been opened with FOPEN. *File#* is the number of the file, and has been returned when FOPEN completed successfully.

FOPEN(filetext,access#)

Opens a text file.

FOPEN opens the file named *filetext*, and returns a file number. The argument *access#* specifies the type of access to allow to the file:

Access#:	Type of access:
1	read/write access
2	read-only access
3	create new file, with read/write access

If the file doesn't exist and access# is 3, FOPEN creates a new file. If it doesn't exist and access# is 1 or 2, or if FOPEN can't open the file, FOPEN returns the error message #N/A!

Chapter 10

FPOS(file#,position#)
Returns position in a text file.
Once a file has been opened with FOPEN and *file#* returned, the FPOS function looks in the file so identified and positions the file (for further activity, such as reading or writing) at *position#* within the file. (The first byte of the file is considered position 1.)

FREAD(file#,#characters)
Reads characters from a text file.
Reads *#characters* from the file *file#*, where file# is the number returned when FOPEN was used to open the file.
     If FREAD is successful, it returns the text read. If file# isn't a valid file number, it returns the error message #VALUE! If FREAD can't read the document, or if it reaches the end of the file, it returns the error message #N/A!

FREADLN(file#)
Reads a line from a text file.
FREADLN starts at the current file position (see FPOS) in the file identified by *file#* and reads till it encounters an End of Line character or equivalent. The file must have been opened with FOPEN, and file# is the number returned by that function.

FSIZE(file#)
Returns the size of a text file.
Returns the number of characters in the file identified by *file#*, which is the number returned by the function FOPEN.
     If file# is not a valid file number, FSIZE returns the error message #VALUE!

FWRITE(file#,text)
Writes characters to a text file.
FWRITE writes the characters in *text* to the file identified by *file#*, starting at the current position (see FPOS). The file must have been opened by FOPEN, which returns file#.
     If file# is not a valid file number, FWRITE returns the error message #VALUE! If it can't write to the file, it returns the error message #N/A!

FWRITELN(file#,text)
Writes line to a text file.
FWRITELN writes the characters specified in *text* to the file identified by *file#*, starting at the current position in that file (see FPOS). The characters written are followed by the character pair carriage return and line feed.

The file must have been opened by FOPEN, which returns file#.

If file# is not a valid file number, FWRITELN returns the error message #VALUE! If it can't write to the file, it returns the error message #N/A!

HELP(helptext)
Displays a customized Help topic.
When used as a macro function, HELP displays the Help topic specified as *helptext*, where helptext is a reference to a topic in a custom help file in the form "filename!topic#". If you omit helptext, HELP displays the normal *Excel* Help index.

INITIATE(applicationtext,topictext)
Opens a channel to another application.
INITIATE opens a DDE channel to another application, but does not start the application. *Applicationtext* is the DDE name of the application you want. *Topictext* describes what you want to access, which can be a filename, or whatever is appropriate for the application.

If INITIATE is successful, it returns the number of the open channel, and all subsequent DDE macro functions will use this number when specifying a channel.

When an application is running, it will have a task number; if more than one instance of the application is running, this task number is necessary to identify which instance you want. If you don't specify a task number and more than one instance is running, INITIATE displays a dialog box, allowing you to identify the instance you want.

INPUT(prompt,type,title,default,xposition,yposition)
Displays a dialog box.
INPUT displays a dialog box, and returns the information in the dialog box. *Prompt* and *type* are required arguments, and

Chapter 10

are text. *Title, default, xposition,* and *yposition* are optional; title is text and the other three arguments must be numbers.

INPUT is one way you can design a custom dialog box, and is particularly useful for prompting the user to enter data.

An INPUT dialog box looks like this:

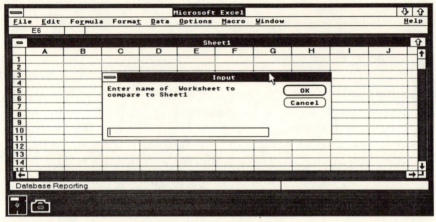

Figure 10-4. An Input Dialog Box

If you omit title, *Excel* assumes it's "Input." If you omit xposition or yposition, *Excel* assumes they are 0 and centers the dialog box.

The argument type refers to the data type that is expected to be entered:

Number:	Data type:
0	formula
1	number
2	text
4	logical
8	reference
16	error
64	array

Excel allows you to indicate a combination of types, by summing the numeric values; that is, if you want the input

322

box to accept numbers, text, or logical values, but not cell references, set type = 7.

When you set type = 8, INPUT returns the absolute cell reference. When you set type = 0, INPUT returns the formula as text, with any references set in R1C1 style.

If the information entered by the user isn't the correct type, *Excel* tries to translate it to the correct type. If it can't, it displays an error message.

MESSAGE(logical,text)

Displays a message in status bar.

Toggles the display or removal of a message (text) in the status bar. Any message displayed with MESSAGE stays in the status bar until removed by another MESSAGE.

If *logical* is True, *Excel* displays *text* in the status bar. If text is the empty text value (""), any message currently displayed in the status bar is removed. If text is False, any message in the status bar is removed and the status bar is re-enabled to handle normal command help messages.

ON.DATA(documenttext,macrotext)

Runs a macro when data is sent to *Excel* by another application.

ON.DATA lets you automatically update a document whenever it receives new data. *Macrotext* is the name of the macro that is started when new data is sent by another application to the document specified by *documenttext*. Macrotext must be a text form of R1C1-style reference.

If the incoming data causes recalculation, *Excel* first does the recalculating, then starts the macro specified.

ON.DATA stays in effect until either you turn it off or you quit *Excel*. If you close the macro sheet containing macrotext, an error message is generated when data is sent to the document named in documenttext. To turn off ON.DATA, omit the macrotext argument.

ON.KEY(keytext,macrotext)

Runs a macro when a particular key is pressed.

ON.KEY lets you set up an autokey initiation of your macro. When you press the key specified in keytext, the macro specified in macrotext is run.

The key specified in *keytext* must be in a form *Excel* can understand. The Appendix on pp. 373-375 of the Microsoft *Excel* Functions and Macros manual explains how to specify keys.

Macrotext must be a text form of R1C1-style reference. If macrotext is empty text (""), nothing happens when the key is pressed. If macrotext is omitted, keytext reverts to its normal meaning.

ON.KEY remains in effect until you turn it off or you quit *Excel*.

ON.TIME(time,macrotext,tolerance,insertvalue)
Runs a macro at a certain time.
ON.TIME lets you set up your worksheet so a macro is run at a specific *time*. It uses the time portion of the serial number that is automatically updated to current date and time when you turn on your machine.

Macrotext is the R1C1-style reference to the macro that is to be run. If *insertvalue* is True or is omitted, the macro will be run at the time specified. If insertvalue is False, any prior requests to execute the specified macro at the specified time are ignored.

The time argument can be a number less than 1; if so, *Excel* assumes that the macro is to be run every day at the time specified. If the specified time occurs and the macro specified is not in memory, the function is ignored. If two identical ON.TIME statements are present, the first is executed, and the second is ignored and returns the error message #N/A!

The *tolerance* parameter is used to allow *Excel* to leave one of the modes where this function can be executed, then return and still run the function. If the specified time occurs and *Excel* is not in READY, COPY, CUT, or FIND mode, *Excel* waits for the length of time specified by tolerance (a date/time serial number). If *Excel* doesn't return to one of these modes within the length of time specified, the request is canceled.

ON.WINDOW(windowtext,macrotext)
Runs a macro when a window is changed.
ON.WINDOW starts the macro specified in *macrotext* when-

ever the window specified in *windowtext* is activated. Both arguments must be enclosed in double quotes.

If windowtext is omitted, *Excel* starts the macro specified whenever any window is activated, except for those windows named in other ON.WINDOW functions.

POKE(channel#,itemtext,datareference)
Sends data to another application.
POKE lets you send data from *Excel* to another application while both *Excel* and the other application are running.

POKE uses the *channel#* returned by the INITIATE function. *Itemtext* is the specification within the other application where the data is to go, and *datareference* is the reference to the cell or cell range where the *Excel* data is to be found.

If POKE is not successful because the channel number was not valid, it returns the error message #VALUE! If POKE is refused, it returns the error message #REF! If the application you are trying to send data to does not respond and you press the Esc key to cancel the request, POKE returns the error message #DIV/0!

REGISTER(moduletext,proceduretext,argumenttext)
Accesses Microsoft Windows library.
This is a very powerful function that returns a text value to be used by the CALL function, which in turn can then be used to access the Microsoft Windows dynamic library.

Basically a system-level command, use it with considerable care, or it could cause system operation errors.

The argument *moduletext* contains the name of the Microsoft Windows dynamic library that contains the procedure you want. *Proceduretext* is the text form of the procedure name you want. *Argumenttext* is a character string with argument codes concatenated with return type codes.

REGISTER is a complex function, requiring system-level understanding of the Microsoft Windows dynamic library. It is discussed in more detail in the companion book, *PC Excel Business Solutions*.

RENAME.COMMAND(bar#,menuposition,commandposition,nametext)
Renames command.

Assigns the name specified in *nametext* to a command at a specified position on a specified menu. *Menuposition* can either be the number of a menu or its name as text. *Commandposition* can either be the number of the command that is being renamed or its title as text. If commandposition is 0, the menu is renamed.

Bar# is either the number of the built-in menu bars or the number returned by the previously executed ADD.BAR function.

If the command specified does not exist, the function returns the error message #VALUE!

REQUEST(channel#,itemtext)

Returns data from another application.

REQUEST gets the data specified by *itemtext* from the application that is connected via *channel#*. *Channel#* is the number of a channel that has already been opened by INITIATE. REQUEST returns data as an array.

If the channel number specified is not valid, REQUEST returns the error message #VALUE! If the request is refused, it returns the error message #REF! If the application is busy, the function returns the error value #N/A! If the application doesn't respond and you press the Esc key to cancel the function, it returns the error message #DIV/0!

SEND.KEYS(keytext,waitvalue)

Sends a key sequence to an application.

SEND.KEYS lets you send a keystroke sequence to another application, just as if you had pressed the keys in that application. The keys should be in the form described in the Appendix, pp. 373-375, of the *Excel Functions and Macros* reference manual.

If *waitvalue* is True, *Excel* waits for the keys to be processed before returning control to the calling macro. If waitvalue is False or omitted, the macro continues without waiting for the other application to process the keys.

SET.NAME(nametext,value)

Defines a name as a certain value.

SET.NAME is the same as equating a named variable with a constant, a logical value, or a reference. If *value* is omitted, the name *nametext* is deleted.

If you use SET.NAME to define nametext as a reference, it will be the text version of that reference, not the value. If you want the value of that reference, use the DEREF function.

SET.VALUE(reference,values)

Enters values in a cell.

SET.VALUE changes the value of the cell or cells specified in *reference* to the *values* specified, unless a cell already contains a formula, in which case it's ignored.

The cells referred to by reference must be cells on the current macro sheet. If reference is a range, then values should be an equivalent size array of numbers. If there is a mismatch, *Excel* expands the array to fit the range.

SHOW.BAR(bar#)

Displays a menu bar.

SHOW.BAR displays the menu bar specified by *bar#*, where bar# can be either one of the built-in menu bars, or the number returned by the previously executed ADD.BAR. If bar# is omitted, *Excel* displays a standard bar, depending on which window is active:

If active window has:	Standard bar:
Worksheet or macro sheet (Full menus)	1
Chart (Full menus)	2
No active window	3
Info window	4
Worksheet or macro sheet (Short menus)	5
Chart (Short menus)	6

STEP()

Single-steps through a macro.

STEP starts single-step processing of a macro, displaying a dialog box for each macro instruction, and letting you choose whether to execute the next instruction, halt the macro, or continue normal processing of the instructions. Single-stepping is particularly useful when debugging a macro.

You can also single-step through a macro by pressing the Esc key while it's running.

Chapter 10

TERMINATE(channel#)
>Closes a channel to another application.
>TERMINATE is the opposite of INITIATE, and closes the channel specified by *channel#*. If TERMINATE is not successful, it returns the error message !VALUE!

WAIT(serialnumber)
>Stops a macro from running.
>WAIT suspends execution of a macro for the amount of time specified in the date/time value *serialnumber*.

Control Functions

ARGUMENT(nametext,datatype#,reference)
>Describes arguments to a macro.
>The ARGUMENT function lets you use named values as arguments in macro functions. These named values will be used wherever the name is referenced in a function macro.
>>*Nametext* is the name you want to assign to the argument. It may also be the name of the cells containing the argument, if you're using reference.
>>*Datatype#* is a code number specifying the type of entry. (See the INPUT function explanation for datatype# values.)
>>*Reference* tells *Excel* where you want it to store the value that will be passed to the macro.

BREAK()
>Gets out of a FOR-NEXT or WHILE-NEXT loop.
>When BREAK is encountered, processing of a FOR-NEXT or WHILE-NEXT loop stops, and macro execution returns to the statement following the NEXT statement at the end of the current loop.

FOR(counter,start#,end#,increment)
>Starts a FOR-NEXT loop.
>A loop in a macro allows you to perform some set of actions a finite number of times. A loop means that a set of instructions is repeated, usually with one or more changes to some counter or other variable, until some specified condition occurs.
>>Looping is a bit like doing situps as part of an exercise program; you repeat the situp exercise until you have com-

pleted a certain number, and then you stop and go on to something else.

A FOR statement begins the loop; a NEXT statement marks the end of the loop and the point at which control either returns to the loop if the end-condition hasn't been yet met, or proceeds with statements outside the loop. Loop processing starts at the begin-point and goes to the last statement before the NEXT statement. When the end-condition has been met, processing is allowed to get past the NEXT statement.

Arguments needed with a FOR-NEXT loop:

Counter is the name of the variable that counts the number of times the loop has been performed; when its value exceeds that of end#, control passes outside of the loop.

Start# (optional) is assumed to be 1 unless specified. Start# is the value to which counter is set when the loop begins.

End# is the value against which countername is compared after each iteration of the loop. Until the value in countername is greater than end#, looping continues.

Increment is the value by which counter is incremented on each pass through the loop.

GOTO(reference)

Jumps to another cell.

The GOTO function works the same as pressing F5; it tells *Excel* to jump to the upper left cell in *reference* and continue processing there.

Reference must be a cell or cell range on an open macro sheet, though it doesn't have to be the same macro sheet as the one on which the GOTO statement occurs.

HALT()

Stops one or more macros from running.

HALT stops all macro action. It's particularly useful for stopping processing when an error occurs.

When you use HALT, you should combine it with a function that produces a message, so the user knows why everything has stopped.

NEXT()
>Ends a FOR-NEXT or WHILE-NEXT loop.
>NEXT is the last statement in a loop. It marks the point at which control either returns to loop processing or continues to other instructions, depending on the current state of the counter. (See FOR and WHILE.)

RESTART(level#)
>Removes return addresses from the stack.
>When you jump from the middle of one macro to the beginning of another, *Excel* stores the address of the last instruction in the macro you left as the return address. If you then jump from the second macro to a third, it keeps track of that return address as well. That list of return addresses is known as a stack.
>
>When you want to return to the calling macro, *Excel* consults this stack. A level 1 return means that control returns to the macro that directly called the macro you're in. If, however, you want to return to another macro that was in the chain of nested calls, you need to specify a different level.
>
>You may wish to remove some return addresses from that stack. RESTART lets you do that by level number, where level 1 is the most recent call, level 2 is the call or set of calls before that, and so on. If the level# argument is omitted, *Excel* removes all return addresses from the stack. Thus, when a RETURN function is encountered, the macro will stop running instead of returning control to the macro that called it.

RESULT(type#)
>Specifies the data type of a function macro's return value.
>RESULT is usually used at the beginning of a macro to specify what kind of return value is expected. The kind of return value is specified by a code number:

Type#	Data type
1	number
2	text
4	logical
8	reference

Type#	Data type
16	error
64	array

Type# can be a sum of the codes, indicating that a combination of types are allowable. For instance, if type# = 7 (the default), the return value may be a number, text, or a logical value.

RETURN(value)
Returns control to whatever started the macro.

RETURN is normally the last instruction in a function or command macro. It tells *Excel* that control is to return to whatever called the macro. This may be the user (using the Macro Run command or a shortcut key), a formula, or another macro.

Use of the argument *value* depends on whether the macro is a command macro or a function macro. In a command macro run by the user, the value should not be specified. In a function macro, value specifies the return value associated with this macro.

WHILE(testvalue)
Starts a WHILE-NEXT loop.

WHILE begins a loop of instructions that ends with a NEXT statement. WHILE continues to loop until *testvalue* is False, unlike a FOR-NEXT loop, where the exit from the loop is determined by a counter.

If testvalue is False the first time, execution skips to the matching NEXT instruction and proceeds with the instruction after it.

Value-Returning Functions
ABSREF(referencetext,reference)
Returns the absolute reference of a cell.

ABSREF lets you determine the reference of one cell by describing its position relative to another cell. *Referencetext* must be in R1C1-style, a relative reference, and in text form: "R[-2]C[-2]". If *reference* is a cell range, referencetext is assumed to be relative to the upper left corner of reference.

Example: Returns:
ABSREF("R[-2]C[-2]",D5)   B3
ABSREF("R[-1]C[-1]",D10:E150)   C9

ACTIVE.CELL()

Returns the reference of the active cell.

ACTIVE.CELL returns the reference of the active cell as an external reference. ACTIVE.CELL is particularly useful when you're working with linked worksheets and need to communicate the value or position of the active cell to an external file.

Normally the value returned by ACTIVE.CELL will be the value contained in the active cell, since that's how it's usually translated. If you want the reference instead, use REFTEXT to convert the active cell reference to text, which can then be stored or manipulated.

CALLER()

Returns the reference of the cell that started the function macro.

Unlike RETURN, CALLER returns the reference of the cell that contained the function which called the currently running macro. If the function was part of an array formula, CALLER returns the range reference. If the currently running macro is a command macro started by the user, CALLER returns the error message #REF!

DEREF(reference)

Returns the value of a cell in a reference.

In most cases, a reference to a cell returns the value of that cell. If, however, you have used a function such as SET.NAME, references are not always converted to values.

In those cases, the DEREF function returns a value. If reference is the reference of a single cell, DEREF returns the value of that cell. If the reference is a range of cells, DEREF returns the array of values in those cells.

DOCUMENTS()

Returns the names of open documents.

DOCUMENT returns the names of all open files in alphabetical order as an array of text values. It is frequently used with INDEX to select individual file names for other uses.

FILES(directoryname)
Returns the names of files in a specific directory.

FILES gives you a horizontal text array of the filenames in the directory you specify. You can use the wildcard characters * and ? in the FILES argument. Up to 256 filenames can be returned.

If *directoryname* is not specified, it is assumed to be *.*.

GET.BAR()
Returns the number of the active menu bar.
Built-in menu bar numbers are:

Number	Built-in menu bar
1	Worksheet and macro menu, Full menus.
2	Chart menu, Full menus.
3	Nil menu (menu displayed when no documents are open).
4	Info window menu.
5	Worksheet and macro menu, Short menus.
6	Chart menu, Short menus.

GET.CELL(infocode,reference)
Returns information about a cell.

GET.CELL tells you about the location, contents, or formatting of the upper-left cell in *reference*. If reference is omitted, it is assumed to be the current selection.

The argument *infocode* specifies what kind of information you want:

Infocode	Result
1	Reference of upper-left cell in area specified, as text.
2	Row number of the top cell in reference.

Chapter 10

Infocode	Result
3	Column number of the leftmost cell in reference.
4	The same as TYPE(reference).
5	Contents of reference.
6	The formula in reference, as text.
7	Format of cell, as text.
8	Cell's alignment: 　1 = General 　2 = Left 　3 = Center 　4 = Right 　5 = Fill
9	If cell has left border, returns True; otherwise False.
10	If cell has right border, returns True; otherwise False
11	If cell has top border, returns True; otherwise False.
12	If cell has bottom border, returns True; otherwise False.
13	If cell is shaded, returns True; otherwise False.
14	If cell is locked, returns True; otherwise False.
15	If cell is hidden, returns True; otherwise False.
16	Column width of the cell, measured in characters of Font 1.
17	Row height of cell, in points.
18	Name of font, as text.
19	Size of font, in points.
20	If cell is bold, returns True; otherwise False.
21	If cell is italic, returns True; otherwise False.
22	If cell is underlined, returns True; otherwise False.
23	If cell is overstruck, returns True; otherwise False.

GET.CHART.ITEM(xyindex,pointindex,code)

Returns the location of a chart element in a chart window. This function returns the vertical or horizontal position of a point on a chart element. The argument *xyindex* is a code number: 1 for horizontal coordinate of the position, or 2 for the vertical coordinate.

Pointindex specifies the point on the chart object, as shown below. If the selected object is a point, pointindex must be 1. If pointindex is omitted, it is assumed to be 1.

The value given for *code* is in text form, and is the same as shown under SELECT, discussed earlier.

If the selected object is any line other than a data line, these values are used for pointindex:

Pointindex	Chart object position
1	Lower left
2	Upper right

If the selected object is a rectangle or an area in an area chart, these values are used for pointindex:

Pointindex	Chart object position
1	Upper left
2	Upper middle
3	Upper right
4	Right middle
5	Lower right
6	Lower middle
7	Lower left
8	Lower middle

If the selected object is an arrow, these values are used for pointindex:

Pointindex	Chart object position
1	Base
2	Head

Chapter 10

If the selected object is a pie slice, these values are used for pointindex:

Pointindex	Chart object position
1	Outermost counter-clockwise point
2	Outer center point
3	Outermost clockwise point
4	Midpoint of the most clockwise radius
5	Center point
6	Midpoint of the most counter-clockwise radius

GET.DEF(definition,document)
Returns a name matching a definition.
Returns the text version of the name that matches whatever is in *definition*, which may be a part of *document*. Definition may be a reference, but if so must be in R1C1 style.

GET.DOCUMENT(infotype,nametext)
Returns information about a document.
Depending on the code you specify in *infotype*, GET.DOCUMENT returns information about the document you identify in *nametext*. If nametext is omitted, it is assumed to be the active document.

Infotype	Result
1	Name of the document as text; does not include drive, directory, or window number.
2	Pathname of directory containing nametext. If nametext has not yet been saved, this infotype returns the error message #N/A!.
3	Returns: 1 if the document is a worksheet. 2 if the document is a chart. 3 if the document is a macro sheet. 4 if the active window is the Info window.

Infotype	Result
4	True if changes have been made to the document since it was last saved; False if no changes have been made.
5	True if access is read-only; False otherwise.
6	True if file protected; False otherwise.
7	True if contents are protected; False otherwise.
8	True if document windows are protected; False otherwise.

The four infotypes shown below apply only to charts:

Infotype	Result

9	Code number indicating type of chart:
	  1 area
	  2 bar
	  3 column
	  4 line
	  5 pie
	  6 scatter

10	Code number (same as above) indicating type of overlay chart. If there is no overlay chart, returns #N/A!
11	Number of series in main chart.
12	Number of series in overlay chart.

The remaining infotype values apply only to worksheets and macro sheets:

Infotype	Result
9	Row number of first row used. If document is empty, returns 0.
10	Row number of last row used. If document is empty, returns 0.
11	Column number of first column used. If document is empty, returns 0.

Chapter 10

Infotype	Result
12	Column number of last column used. If document is empty, returns 0.
13	Number of windows.

14	Code number indicating calculation mode:
	  1 automatic
	  2 automatic except tables
	  3 manual

15	True if iteration is enabled; otherwise False.
16	Maximum number of iterations.
17	Maximum change between iterations.
18	True if updating remote reference is enabled; False otherwise.
19	True if set to Precision as Displayed; False otherwise.
20	True if document is using 1904 date system; False otherwise.
21	4-item horizontal text array of the names of the four fonts
22	4-item horizontal number array of the sizes of the four fonts.

GET.FORMULA(reference)
Returns the contents of a cell.
GET.FORMULA returns the contents of *reference* as it would appear in the formula bar. The contents are returned as text. If the formula contains references, they are returned in R1C1-style.

GET.NAME(nametext)
Returns the definition of a name.
GET.NAME returns a name's definition as it would appear in the Refers to text box Formula Define Name command. *Nametext* can be a name on a macro sheet, or an external reference to a name defined on a document.

If the definition of nametext contains references, they are returned in R1C1-style.

GET.NOTE(cellreference,start,count)

Returns characters from a note.

GET.NOTE returns count number of characters from the cell identified by *cellreference*, beginning at the character numbered start. If *start* is omitted, it assumed to be 1. If *count* is omitted, it is assumed to be the length of the note attached to cellreference.

GET.WINDOW(infotype,nametext)

Returns information about a window.

Depending on the code you specify in *infotype*, GET.WINDOW returns information about the window you identify in *nametext*. If nametext is omitted, it is assumed to be the active window.

Use infotype to specify what kind of information you want. Infotypes 1 through 7 apply to all windows, and 8 through 17 apply to worksheets and macro sheets. Infotypes 13 through 17 return numeric arrays that specify what rows or columns are at the edges of the panes in the specified window.

Infotype	Results
1	Name of document in the window specified in nametext, as text.
2	Number of window specified.
3	Number of points from the left edge of your screen to the left edge of the window (x position).
4	Number of points from the top edge of your screen to the top edge of the window (y position).
5	Width, measured in points.
6	Height, measured in points.
7	True if window is hidden; otherwise False.
8	True if formulas are displayed; otherwise False.
9	True if gridlines are displayed; otherwise False.
10	True if row and column headings are displayed; otherwise False.

Infotype	Results
11	True if zeros are displayed; otherwise False.
12	Code number 0-8 giving the color of gridlines and headlines, corresponding to colors shown in the Options Display dialog box. (0 is equivalent to the Automatic Display option.)
13	The leftmost column of each pane, as an array.
14	The top row of each pane, as an array.
15	The rightmost column of each pane, as an array.
16	The bottom row of each pane, as an array.
17	Returns the active pane number.

GET.WORKSPACE(infotype)

Returns information about the workspace.

Depending on the code you specify in infotype, GET.WORKSPACE returns information about your workspace.

Use infotype to specify what kind of information you want.

Infotype	Result
1	Name and version number of the environment in which *Excel* is running, as text.
2	Version number of *Excel*, as text.
3	If auto-decimal is set, returns the number of decimals; otherwise 0.
4	True if in R1C1 mode; False if in A1 mode.
5	True if scroll bars are displayed; otherwise False.
6	True if status bar is displayed; otherwise False.
7	True if formula bar is displayed; otherwise False.

Infotype	Result
8	True if remote requests are enabled; otherwise False.
9	Returns alternate menu key as text; returns #N/A! if no alternate menu key is set.

10	Special mode code number:
	  1 Data Find
	  2 Copy
	  3 Cut
	  0 No special mode

11	Number of points from the left edge of your screen to the left edge of the *Excel* window (x position).
12	Number of points from the top edge of your screen to the top edge of the *Excel* window (y position).
13	Usable workspace width, in points.
14	Usable workspace height, in points.

15	Maximize/minimize code number:
	  1 *Excel* is neither maximized nor minimized.
	  2 Minimized.
	  3 Maximized.

16	Number of Kbytes of memory free.
17	Total number of Kbytes of memory available to *Excel*.
18	True if math coprocessor is present; otherwise False.
19	True if mouse is present; otherwise False.

LINKS(docname)

Returns the names of all linked documents.

LINKS returns a horizontal array of the names of all documents referred to by external references in the document specified by *docname*. If docname is omitted, it is assumed to be the active document. If the document identified by docname contains no external references, LINKS returns the error message #N/A!

Chapter 10

NAMES(docname)
Returns an array of defined names on a document.
NAMES returns a horizontal text array of all names that are defined on *docname*. If docname is omitted, it is assumed to be the active document.

OFFSET(reference,rows,columns,height,width)
Returns a reference offset from a given reference.
OFFSET returns the reference height rows high and width columns wide that is *rows* rows and *columns* columns offset from reference. If *height* or *width* are omitted, they are assumed to be the same dimensions as *reference*.

If the offset parameters go over the edge of the worksheet, OFFSET returns the #REF! error message. If reference is a multiple value, the function returns the error message #VALUE!

REFTEXT(reference,a1)
Converts a reference into text.
Converts *reference* to an absolute reference, as text. If *a1* is True, REFTEXT returns it in A1-style; if False or omitted, REFTEXT returns it in R1C1-style.

RELREF(reference,comparison)
Returns a relative reference.
RELREF compares *comparison* to *reference* and returns a relative reference, in R1C1-style, as text.

Example:	Returns:
RELREF(B3,C4)	"R[-1]C[-1]"

SELECTION()
Returns the reference of a selection.
SELECTION returns the reference of a selection as an external reference.

Normally the value returned by SELECTION gets converted to a value, rather than stored as a reference. If you want the reference rather than the value, use REFTEXT to convert the reference to text, which can then be further manipulated.

TEXTREF(text,a1)
Converts text to a reference.
Converts the *text* specified to a cell reference. If *a1* is True, text is assumed to be in A1-style; if a1 is False or omitted, text is assumed to be in R1C1-style.

WINDOWS()
Returns the names of open windows.
WINDOWS returns a horizontal text array of all windows on your screen, in order by level. The active window is the first named; the window directly under that is the second, and so forth.

Chapter 11
Excel and Other Programs

An *Excel* worksheet can share data with a wide variety of other programs—with another worksheet or set of worksheet files, with another program running under Microsoft *Windows,* or with other non-Microsoft programs, including the more popular spreadsheet and database programs. Additionally, it can share data with other computers over a Local Area Network, or even a direct connection. This chapter looks at some of the ways *Excel* shares data.

Sharing Data Between Microsoft *Windows* Applications

It's easy to share data with another application running under Microsoft *Windows* (version 2.0 or higher). In many cases, you can use the Clipboard (discussed in Appendix D) as the temporary storage area while you pass data between *Excel* and the other application.

If you copy or cut data from an existing worksheet and display the Clipboard (press Alt + Space bar for the Control menu, then choose the Run command, and in the dialog box choose Clipboard), you'll see a list of terms, such as Picture, Printer_Picture, Bitmap, and so forth, followed by an R1C1-style description of the cell or cells that have been selected. The list of terms is a list of file formats which *Excel* can use to send whatever has been put on the Clipboard to another application. You can send your data in any of these formats, or even send it in more than one format.

To send data from *Excel* to another application running under Microsoft *Windows,* open the window you want, select the cells involved, then choose Copy or Cut as appropriate. If you display the Clipboard at that point, you'll see the selected cells indicated by address. Next, open the receiving application, and use the appropriate commands to retrieve the cells from the Clipboard.

Sharing Data with Other *Excel* Worksheets

In Chapter 4 we discussed the concept of linking, the term *Excel* uses to describe a situation where data in one worksheet is shared with one or more *Excel* worksheets. This is one way of sharing data between worksheets, a way that tells *Excel* that these worksheets are linked and hence any change to data in one should be reflected in changes to the appropriate cells in the other(s).

Any cell references involved in such an exchange are considered *external references* and are subject to some limitations, which we discussed in earlier chapters.

There is a more direct way to share data between *Excel* worksheets: You can use the Copy or Cut command to share data between currently open worksheets by moving back and forth between them with the *Windows* menu—and then use the Paste command to put data in place.

Dynamic Data Exchange (DDE)

The Dynamic Data Exchange (a method for communicating between *Windows* applications) allows you not only to get data from and send data to other applications, but it also allows you to start and carry out commands in other applications, and to respond to requests initiated by other applications.

In order to respond to DDE requests from other applications, use the Options Workspace command, and be sure the Ignore Remote Requests check box is turned off. To disable those requests, turn on the check box.

Applications using the DDE method must have defined three elements:

App	The name of the application. In the case of *Excel*, use the text value *"Excel."* If more than one instance of *Excel* is running, you'll need to append the task identification number.
Topic	Either the word "System" or the text version of the name of any currently open file, as it appears in the title bar.
Item	A reference, or the name of a reference.

You can ask *Excel* for specific information with the "System" topic:

"SysItems"	Returns a list of all the items you can use with the "System" topic: SysItems, Topics, Status, and so forth.

"Topics"	Returns a list of all currently open documents, including their pathnames.
"Status"	Returns " "Ready" if *Excel* is ready to execute commands; otherwise "Busy."
"Formats"	Returns a list of all the Clipboard formats supported by *Excel*.
"Selection"	Returns a list of all external references of all currently selected ranges in *Excel*. References are given in absolute R1C1 style.

Values returned are in CF_TEXT format (ASCII text), with items separated by tabs.

To execute a command looking for an item, use a text value that includes *Excel* command-equivalent macro functions, enclosing each function in brackets. For example:

"[OPEN("C:\\WINDOWS\\EXCELCBT\\ADDRESS.XLS")]"

opens the worksheet file ADDRESS.XLS in the EXCELCBT subdirectory of the WINDOWS directory.

Macro functions used in the item must be command-equivalent macro functions. Arguments must be constants, and references must be in R1C1-style.

Data Exchange Formats

Excel can recognize (read and write) files in a number of formats other than .XLS, .XLM, .XLC, and .XLW:

Format	File Extension
Text (ASCII)	.TXT
Comma separated values	.CSV
Symbolic link	.SLK
Lotus 1-2-3 version 1A	.WKS
Lotus 1-2-3 version 2.0 or higher	.WK1
Data interchange	.DIF
dBase II and dBase III	.DBF

In addition, a number of other Clipboard formats are supported:

Chapter 11

Format	Clipboard type identifier
Microsoft *Excel* file	CF_BIFF
Symbolic link	CF_SYLK
Lotus 1-2-3 version 2.0	CF_WK1
Data Interchange	CF_DIF
Picture	CF_METAFILEPICT
Bitmap	CF_BITMAP

When you examine the file exchange formats supported by *Excel* more closely, a number of possibilities crop up. For example, since some Postscript-capable illustration programs for the Macintosh allow the user to save a bitmapped file, you could create an illustration as a bitmapped file on a Macintosh computer. Then you could use that computer's Clipboard to transfer the illustration from the Macintosh (over a LAN such as Appletalk) to an IBM-AT, and then into *Excel* for use with a chart. Chart formats are discussed shortly.

Figure 11-1 shows how *Excel* tries to interpret external files and convert them to a format it can use.

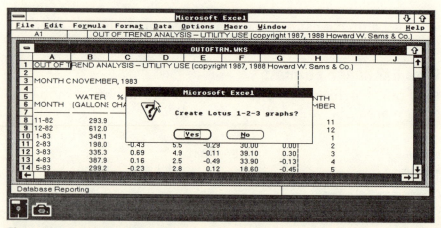

Figure 11-1. Importing *Lotus* Charts

Generally, if you want to exchange illustrations with another computer or set of software, you only need to find out whether the program you want to use produces files that can be transferred into *Excel*. Even if that particular file format isn't directly translatable, look at your other programs to see if one of them can translate the file into something that can eventually be used by *Excel*.

(To see how this works, look at the following example shown under "Copying Pictures," where a file was transferred from Borland's *Quattro* into *Lotus 1-2-3* format, and then into *Excel*.)

Other Databases

Several dedicated database formats are among the file transfer formats supported by *Excel*. Thus, it's possible to import information from an already existing database into *Excel* for use with a preexisting worksheet. In addition, you can export data from an *Excel* database to another, more powerful database format for use with one of the popular stand-alone database programs.

Besides the dedicated database formats supported by *Excel*, there are also a number of spreadsheet packages that contain at least a minimal database capability. As a result, you can exchange database information with a variety of other spreadsheet programs.

One result of this capability is that while it may not be possible to directly access the information stored in an outside database, it is quite possible to import that database information into *Excel*. From here, you can reformat it as necessary to conform with the needs in your worksheet and then copy it from one worksheet to another, using the windowing capability of *Excel*.

Excel's database capabilities can also serve as a temporary storage mechanism, allowing the transfer of information from a database on a much larger worksheet into a temporary *Excel* worksheet. That export can then be transferred into an outside database that is used somewhere else, possibly with a much larger and more comprehensive database program.

Copying Pictures

Excel can import and export a variety of chart file formats. Since the .WKS, .WK1, and .SLK file formats are all supported by *Excel*, it is quite possible to move or copy a chart from one program to another within your network.

Chapter 11

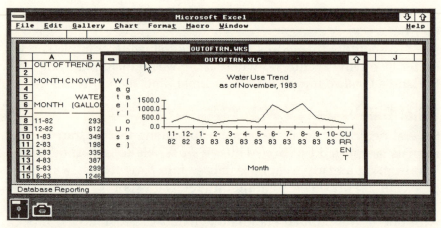

Figure 11-2. A *Lotus*-format Chart in *Excel*

The above spreadsheet and accompanying chart were not created in *Lotus 1-2-3*. While the .WKS file format was used as the transfer medium, both files were originally generated in Borland's *Quattro* spreadsheet program. They were then saved in a .WKS file format, imported into *Excel*, and opened in the XLS/XLC formats.

You can do this sort of thing with more than just the Lotus formatting. Since *Excel* also supports a number of other file formats, it is also quite easy to import and export charts in a number of other formats, as well as translating them from one format to another with little or no effort.

One of the more important things to remember is that the file formats supported by *Excel* extend to more than just the IBM-related formats. If you are using a LAN, depending on the other computers that are attached, you may find yourself dealing with several things: Macintosh formatting, information coming from a mainframe, or some other esoteric format that doesn't, at first glance, appear to be something you could possibly run on an IBM-compatible computer.

The key is to use the appropriate file format. This mechanism means that you can use quite a few of these supposedly unusable formats. The Macintosh, as an example, uses (among others) .SLK formatting. Some of the other formats are supported for opening and/or saving the file format, while others are supported in clipboard exchange format.

Consult the *Excel Reference Guide,* and the appropriate reference material for the program you'll be working with for further details. However, chances are good that you can transfer most files for use with *Excel*.

Excel and Lotus 1-2-3

Excel can read and write *Lotus 1-2-3* worksheet files, and can deal with charts produced by *Lotus 1-2-3*. In addition, there is a Help *Lotus 1-2-3* command in *Excel* that lets you get online help about the *Excel* equivalent of *1-2-3* commands. You'll also be able to find help about the *Excel* equivalent of *1-2-3* functions. Finally, the Macro Translation Assistant lets you convert most *1-2-3* macros into *Excel* macros.

Excel can read and write files in both .WKS and .WK1 formats, the formats *Lotus 1-2-3* worksheets use. (*Lotus 1-2-3* version 1A produces files in .WKS format; version 2.0 or higher produces files in .WK1 format.)

When preparing to read a file from *Lotus 1-2-3*, choose the File Open command, and in the File Name box type:

.wk

Press Enter and in the list box, the files with either .WKS or .WK1 extensions will be shown. Choose the filename you want to open, and press the OK bar. The file is automatically translated, and the data appears as an *Excel* worksheet.

If you want to save an *Excel* worksheet as a *1-2-3* file, choose File Save As, and then choose the Options button. Under File Format, specify either .WKS or .WK1, as appropriate to the file's destination. Then type the filename you want to use. *Lotus 1-2-3* uses the same filename rules as *Excel*. When you've specified everything as you want it, choose the OK bar, and the file is saved in appropriate *1-2-3* format.

(You can then go ahead and resave the file in another format, if you want to use it with *Excel* or with yet another program.)

Excel tries to convert all *Lotus 1-2-3* formulas into *Excel* formulas when reading a *1-2-3* file, and tries to convert *Excel* formulas into *1-2-3* formulas when writing a *1-2-3* file. If a conversion is impossible, you'll see a message giving the reference of the cell containing the formula. When conversion can't be done, *Excel* saves the value of the formula.

Numbers and text convert directly, including text used as

constants in cells. *Excel* and *1-2-3*, version 2.0 and higher, allow text constants to be used in formulas and formulas that produce text. *1-2-3* version 1A does not.

Excel and *1-2-3* use many of the same operators, but there are a few differences, and the order of evaluation is different. Check the *Excel Reference Guide*.

Excel and *1-2-3* handle the logical values True and False somewhat differently. They also handle error values differently; consult the *Excel Reference Guide* for details.

While *Excel* can handle arrays, *1-2-3* does not support them, so *Excel* formulas involving arrays are not converted.

Excel can handle references to single cells, to cell ranges, and to multiple ranges. *Lotus 1-2-3* can handle references to single cells and to cell ranges, but not to multiple ranges. *1-2-3* version 1A does not allow functions that produce references as a result.

Excel's standard worksheet is 16,384 rows by 256 columns. Worksheets for *Lotus 1-2-3* version 1A are 2,048 rows by 256 columns; worksheets for version 2.0 or higher are 8,192 rows by 256 columns. Thus, size may be a problem when converting an *Excel* worksheet to a *1-2-3* file.

Excel also supports references to worksheets external to the current one. Neither version of *Lotus 1-2-3* supports external references, so attempting to convert linked *Excel* worksheets to *1-2-3* formats may cause problems.

Excel supports range names for single cells and cell ranges, as well as names for constant values, formulas, and references to multiple selections. *1-2-3* supports names for cells and ranges only. Named constants and formulas in *Excel* are converted in *1-2-3* files to the constant or formula, enclosed in parentheses.

Lotus 1-2-3 allows you to calculate by rows, by columns, or in natural order (order according to dependent formulas). *Excel* allows calculation only in natural order.

Generally, all cell alignments convert. However, nontext cells are right-aligned in *1-2-3* files, whereas in *Excel* you can specify the alignment.

Protection is allowed in both *Excel* and *1-2-3*, as is hiding of cell formulas.

Tables are handled differently by *Excel* and *1-2-3*. *Excel* tables are formulas, but in *1-2-3* tables must be calculated with a command or function key, and there are restrictions on where the data can be.

For comments on how *Excel* and *1-2-3* handle databases, see the "Other Databases" section in this chapter.

Most *1-2-3* macros can be converted to *Excel* macros with the Macro Translation Assistant. (Note: you'll need a lot of free memory to run the Translation Assistant; close any unnecessary windows, including Help windows, while it's running.)

Charts and graphs from *1-2-3* files can be converted to *Excel* files, but *Excel* charts don't convert to *1-2-3* files. See the "Copying Pictures" section in this chapter.

Excel and Multiplan

Excel can read and write *Multiplan* worksheet files. In addition, there is a Help *Multiplan* command in *Excel* that lets you get on-line help about the *Excel* equivalent of *Multiplan* commands. However, macros cannot be converted, nor can window and worksheet aspects such as splitting, freezing of row or column titles, the current selection, or the position of the scroll bars.

Excel can read and write files in SYLK (Symbolic Link) format, the format used by *Multiplan*. When preparing to read a *Multiplan* file, choose the File Open command, and in the File Name box type:

*.slk

Press Enter and in the list box, the files with that extension will be shown. Choose the filename you want to open, and press the OK bar. The file is automatically translated, and the data appears as an *Excel* worksheet.

If you want to save an *Excel* worksheet as a *Multiplan* file, choose File Save As, and then choose the Options button. Under File Format, choose SYLK. Then type the filename you want to use. Choose the OK bar, and the file is saved in a format that can be read by *Multiplan*.

Excel can convert most *Multiplan* formulas into *Excel* formulas. If a conversion is impossible, you'll see a message giving the reference of the cell containing the formula. When conversion can't be done, *Excel* saves the value of the formula.

However, *Excel* formulas are not converted into *Multiplan* formulas when writing a SYLK file. Rather, they are stored in the SYLK file exactly as they appeared in *Excel*. If *Multiplan* can't understand a formula, it will either ignore the formula or produce an error message.

Most numbers and text convert directly, including text used as constants in cells. However, *Excel* allows dates as a number format, and percentages enclosed in double quote marks, whereas *Multiplan* does not. Further, *Excel* supports arrays; *Multiplan* doesn't.

Excel and *Multiplan* have the same operators, and the same order of evaluation, except for range (:) and intersection (,). In *Excel*, range is evaluated before intersection; in *Multiplan*, intersection is evaluated before range. Further, *Excel* allows you to compare arguments of any type: number, text, logical. With *Multiplan*, however, you can't use comparison operators with logical arguments.

Excel and *Multiplan* handle the logical values (True and False) the same, and also handle error values the same.

Both *Excel* and *Multiplan* can handle references to single cells, to cell ranges, and to multiple ranges. *Excel*'s standard worksheet is 16,384 rows by 256 columns. *Multiplan* worksheets are 4,095 rows by 255 columns.

Both programs also support references to worksheets external to the current one; however, they do it differently. See the *Excel Reference Guide* for details.

Excel supports all of *Multiplan*'s functions except the DELTA and ITERCNT functions, but *Multiplan* won't recognize *Excel* functions that are different from its own set. Some of the *Excel* functions that look like the *Multiplan* equivalent work slightly differently.

Iteration is controlled differently by the two programs. *Multiplan* offers the Iteration and Completion Test At settings in the Options, along with the ITERCNT and DELTA functions. *Excel* lets you control iterations with the dialog box options on the Options Calculation command.

Cell alignments convert. So do column width formats. Number formats are generally the same, except for *Multiplan*'s Bar Graph format, which *Excel* converts to General.

Summary

This chapter has shown you some of the ways in which you can transfer data between *Excel* and other programs, including examining just how transfer works for both *Lotus 1-2-3* and *Multiplan*.

Appendix A
Shortcut Key Quick Reference

Shortcut Keys

F1	Help
Shift + F1	Context-sensitive Help
Alt + F1	File New command (Chart)
Alt + Shift F1	File New command (Worksheet)
Alt + Ctrl F1	File New command (Macro)
F2	Activate Formula bar, Edit mode
Shift + F2	Formula Note command
Ctrl + F2	Window Show Info command
Alt + F2	File Save As command
Alt + Shift + F2	File Save command
Alt + Ctrl + F2	File Open command
Alt + Ctrl + Shift + F2	File Print command
F3	Formula Paste Name command
Shift + F3	Formula Paste Function command
Ctrl + F3	Formula Define Name command
Ctrl + Shift + F3	Formula Create Names command
F4	Formula Reference command
Ctrl + F4	Control Close command (document window)
Alt + F4	Control Close command (application window)

Appendix A

F5	Formula Goto command
Shift + F5	Formula Find command (specific contents)
Ctrl + F5	Control Restore command (document window)
Alt + F5	Control Restore command (application window)
F6	Next pane
Shift + F6	Previous pane
Ctrl + F6	Next document window
Ctrl + Shift + F6	Previous document window
F7	Formula Find command (next cell)
Shift + F7	Formula Find command (previous cell)
Ctrl + F7	Control Move command (document window)
Alt + F7	Control Move command (application window)
F8	Toggles EXTEND on or off
Shift + F8	Turns on Add
Ctrl + F8	Control Size command (document window)
Alt + F8	Control Size command (application window)
F9	Options Calculate Now command
Shift + F9	Options Calculate Document command
Alt + F9	Control Minimize command (application window)
F10	Activate Menu bar
Ctrl + F10	Control Maximize command (document window)
Alt + F10	Control Maximize command (application window)

F11	File New command, Chart
Shift + F11	File New command, Worksheet
Ctrl + F11	File New command, Macro
F12	File Save As command
Shift + F12	File Save command
Ctrl + F12	File Open command
Ctrl + Shift + F12	File Print command
Ctrl + ~	Format Number, general format
Ctrl + !	Format Number, 0.00 format
Ctrl + @	Format Number, h:mm AM/PM format
Ctrl + #	Format Number, d-mmm-yy format
Ctrl + $	Format Number, $#,##0.00 format
Ctrl + %	Format Number, % format
Ctrl + ^	Format Number, 0.00E+00 format
Ctrl + 1	Format Font, font 1
Ctrl + 2	Format Font, font 2
Ctrl + 3	Format Font, font 3
Ctrl + 4	Format Font, font 4
Ctrl + ?	Formula Select Special, notes
Ctrl + *	Formula Select Special, current region
Ctrl + /	Formula Select Special, current array
Ctrl + \	Formula Select Special, row differences
Ctrl + |	Formula Select Special, column differences
Ctrl + [	Formula Select Special, precedents: direct only
Ctrl + {	Formula Select Special, precedents: all levels
Ctrl +]	Formula Select Special, dependents: direct only

Appendix A

Ctrl + }	Formula Select Special, dependents: all levels
Ctrl + =	Options Calculate Now
Ctrl + '	Options Display, formula/values
Alt + Hyphen	Control menu, document
Alt + Space Bar	Control menu, window
Alt + Hyphen + M	Control Move command, document
Alt + Hyphen + R	Control Restore command, document
Alt + Hyphen + S	Control Size command, document
Alt + Hyphen + T	Control Split command, document
Alt + Hyphen + X	Control Maximize command, document
Alt + Space Bar + C	Control Close command, window
Alt + Space Bar + M	Control Move command, window
Alt + Space Bar + N	Control Minimize command, window
Alt + Space Bar + R	Control Restore command, window
Alt + Space Bar + S	Control Size command, window
Alt + Space Bar + U	Control Run command, window
Alt + Space Bar + X	Control Maximize command, window
Shift + Backspace	Select rows containing selected cell or range
Shift + Ctrl + Enter	Move between selected ranges
Shift + Ctrl + Tab	Move between selected ranges
Shift + Del	Cut selection
Shift + Arrow key	Extend selection in direction chosen
Shift + End	Move to end of window
Shift + Enter	Move up one cell in the selection

Shift + Home	Move to beginning of window
Shift + Ins	Paste selection
Shift + PgUp	Extend selection up one window
Shift + PgDn	Extend selection down one window
Shift + Space Bar	Select row
Ctrl + Space Bar	Select column
Shift + Tab	Move one cell left in the selection
Alt + Backspace	Undo last action
Alt + Enter	Repeat last action
Alt + Esc	Select Spooler when printing
Alt + Z	Choose Zoom button when previewing

Appendix B

The Models in *Excel*

Files from EXCELCBT Directory

ACCOUNT.XLS

This is a customer-accounting spreadsheet that keeps track of both account numbers and balances. It's a good example of how a spreadsheet can be presented without gridlines and with some interesting formatting.

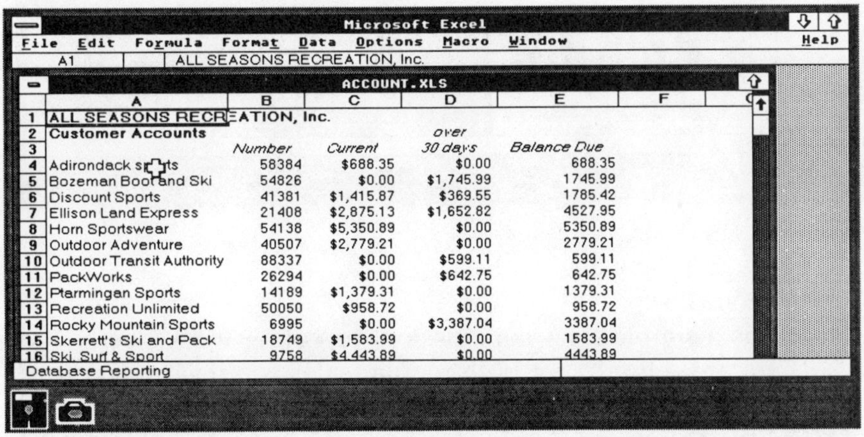

	A	B	C	D	E
1	ALL SEASONS RECREATION, Inc.				
2	Customer Accounts			over	
3		Number	Current	30 days	Balance Due
4	Adirondack s[illegible]ts	58384	$688.35	$0.00	688.35
5	Bozeman Boot and Ski	54826	$0.00	$1,745.99	1745.99
6	Discount Sports	41381	$1,415.87	$369.55	1785.42
7	Ellison Land Express	21408	$2,875.13	$1,652.82	4527.95
8	Horn Sportswear	54138	$5,350.89	$0.00	5350.89
9	Outdoor Adventure	40507	$2,779.21	$0.00	2779.21
10	Outdoor Transit Authority	88337	$0.00	$599.11	599.11
11	PackWorks	26294	$0.00	$642.75	642.75
12	Ptarmingan Sports	14189	$1,379.31	$0.00	1379.31
13	Recreation Unlimited	50050	$958.72	$0.00	958.72
14	Rocky Mountain Sports	6995	$0.00	$3,387.04	3387.04
15	Skerrett's Ski and Pack	18749	$1,583.99	$0.00	1583.99
16	Ski, Surf & Sport	9758	$4,443.89	$0.00	4443.89

Figure B-1. ACCOUNT.XLS

AD.XLW

A linked series of worksheets, this workspace includes both the ADS.XLS and FACILITIES.XLS files.

ADDRESS.XLS

This database contains a complete address-book file. As a result, it can readily be used for your purposes if necessary with little or no modification.

ADS.XLS

This is an advertising-budget file. This file is part of the AD.XLW workspace.

CARPOOL.XLS

This is a car pooling–management database. Each record contains a name, a phone number, an area where the person

Appendix B

works, and the time that person arrives at work. From this information, a car-pooling schedule can be compiled.

CHART.XLC

This is a quarterly-sales chart showing month-by-month breakdowns. This chart is run from the REGION.XLS worksheet.

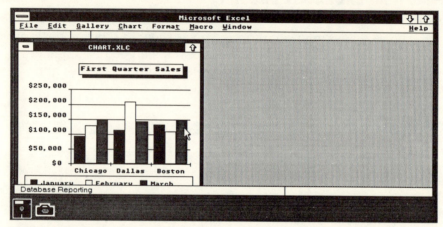

Figure B-2. CHART.XLC

COMMISS.XLS

This is a simple sales commission–reporting worksheet. There are columns for both regular sales commissions and bonuses.

COMPARE.XLS

This is an income/expenses comparison. It can be used to show cashflow from one from one month to another and to highlight certain critical cases.

EXPENSES.XLS

This is an expense-tracking worksheet, used to show where individual departmental expenses are being charged.

FACILITY.XLS

This is a facilities-expenses worksheet. This is part of the AD.XLW workspace.

FIRSTQTR.XLS

This is a basic quarterly sales report showing total quarterly sales for several items, as well as a month-by-month breakdown.

The Models in Excel

FORM.XLS
A sales-order form this shows locations for standard customer information as well as the actual sales order.

INCCAT.XLS
This worksheet shows catalog sales and costs, giving a rough income balance. It is part of both the MWPRA1.XLW and MWPRAC.XLW workspaces.

INCOME.XLS
This is a basic income statement, showing room for regional sales reports. It is also a part of the MWPRA1.XLW and MWPRAC.XLW workspaces.

KWWHAT.XLM
A demonstration macro, this is used with the Help topics.

LISTINGS.XLS
A home sales–listing file, this should be used more as a database than anything else, though it can be used for some elementary sales analysis.

MACRO.XLM
A basic demonstration macro, this is used to show how macro programming works.

MACRO9.XLM
Another demonstration macro, this one is used to demonstrate how it is possible to automate some features of your usage.

MAILER.XLM
A mailer-creation macro, this uses an an outside data file to create a mass-marketing mailer.

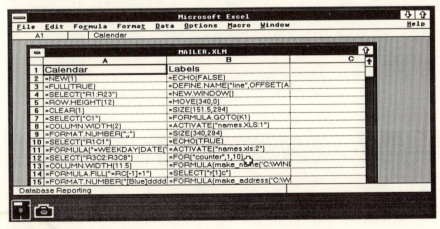

Figure B-3. MAILER.XLM

Appendix B

MONTHLY.XLS

A monthly sales–projection worksheet, this uses monthly-sales projections for individual products to create total monthly sales projections for a company.

MWPRA1.XLW

This workspace includes both the INCOME.XLS and INC-CAT.XLS files and is used to demonstrate basic worksheet linking principles.

MWPRAC.XLW

This workspace is used to demonstrate the effects of highly linked worksheets. It includes the INCOME.XLS, REGION1.XLS, REGION2.XLS, REGION3.XLS, and INC-CAT.XLS.

NAMES.XLS

A contribution-listing file, this can be used to track a number of things, such as total contributions or people who should be contacted at a later date.

ORDER.XLS

A sales order–compilation file, this can be used to create billing receipts for use with shipped products.

PAYROLL.XLS

A basic payroll worksheet, this can be used both to generate employee gross pay and to track employee productivity and overtime hours.

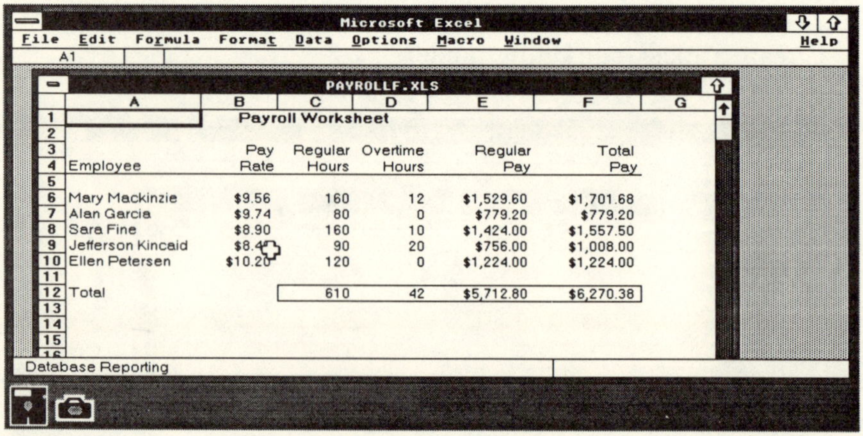

Figure B-4. PAYROLL.XLS

PAYROLLF.XLS
  A final, formatted payroll worksheet, this is a presentation level of payroll worksheet—the type that might be used for records or to show a superior.

QUARTER.XLS
  A quarterly sales report worksheet, this shows not only the previous quarter's sales, but also the sales for the present month.

RACKCHRT.XLS
  This is a worksheet specially prepared to be used for a demonstration of how to create a chart.

RACKS.XLS
  This file shows a set of sales breakdowns for several products from various sales regions. It is a part of the RACKS.XLW workspace.

RACKS.XLW
  This workspace contains the sales breakdowns for a particular product, showing reporting for a number of sales regions. It includes the RACKS.XLS, REGION1.XLS, and REGION2.XLS files.

RACKSLS.XLS
  A month-by-month breakdown of several products' sales, this is used to demonstrate several basic functions.

REGION.XLC
  A chart showing another format for local-sales breakdowns, this breaks down the sales by region and then time, instead of the other way around.

REGION.XLS
  A regional-sales-office breakdown, this file can be used to generate the REGION.XLC chart.

REGION.XLW
  This is a regional-sales-reporting workspace that includes both the REGION1.XLS and REGION2.XLS files.

REGION1.XLS
  This file contains a single sales region's financial reports. It is a part of both the MWPRAC.XLW and RACKS.XLW workspaces.

REGION2.XLS
  This file contains the Central-region sales figures for the MWPRAC.XLW workspace. It is also used in the RACKS.XLW workspace.

REGION3.XLS

The final set of sales figures for the MWPRAC.XLW workspace, this is an incomplete practice file.

REGSALES.XLS

An individual sales–breakdown worksheet that you might see as a precursor to a regional, and then a national, sales report.

SALES.XLS

An extremely basic local-sales worksheet, this can be used to practice basic data-entry and tabulation skills for *Excel*.

SAMPLES1.XLS

This is a demonstration of how to create a basic productivity analysis. As always, you need to define what your productivity criteria are before trying to analyze them.

SHEET.XLS

A payroll-tracking worksheet, this is much like a corporate cashflow sheet, with the exception that it is used to track employee payroll instead.

SLSPROJ.XLS

A complete sales-projection worksheet for a product line, this can be used alternatively to track product sales.

SUMMARY.XLS

An executive-expenses summary, this could be used to show the basic expenses associated with a variety of different departments.

TAXES.XLM

A city sales tax–generation macro, this can also be used to generate any number of other values that make use of a common value.

THIRDQTR.XLS

A comprehensive quarterly sales report, this provides breakdowns for quantities sold, amounts received, and regional contributions to the sales total.

TUTOR.XLM

This is one of the macros designed to work with the Help software. This is used to structure data entry into the formats wanted for the individual lessons. This macro makes a good study in how to restrict data entry.

TUTOR2.XLM

Another tutoring macro, this also works with the Help software of *Excel*.

ZEBRA.XLM
This is the last of the tutorial macros for the Help software. This macro fulfills a variety of tasks from within a single macro.

Excel LIBRARY Directory Files

AMORTIZ3.XLS
This is a mortgage-loan-analysis spreadsheet that allows you to input a variety of variables to create a comprehensive amortization table.

AR.XLM
This is a macro designed to work with the AR.XLS spreadsheet. It is designed to add an invoice to the database in the accompanying spreadsheet.

AR.XLS
This is an accounts receivable worksheet, and it also includes a database to help keep track of the customers.

AUDIT.XLM
This is a macro designed to assist in auditing spreadsheets. There are a large variety of commands included in the macro, allowing you to do a number of different operations in a much more efficient manner.

AUSTRAL.XLS
This is an inventory-control worksheet linked with several other files to provide a demonstration of the information-transfer capabilities of *Excel*.

BALANCE.XLS
This is a linked balance sheet used to demonstrate how information can be provided by one worksheet to another to keep certain data current.

BEARING.XLM
This is a macro used to help compute the bearing of any set of x,y coordinates from the origin.

BONUS.XLM
This is a macro used to calculate bonuses on sales commissions. It can also be used in a somewhat-modified form to keep track of employee productivity.

BREAKEVN.XLC
This is a chart showing the elements used to determine the profit/loss curve for a particular project. It also includes the actual profit/loss curve, used to show where the break-even point is.

Appendix B

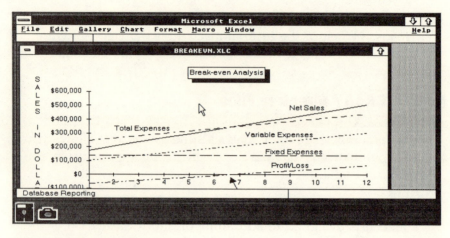

Figure B-5. BREAKEVN.XLC

BREAKEVN.XLS
This is a spreadsheet used to demonstrate the break-even point for a project, given various assumptions. It is linked to the CASHBUDG.XLS file, allowing the spreadsheet to use values derived somewhere else.

CALENDAR.XLM
This is a macro associated with the CALENDAR.XLS file. It is used to set up a calendar and add important dates to it.

CALENDAR.XLS
This is a worksheet containing a complete 12-month calendar. The associated macro file, CALENDAR.XLM, is used to post dates and maintain the calendar.

CAPTURE.XLS
This is a file containing a Capture session from CompuServe. The actual Capture script can be written by, run under, and the resulting data used by *Excel*.

CASHBUDG.XLS
This is a cash-outlays budget for a project. This file is linked to the BREAKEVN.XLS file, providing a number of important values for that file to use.

CASHTMP.XLS
This is a basic cash-budget worksheet. It provides a rough cash budget–approximation format.

COMMCALC.XLS

This is a basic commission-calculator data file. This worksheet contains a simple lookup chart of a variety of sales-commission rates.

COMMTEMP.XLS

This is a commission-calculation worksheet. It uses the COMMCALC.XLS data file and the BONUS.XLM macro to work out the per-item and total sales commission earned by a given person.

COMPARE.XLM

This is an automated file-comparison macro designed to look at a file and to search for certain critical information.

CONSOL.XLM

This is an automated file-consolidation macro designed to work around certain sensitive parameters.

CONSTANT.XLM

This is a simple currency-exchange macro designed to speed up currency exchange problems for different countries.

CORRECT.XLM

This is a simple database-correction macro designed to work with a database, storing reports from a scientific instrument.

CROSSTAB.XLM

This is a cross-tabulation macro designed to be used with a specially formatted database.

CUSTOMER.XLS

This is a customer-listing database. If you use this one for personnel purposes, you'll find that it includes all of the basic elements you might need.

DATA.XLS

This is a database and report-isolation worksheet containing collected gravimeter readings.

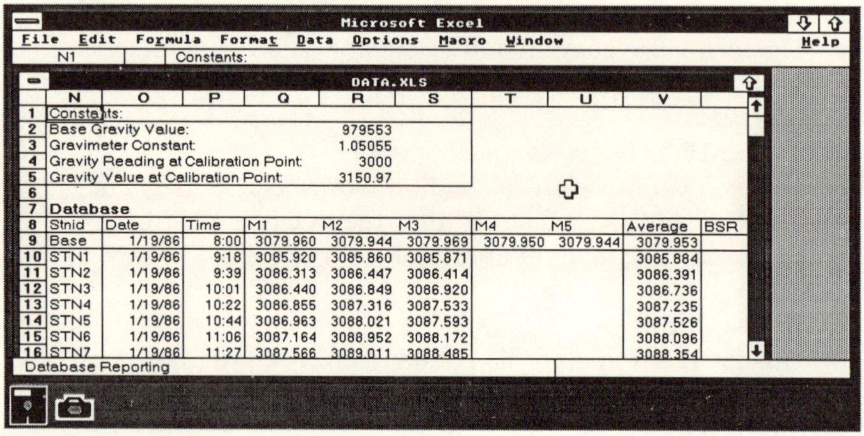

Appendix B

Figure B-6. DATA.XLS

DBREPORT.XLM

This is a report-generation macro. This is designed to work with one of several databases.

DEBUG.XLM

This is a macro-debugging macro. This can be used to test out your new macros to see whether they work.

FORMVIEW.XLM

This is a macro designed to allow the user to create a form-viewing capability.

GOALSEEK.XLM

This is a macro designed to search for a particular target value starting from a user-defined cell.

GREATBRT.XLS

This is another of the files linked with AUSTRAL.XLS. It is one of four "regional" spreadsheets that contribute to a final, multinational financial report.

INCOME.XLS

This is a basic income statement. This worksheet is referenced by the CASHBUDG.XLS worksheet as one of its source files.

INVENTRY.XLS

This is an inventory-management worksheet. This particular file can be used in a number of ways, depending on your needs.

INVOICE.XLM

This is an invoice-management macro. This macro is used to create the individual invoices.

INVOICE.XLS

This is an invoice listing. It is used as long-term data storage by the INVOICE.XLM and INVTMP.XLS files.

INVTMP.XLS

This is the output invoice associated with the INVOICE.XLM macro and the INVOICE.XLS worksheet. It stores the actual invoice.

JAPAN.XLS

This is the third of the inventory-management files. This worksheet is also part of the group formed by GREAT-BRT.XLS and WESTGERM.XLS.

LABEL.XLM

This is a label-generation macro.

MONTHCAL.XLS

This is an individual monthly calendar. It can be used to set up appointments and such. It's also associated with CALEN-DAR.XLS and CALENDAR.XLM.

PORTFOL.XLS

This is a stock-portfolio worksheet. This file uses the STOCKS.XLM file to download current quotes on a variety of stocks.

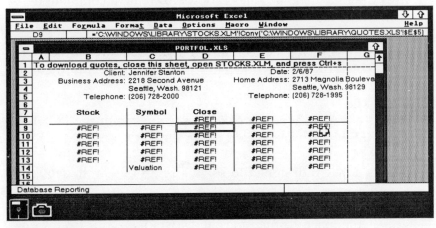

Figure B-7. PORTFOL.XLS

Appendix B

QUARTER.XLW

This is a quarterly-sales workspace. This file uses the AUSTRAL.XLS, GREATBRT.XLS, JAPAN.XLS, and WESTGERM.XLS files to maintain individual financial reports, updating information into the master file.

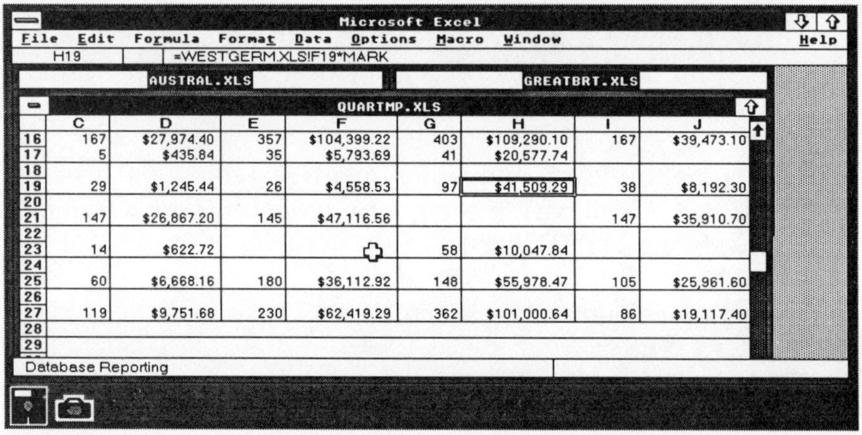

Figure B-8. QUARTER.XLW

QUARTER3.XLS

This is the quarterly cumulative sales–report spreadsheet. It uses the four national sales reports to create a complete financial picture.

QUARTMP.XLS

This is the spreadsheet containing the essential analyses for the QUARTER.XLW workspace. It's also linked into the four individual data files.

QUOTES.XLS

This is a downloaded set of quotes for use with the PORTFOL.XLS file. It was created using the STOCKS.XLM macro.

SIMEQ.XLM

This is a macro designed to solve a series of simultaneous equations.

STOCKS.XLM

This is the macro containing the Download script from CompuServe designed to work with the PORTFOL.XLS file. It creates the QUOTES.XLS text file.

WESTGERM.XLS
This is the last of the nationally based–sales-report files used with QUARTER.XLW and QUARTER3.XLS

WHATIF.XLM
This is a what-if creation macro. It is designed to be used with just about any worksheet that you want.

YEARCAL.XLS
This is the year calculation for use with the CALENDAR.XLS and CALENDAR.XLM files. It is a data file containing information needed by those two files.

Appendix C
Using the Clipboard and Control Panel

The Clipboard

The Clipboard is a place where you can temporarily store data that is being copied or moved within an *Excel* worksheet or macro sheet, from one *Excel* worksheet or macro sheet to another, or from one application running under Microsoft *Windows* (version 2.0 or higher) to another such as *Excel*.

To display the Clipboard:

- Choose the Control Run command (Alt + space bar + U).
- Select Clipboard.
- Choose OK.

If you have cut or copied anything from an active document, you'll see specific Clipboard information.

Notice that the top part of the Clipboard contains items describing Clipboard file formats. You can specify any of these when pasting information to another application. If you're pasting to another *Excel* worksheet or macro sheet, ignore these formats, since *Excel* takes care of that.

In the section describing the file formats is a listing of what is currently on the Clipboard. In the example above, only one item is there—the unnamed cell range that is one row high and five columns wide.

Once data is on the Clipboard, you can paste it into the same or another document using the Paste command in an *Excel* document or its equivalent in another application. If the application has an insertion point, the data from the Clipboard appears to the left of the insertion point. If you've selected cells on the destination document or application, the cells from the Clipboard replace the selected cells.

The data on the Clipboard stays there until you Cut or Move different cells, allowing you to Paste the same cells in several dif-

Appendix C

ferent places. In most cases, however, formatting information doesn't get stored on the Clipboard, so you may have to reformat the data after it's been pasted in place.

To remove the Clipboard from your screen, choose Control Close (Alt + space bar + C). The Clipboard remains active, however, until you close the document, even though it's not visible unless you specifically ask to see it.

The Control Panel

The Control Panel, another option on the Control menu, lets you change system settings such as date and time, the insertion point, the double-click rate used with your mouse, printer assignments, and colors that appear in various places in your windows.

The Control Panel is a program module that is part of Microsoft *Windows* and is furnished with the modified version of *Windows* that comes with *Excel*.

Changes that you make with the Control Panel are stored in the initialization file, WIN.INI. However, these changes don't affect certain other settings, such as the graphics card designation or graphics resolution. These latter changes are governed by the SETUP program that you run when you first install *Excel*.

When you choose the Control Panel (press Alt + space bar + U and select Control Panel), you see a menu bar and, below it, a box with four sections. The menu bar lists the commands Installation, Setup, and Preferences; each command has its own menu of subcommands, which we'll look at shortly. The box, however, lets you change certain other system information.

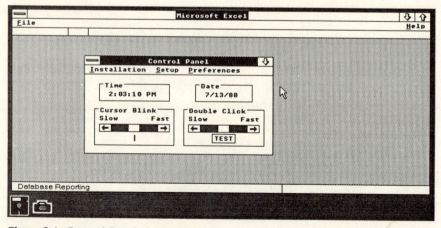

Figure C-1. Control Panel, Initial Box

The Time box shows the current time as determined by your system clock. If you want to change this, press Tab to move to the Time section and use the right- or left-arrow keys or click with your mouse to select the section of the time (hours, minutes, seconds) you want to change. Use the up-arrow key or click your mouse's up scroll arrow to increase the number; use the down-arrow key or click with your mouse's down scroll arrow to decrease the number. When you've finished, press Enter, or with your mouse click anywhere outside the Time box.

The Date box shows the date stored by your system. You change it the same way you change the data in the Time box.

The Cursor Blink box controls how fast the bar at the insertion point in a formula or text box blinks. To change the blink rate, press the Tab key to move to the Cursor Blink section and use the right- or left-arrow on your keyboard or drag the scroll box with your mouse to speed up or slow down the blink rate.

The Double Click rate controls how long *Excel* waits for the second click before executing a command when you double-click your mouse. If you have a relatively slow double-click time, *Excel* waits that amount of time to execute the command. If your double-click time is faster, however, and you take longer than the set amount to click the second time, you'll probably wind up executing some wrong commands, since *Excel* will interpret the clicks as two separate choices.

You can test the double-click setting by double-clicking the Test button. The button color changes if *Excel* interprets your action as a double-click.

The Installation Menu

The first of the Control Panel menus governs installation of various options for use with your printers. Covering fonts and printer drivers, this menu is used both to install and to deinstall the drivers that determine your printing capabilities.

The first entry on the Installation menu is used to install new printer drivers for use under your *Windows* environment. To install a new printer driver, simply insert the disk with the printer-driver file into the appropriate disk drive; then enter the path and filename that are needed to load the printer driver. Once you have done this, simply press the Enter key, and the new printer is installed in your operating environment.

Next is the Delete Printer command. This is used to deinstall a printer that has already been installed to your WIN.INI file. Use

Appendix C

the Delete Printer box to highlight the printer you want removed, and press the Enter key. The printer driver is immediately removed.

The third and fourth commands on the Installation menu deal with adding and removing fonts. Just like the printer drivers, the font drivers can be removed and installed using these two commands. Fortunately, the procedure for installing or removing a font set is identical to the procedure used to install or remove a printer driver.

The last two commands on the Installation menu are, respectively, the Exit and About Control Panel commands. The first of these is used to exit the Control Panel, while the second provides a small window containing some information about the Control Panel software.

The Setup Menu

The second of the menus on the Control Panel, Setup, is used to describe the various hardware hookups that *Excel* can use. Included in this is the description of which printers are linked to which communications ports, which printer is being used as the default printer, and which port is being used for external telecommunications.

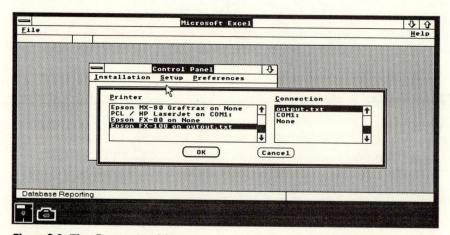

Figure C-2. The Connection Menu

The first entry on the menu, Connections, is used to tell *Excel* which printer is hooked up to which external communications port. If a printer has already been defined as being connected to a given port, then in the Printer box it shows up as connected to that port. Otherwise, the printer is shown as being connected to *None*. If you want to change the connection for a printer, highlight that printer on the Printer box, and then select the appropriate communications port in the Connections box.

If you select the Printer selection box, you're asked to choose the default printer that will be used when you print something from within *Excel*. To change the default printer, simply highlight a different printer in the selection box. If you want to change the printer timeouts that are used, you can also enter new values for those by simply selecting the appropriate setting and entering the new value in seconds.

The last entry on the Setup menu is for something that normally isn't dealt with by spreadsheet packages: communications. When you open this window, you are presented with a complete set of communications-protocol selections that you can use to set what you want to use with your telecommunications equipment. Choose the selections that are appropriate for your equipment, software, and the system you will be logging on to. Once you have finished entering these values, they can be activated by just pressing the Enter key.

The Preferences Menu

The Preferences menu is used to control how your screen looks. From the screen colors to the different national settings used to such minor changes as the border widths, all of the user-definable onscreen settings are altered from this one place.

If you are using a monitor that has color capabilities, it is quite possible to alter the screen colors used for a number of the different screen elements.

Appendix C

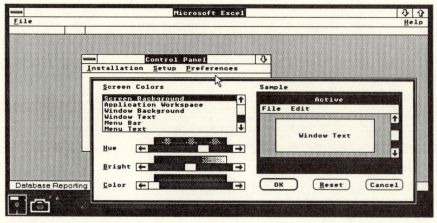

Figure C-3. Screen Colors Window

So that you can view the effects of what you are doing, there is a sample screen displayed in the right side of the window. To change a given element, first pick the item that you want to change. Make sure that it is selected by moving the Screen Colors selection up and down until the item you want to change is highlighted. Then change the color, brightness, and hue of that item until it appears as you want it to. Once you have finished making changes, press the Enter key to activate the changes.

The next entry on the Preferences menu is for border widths. When you select this, you are presented with a simple dialog box allowing you to thicken or reduce your border widths. If you wish to change the widths used for your borders, enter the value that you want to use for your new border. The larger the value, the larger the border.

The third entry on this menu is for the Warning Beep. As long as this entry is checked, the beep on your computer is turned on. If you would like to turn the beep off, turn off this entry. As a rule, whenever you select the Warning Beep option, you will change the status of the beep either from *on* to *off* or from *off* to *on*.

The last of the Preference menu options is for the Country Settings. Depending on what you want to use, you can either use the Country Settings box to pick a preset group of settings or set the various options directly to what you want them to be, for a custom batch of settings.

To create your own group of settings, first select the Other

Country option in the Country Settings box. Next, select the various options that you want to use, such as the correct currency symbol and position and the correct time format.

To return to the settings you were using before, select the Reset option.

When you have finished with the Control Panel, put it away by choosing Control Close for the Control Panel window (Alt + space bar + C).

Index

\ *See* backslash
! *See* exclamation mark
A1.R1C1 305
ABS 156
ABSREF 331–32
ACOS 158
ACTIVATE 305
ACTIVATE.PREV 305
Activate Window command 127, 130
active cell 6–7, 24–25, 41
ACTIVE.CELL 332
ADD.BAR 312–13
ADD.COMMAND 313
ADD.MENU 313
Add Legend command 272
Add New Printer command 220
ALERT 314
alignment 50–51, 112
AND 153–54
annuities 172–75, 177–78
APP.ACTIVATE 314
application window 121
   types 123–25
Apply Name command 92
AREAS 180
argument 146–48
   for database functions 200
   function statement 297
ARGUMENT 328
Arrange All command 127–28, 130
array 189, 190, 204–205
ASCII character 193
ASCII code 193
ASCII format file 219
ASIN 158
ATAN 159
ATAN2 159
Attach Text command 277
AVERAGE 160
axis labels 96

backslash 68–69
backup 71
.BAK extension 71
BEEP 314
borders 41, 114
   adding 56
boxes 95
BREAK 328

Calculate Now command 138
Calculation command 138
calendar, producing 10
CALENDAR.XLM 10
CALL 315
CALLER 332
CANCEL.COPY 305
CANCEL.KEY 315
Category Axis 285
CELL 180–81
cell 40–41, 44, 200
   addresses 40
   hiding and locking 57–58
   copying 105–107
   deleting 97–98
   naming 58–64
   nonblank 107
   search and replace 132–37
   selection of 133
   transposing 107
CHAR 193
chart 10, 26–28, 78
   area 256–57, 289
   bar 251, 258–59, 289
   changing axes of 273–77
   changing background of 270–71
   changing legend of 272–73
   changing plot area of 272
   changing text format of 280–81
   changing text of 277
   column 260, 289
   combination 266–67
   copying data from another chart 110
   copying data from a worksheet 110–111
   creation of 251–55
   customizing of 268–86
   deleting text 283
   editing text 280
   formatting 288–90
   importing and exporting 350
   line 261–62, 289
   moving and resizing arrows 283–84
   moving unattached text 281–82
   pie 4, 251, 263–64, 289
   printing 226–28
   removing data from 97
   resizing unattached text 282
   saving 290–91

Index

chart (*continued*)
  scatter 251, 265–66, 289
  selecting 94–96
  selecting objects 269–70
  text justification 112
  using gridlines in 284–86
  window 122
check boxes 18
CHECK.COMMAND 315
CHOOSE 187
CLEAN 193
Clear command 91, 97
clearing 96–98
Clipboard 88, 345, 375–76
  formats 347–48
  window 124
Close command 70, 72, 291
CODE 193
color monitor 56
colors 48
column 200
  changing width of 51–52
  deleting 97
  inserting 99
  labels 214–15
  making double lines 116
  removal of identifiers 116
  COLUMN 181–82
commands
  control 21
  document-control 24
  editing 91–92
  file 65
  issuing 14–16
  naming 59
  saving 70
  window 126–30
comments 297
communications, setting up 378–79
Compaq Deskpro 286 8
Connections command 220
Connections Port command 209
constants 143
control characters 193
Control Move command 119
Control Panel 207–209, 376–81
  installation menu 377–78
  preferences menu 379–81
  setup menu 378–79
  window 124
Control Run command 125
Control Split command 127
COPY.CHART 305
Copy command 91, 100, 105

copying 100–105
  into Formula Bar 108
  pictures 349–51
Copy Picture command 92
COS 159
COUNT 160
COUNTA 161
Create Name command 60, 92
criteria 200
  comparison 242–43
  computed 242, 244–47
criteria matching 240
criteria range 241
Cut command 91, 100, 105

data
  displaying 45–46
  entering 37–64
  protection of 56–58
  selection of 31
  types of 37
DATA.FIND.NEXT 306
DATA.FIND.PREV 306
database 200, 229–50
  creation of 233
  deleting 238–39
  editing 235, 238–39
  extracting data from 249–50
  importing into *Excel*'s worksheet 349
  searching 240–41
  setting up 230–32
  sorting 247–49
database form 235–37
  defining 235–37
  deleting 238–40
  editing 238–40
  moving within 237
  searching 240–41
database range 230
Database Set Range command 230
Data Delete command 34
Data Extract command 34
Data Form command 235
Data Parse command 88
data series 42–44
  editing definitions 287–88
  selecting 252–54
Data Series command 42–44
Data Set Criteria command 200
Data Set Database command 200
DATE 149
DATEVALUE 149–50
DAVERAGE 201
DAY 150

384

DCOUNT 201–202
DCOUNTA 202
DDB 171
DDE 88, 346–47
debugging 24
default values 111
Define Name command 92
DELETE.BAR 316
DELETE.COMMAND 316
DELETE.FORMAT 306
DELETE.MENU 316
Delete command 91, 97
Delete Printer command 377
deleting 96–98
dependents 24, 26, 137
DEREF 332
dialog box 15–19
   Data Series 43–44
   Font 16–17, 55
   macro functions 304–305
   style 18
   text 18
DIALOG.BOX 316–17
directories 66–69
   root 67
DIRECTORY 306
DISABLE.INPUT 317
discounted value 176
discounting 176
disks
   floppy 13–14
   hard 13
   Setup 13–14
DMAX 202
DMIN 202
Document Control menu 21
DOCUMENTS 332
DOLLAR 193–94
double-declining balance. *See* DDB
DPRODUCT 203
DSTDEV 203
DSTDEVP 203
DSUM 203
DVAR 203
DVARP 204
Dynamic Data Exchange. *See* DDE

ECHO 317
editing 91–141
ENABLE.COMMAND 317
ERROR 318
error messages 37
error values 37, 103
EXACT 194

Excel 1–12
   and exchanging illustrations 348
   Functions and Macro manual 9
   Getting Started and Quick Reference
      manual 9
   installation of 13–14
   keyboard and screen 14–34
   models 361–73
   Reference Guide 9, 21, 50, 350, 352,
      354
   Sampler and Idea Book 9
   sharing with other programs 345–54
   tutorial 8
   worksheet 5–8
exclamation mark 81
EXEC 318
EXECUTE 319
Exit command 70, 72
EXP 156
extension 66
   .BAK 71
extract range 249

FACT 156
FALSE 154
FCLOSE 319
Feature Guide 8
field 200, 231, 236
   computed 231, 236
   name 231
File Close All command 72
File Delete command 34
filename 65–66
File Page Setup command 56, 120
File Print command 117, 120, 216
File Printer Setup command 209–211
File Print Preview command 215
FILES 333
files 65–90
   associated 76
   from EXCELCBT directory 361–67
   from LIBRARY directory 367–73
   linked 81–85
   output 219–21
   protecting 80–81
   retrieving 77–87
   saving 69–73
File Save As command 64
File Save command 64
Fill command 105
Fill Down command 91, 105
Fill Left command 91, 105
Fill option 51
Fill Right command 91, 105

Index

Fill Up command 92, 105
financial analysis 11
FIND 194–95
Find command 92, 133–34
FIXED 195
fonts 16–17, 377–78
  selecting 54–55
  size 53–55
FOPEN 319
FOR 328–29
Format Alignment command 51, 112
Format Border command 56, 114
Format Cell Protection command 58, 140
Format command 199, 288
Format Font command 54
Format Justify command 51, 113–14
Format Numbers command 47–48, 51, 195
Format Row Height command 52
formats
  creating own 49–50
  data exchange 347
  dedicated database 349
  number 47–49
  SYLK 353
  text 50
Format Text command 50, 112
formatting 111–17
  options 47–56
formula 81, 143, 297
  construction of 29
  copying 108–110
  editing 92
  naming 61–62
FORMULA 306–307
Formula Apply Names 63
Formula bar 6, 29
Formula Define Name command 59, 245
Formula Find command 103
Formula Note command 26, 118, 120
Formula Paste Function command 108–109
Formula Paste Name command 61–62, 108
Formula Select Special command 26, 120
FORMULA.ARRAY 307
FORMULA.FILL 307
FORMULA.FIND 308
FORMULA.FIND.PREV 308
FPOS 320

FREAD 320
FREADLN 320
Freeze Pane command 131–32
FSIZE 320
functions 146–48
  database 200–204
  date and time 149–53
  financial 171–79
  information 180–87
  logical 153–55
  lookup 187–93
  macro 301–343
  mathematical 156–58
  matrix 204–206
  pasting 148
  statistical 160–71
  text 193–200
  trigonometric 158–60
FV 172
FWRITE 320
FWRITELN 321

Gallery 267–68, 288
GET.BAR 333
GET.CELL 333–34
GET.CHART.ITEM 335–36
GET.DEF 336
GET.DOCUMENT 336–38
GET.FORMULA 338
GET.NAME 338
GET.NOTE 339
GET.WINDOW 339–40
GET.WORKSPACE 340–41
GOTO 329
Goto command 92, 132–133
graphics resolution 211
graphs 228
gridlines 56, 114, 116, 212, 284–86
  major 286
  minor 286
GROWTH 161–62

HALT 329
headers and footers 211–12
headings 114, 212
HELP 321
Help menu 8–9
Help window 123
Hide command 127, 129
hiding cells 57–58, 140
highlighting 41, 95
HLINE 308
HLOOKUP 187–188

HOUR 150
HPAGE 308
HSCROLL 308–309

IBM PC AT 8
IBM PC XT 8
IBM Personal System/2 series 8
IF 154, 187
INDEX 189
INDIRECT 182
Info Window 24–25, 120, 123
INITIATE 321
INPUT 321–23
Insert command 91, 98, 235
inserting data 98–100
insertion point 98
installing printer driver 207–209
INT 156–57
IPMT 173
IRR 173–74
ISBLANK 182
ISERR 182
ISERROR 183
ISLOGICAL 183
ISNA 183
ISNONTEXT 184
ISNUMBER 184
ISREF 184
ISTEXT 184
iteration 138–39

justification 112

keyboard
   and moving around the worksheet 30
   and moving within a selection 31–32
   and scrolling within an active window 32
   and selecting data 31

LAN 345, 350
Landscape mode 209
LEFT 195
legend 96, 272–73
LEN 196
LINEST 162–64, 168
linking 81–87, 345
   to non-*Excel* program 88–90
LINKS 341
Links command 81–84
LN function 157

Local Area Network. *See* LAN
locking cells 57–58, 140
LOG 157
LOG10 157
LOGEST 164–65
logical values 37
LOOKUP 187, 190
Lotus 1-2-3 14, 351–53
LOWER 196

Macintosh 348
Macro Record command 298
macros 293–343
   action equivalent functions 305–312
   and documentation 297
   and stepping 296
   command 293, 296
   command equivalent functions 301–304
   control functions 328–31
   conversion of 125
   customizing functions 312–28
   dialog box functions 304–305
   function 109, 293, 297
   using the Recorder 298
   value-returning functions 331–43
   writing 297
macro sheet 78–79, 294
   construction of 299–301
   window 122–23
Macro Stop Recorder command 298
Macro Translation Assistant 125, 351
margins 212
MATCH 190
MATCHTYPE 191–92
MAX 166
Maximize command 23
MDETER 204–205
Menu bar 6–7, 14
menus 15–16
   chart 26–28
   control 20–24
   Gallery 28
   Info 24–26
   short 19–20
MESSAGE 323
Microsoft, support program 9
MID 196–97
MIN 166
Minimize command 23
minus sign 39
MINUTE 151
MINVERSE 205

Index

MIRR 174–75
MMULT 205
MOD 157–58
modes 28–30
  edit 28–29
  enter 28–29
  point 28–29
  ready 28
MONTH 151
More Windows command 127
mouse 32–34
moving 100–105
Multiplan 353–54

NA function 185
NAMES 342
naming cells 58–64
Net Present Value function. *See* NPV
network 80
New command 78
New Window command 127
NEXT 329–30
Next command 216
N function 184–85
NOT 155
Note command 92
notes
  addition of 118
  duplicating 119
  editing 120
  printing 120
NOW 151
NPER 175
NPV 176
numbers 184, 193, 195, 200
  alignment of 50–51, 112
  entering 41–42, 44–45
  formats 47–49
  in text strings 46
numeric data 37, 88

OFFSET 342
ON.DATA 323
ON.KEY 323–24
ON.TIME 324
ON.WINDOW 324–25
Open command 79–80
operators
  numeric 244
  types of 144–45
Options Display command 56, 116
Options Protect Document command 58, 140

Options Set command 117
Options Set Print Titles command 215
Options Unprotect Document command 140
OR 155

page breaks 213
  horizontal 213–14
  manual 213
  vertical 213–14
page layout 209
pane 50
password 58, 71, 80
password protection 139–41
Paste command 91, 100, 108
Paste Function command 92
Paste Link command 91
Paste Name command 92
Paste Special command 91, 105, 110
pathname 67–68
Patterns command 271
PC Excel Business Solutions 297–98
PI 158
PMT 176–77
point 52
POKE 325
Portrait mode 209
position indicator 236
precedents 24, 26, 137
Precision as Displayed option 45–46
previewing 215–16
Previous command 216
printer driver, installation of 207–209, 377–78
Printer Setup command 211
printers, networking 224–26
printing 207–228
  automatic sheet-feeding 210
  charts 226–28
  complete document 216–17
  formats 117
  graph 213
  manual loading 210
  multiple-feed capability 210
  part of a spreadsheet 217–19
  ranges 218
  to a file 219
Priority Exit command 224
PROPER 197
protecting
  charts 141
  data 56–58, 139–41
  window 141
PV 177

queue 221
Queue Resume command 224
Queue Terminate command 224

R1C1 style 40
RATE 178
recalculation 137–139
Record mode 296
records 200, 231
Reference command 92
references 102, 184, 189
   absolute 40–41, 145, 244
   circular 138
   external 85–86, 278, 346
   relative 40–41, 145, 244
reference values 143
REFTEXT 342
REGISTER 325
RELREF 342
Remove Page Break command 214
RENAME.COMMAND 325–26
Repeat command 91
repetition 197
REPLACE 197–98
Replace command 92, 134–35
REPT 197
REQUEST 326
RESTART 330
Restore command 23
RESULT 330–31
retrieving files 77–87
RETURN 331
RIGHT 197–98
ROW 185–86
rows 185, 200
   changing height of 52–53
   deleting 97
   labels 214–15
   removal of identifiers 116
ROWS 186

Save As command 64, 70, 291
Save command 64, 70, 72, 291
Save Workspace command 72–73, 83, 291
saving 64, 69–73
   associated files 76–77
Scale command 275
screen 5–8, 379–81
   splitting 130–32
scroll bar 6–7
scrolling 32
SEARCH 198
SECOND 152

SELECT 309–310
SELECT.END 310
SELECT.LAST 311
selecting
   cells 133
   on a chart 94–96
   on a worksheet 93
   within the formula bar 94
SELECTION 342
Select Special command 92, 136–37
SEND.KEYS 326
Set Database command 233
SET.NAME 326–27
Set Page Break command 214
Set Print Area command 218
SET.VALUE 327
shading, addition of 56
shortcut keys 355–59
SHOW.ACTIVE.CELL 311
SHOW.BAR 327
SHOW. CLIPBOARD 311
Show Document command 25, 128
Show Info command 25, 127–28
SIN 159
single-stepping 327
Size command 21, 23
SLN 178–79
sorting keys 247
specific data search 240
Split command 130
splitting the screen 130–32
Spooler utility 125, 221–24
   disabling 222–23
Spooler window 125
spreadsheet 1–4, 227
   creation of 38–39
   uses for 9–12
standard deviation 166–67, 170, 203
Status bar 6–7, 15, 29
STDEV 166–67
STDEVP 167
STEP 327
straight-line depreciation. *See* SLN
STYLE 311
STYLE? 311
subdirectories 67
SUBSTITUTE 198–99
SUM 39, 147, 167–68
SYD 179
SYLK (Symbolic Link) format 353

tally line 39
TAN 159
tax tables 188, 192

Index

templates 77
TERMINATE 328
TEXT 199
text 37, 184, 193–200
   alignment and justification of 51, 112–13
   attached 277
   entering 46–47
   for charts 277–83
   unattached 279–82
text constant 232
TEXTREF 343
T function 186
TIME 152
TIMEVALUE 152
TRANSPOSE 205–206
TREND 168–69
TRIM 199
TRUE 155
TYPE 186–87

underlines 115
Undo command 34–35, 91, 99, 103
Unfreeze Pane command 132
Unhide command 127, 129
UNLOCKED.NEXT 311
UNLOCKED.PREV 311
UPPER 199

VALUE 200
Value Axis 285
value, reformatting 199
VAR 169, 170
variance 169–70, 203–204
VARP 169, 170
vector 190

viewing cell names 61
VLINE 312
VLOOKUP 192
VPAGE 312
VSCROLL 312

WAIT 328
WEEKDAY 153
WHILE 331
wildcard 242–43
window
   application 21, 121, 123–25
   changing the size of 21–23
   chart 122
   commands 126–30
   creation of 78
   document 23–24, 121
   Info 24–25, 120, 123
   macro sheet 122–23
   using 120–25
Window Control command 130
Window New Window command 78
Windows 67, 87–88, 120, 124, 343, 345, 375–77
Window Show Info command 120
WIN.INI 73, 219–20, 376–77
worksheet
   creation of 37–64
   linking 85–87
workspace
   saving 72–73
   using 74–77

YEAR 153

Zoom command 216